MEDALS
The Researcher's Guide

MEDALS
The Researcher's Guide

WILLIAM SPENCER

✦

FOREWORD BY
Major General Michael Tillotson
CB, CBE

The National Archives

First published in 2006 by The National Archives, Kew,
Richmond, Surrey, TW9 4DU, UK

www.nationalarchives.gov.uk

This paperback edition published in 2008

The National Archives brings together the Public Record Office,
Historical Manuscripts Commission, Office of Public Sector
Information and Her Majesty's Stationery Office.

A catalogue card for this book is available
from the British Library.

ISBN 978 1 905615 35 3

Typographic design by Ken Wilson and Goldust Design
Typesetting by Goldust Design

Cover design by Penny Jones and Michael Morris
and Goldust Design

Printed in Singapore by KHL Printing Co Pte Ltd

Front cover: (above) the medals of Air Marshal Sir Bertine Sutton
KBE, CB, RAF (see Plate 31); (centre) photograph of Sir Bertine
Sutton; (below) medal roll containing the recommendation of a
Distinguished Service Order for Sir Bertine Sutton, 1917.
Back cover: The South Atlantic Medal awarded to the author
for service in the Falklands War, 1982.

Frontispiece
The orders, decorations and medals of Air Marshal Sir Bertine
Sutton KBE, CB, comprising: (far left) Knight of the British
Empire (KBE) neck badge and breast star; (far right) Commander
of the Order of the Bath (CB) neck badge; (medals, left to right)
medal bar with Distinguished Service Order, Military Cross,
1914/15 Star, British War Medal, Victory Medal with MiD oakleaf,
IGS 1908-35 with clasp MOHMAND 1933 and MiD oakleaf,
Defence Medal 1939–45, War Medal 1939–45, 1935 Jubilee
Medal, 1937 Coronation Medal and Belgian Croix de Guerre.

Contents

PART TWO

Foreword
Major General Michael Tillotson CB, CBE

In producing *Medals*, William Spencer has rendered an invaluable service to authors, historians and journalists. Acquired over many years, his ability to find a way through labyrinthine routes to citations for decorations and entitlements to medals of many varieties is remarkable. Now he has put this experience at the disposal of anyone who needs to take those paths in their work.

Medals, dealing equally with civilian and service awards, will ease the anxieties of people asked to deliver eulogies at memorial services or write obituaries for newspapers. An inquiry to a family for the background to an individual's decoration or medal only too often elicits the reply, 'We have no idea, he never spoke about it.' This guide can help to solve such a dilemma.

The book will also be of great interest to the general public because it throws light on some of the anomalies that have arisen in the awards of decorations and campaign medals. While unfairness is never the intention, popular acclaim for some events has undoubtedly led to over-generous recognition for the people involved, compared to others which were equally dangerous or demanding, but less well publicized.

Race and colour are revealed as sources of inequality. Sergeant George Williams, a Christian Sudanese soldier of the King's African Rifles, was recommended for the Victoria Cross, only to be denied the highest award for valour because he was a black African. That was during the Great War of 1914–18. By the time millions from the Empire and Commonwealth were mobilized for the Second World War, this exclusion had been removed, as it was for the Indian and Gurkha soldiers of the Indian Army.

William Spencer offers his readers a variety of practical, accessible routes to the information they seek. Among the options likely to seize the attention of some are the facilities of the *London Gazette* online. In this electronic age it is no longer is it necessary for those in urgent need of information to have to search through books and microfilm – although some will always prefer the challenge and sense of achievement of these well-tried methods.

Spencer, one of whose relatives, George Spencer, is featured in the book, joined the Fleet Air Arm in 1980. He saw operational service with 848 Squadron during the Falkland Islands War of 1982 and joined the Public Record Office, now the National Archives, in 1993. He holds an MA in War Studies from King's College, London, and has been the National Archives' Senior Military Specialist since 1996. His other publications include *Army Records, Air Force Records, First World War Army Service Records* and *Family History in the Wars*.

MICHAEL TILLOTSON

About This Guide

Orders, decorations and medals are more than just items worn by people at parades and important events – they are signposts to the past. In many cases, they provide the only tangible pieces of evidence between the present and the event they represent or commemorate. The more you can find out about a medal's original recipient, the more interesting and valuable it becomes.

Most British campaign and long service medals are named around the edge or on the reverse, as are many gallantry awards. It is this attribution, together with the design of the medal and its ribbon, that will help you discover what it represents, to whom it was awarded and why.

A number of medal-related terms are used in this guide and it may be helpful to mention them here. Most medals consist of a cross, star or circular device that is made of metal, usually bronze, silver or cupronickel bronze, and is fashioned into a design on both front and back. The front of a medal is called the obverse, and this usually carries an effigy or cipher of the monarch of the time. The back of the medal is called the reverse. This usually carries a design that either tells you specifically what the medal is or something that will provide you with information about the campaign for which it was awarded. Images of most British medals can be found in the *Medal Yearbook* by Token Publishing.

Nearly all British medals are hung from a ribbon, and the medal is joined to it by something called a suspension. Many ribbons on campaign medals are symbolic and represent something connected with that campaign. For example, the Egypt Medal 1882–9 hangs on a ribbon of five stripes, three blue and two white, which represent the Blue and White Nile rivers of the region.

On the ribbon of many campaign medals there will be found strips of fashioned metal known as clasps. A clasp usually records a particular battle or date in which the recipient of the medal participated. Some campaign medals were issued without a clasp, other medals were not. For further information, see *British Battles and Medals.*

Other strips of metal may be found on the ribbons of awards for gallantry or long service. Usually called bars, they represent a further award of the same medal upon which the bar is suspended.

For the first time, this guide brings together information about the most important archival sources relating to orders, decorations and medals held by the National Archives and in the India Office Collection at the British Library. It is split into three distinct parts: Part I covers campaign medals and awards for gallantry or meritorious service; Part II covers long service awards, coronation and jubilee medals and miscellaneous medals; and Part III covers research techniques and the rapidly expanding online resources. Appendices offer details of societies and where to see medals, as well as advice on published sources and further reading.

The variety of records of central government and the bureaucracy relating to medals – from the decision to create one and the lists of those entitled to receive one to the design and manufacture of the medal and the overall cost of the whole enterprise – means that there are many places where information relating to medals can be found. Most of the key records series are covered in this guide.

The records are brought to life by over a dozen case studies, each a unique story of the recipient and how the records were used to trace them or their medals. From the Knight Air Marshal and the Canadian who fought in the Indian Mutiny to the soldier who got the Army to pay him twice, from the nurse who was decorated by King George V to the African child bugler of the King's African Rifles, they are but a very small range of different stories that can be discovered by using the records described. The guide is not only about medals awarded to men and, in particular, servicemen; it also covers awards to civilians and to women.

This guide is not only aimed at medal collectors. It is designed to be helpful to all researchers, especially those tracing the careers of service personnel and other medal recipients, as well as family historians, biographers and military obituarists. I hope that it will prove as valuable in use as it was fascinating to compile.

USING THE NATIONAL ARCHIVES AND
THE BRITISH LIBRARY

The National Archives

The National Archives, Ruskin Avenue, Kew, Richmond, Surrey TW9 4DU
All of the records of the National Archives discussed in this guide are held
at Kew. Access to the archives is by Reader's Ticket, which can be applied for
in person at Kew or online, but they are issued upon production of a form
of identity such as a passport, driving licence, bank or credit card when
you arrive.

The National Archives is open six days a week:

Monday	09:00–17:00
Tuesday	09:00–19:00
Wednesday	10:00–17:00
Thursday	09:00–19:00
Friday	09:00–17:00
Saturday	09:30–17:00

The National Archives is closed on a number of days throughout the year. For
further information see **www.nationalarchives.gov.uk** or ring 020 8876 3444.

How to get there
The nearest station is Kew Gardens on the District Line, also served by the
London Overground. The R68 Bus from Richmond terminates at Kew Retail
Park, a short walk from the Archives. For motorists, it is just off the South
Circular Road (A205). There is a car park onsite.

The British Library (India Office Records)

The British Library, 96 Euston Road, London NW1 2DB
Access to the Library is by Reader's Ticket and these can be applied for online
and in person upon production of a valid form of identification. See
www.bl.uk/services/reading/admissions.html for further information.

For information about opening times etc. see **www.bl.uk** or ring
0870 444 1500.

Liverpool Central Library

Liverpool Central Library, William Brown Street, Liverpool L3 8EW
The Library is open:

Monday to Friday	09:00–18:00
Saturday	09:00–17:00
Sunday	12:00–16:00

For further information see www.liverpool.gov.uk/libraries or ring 0151 233 5829.

Imperial War Museum (Department of Documents)

The Imperial War Museum, Lambeth Road, London SE1 6HZ
The Department of Documents is housed in the main museum building.
The Museum is open 7 days a week from 10:00–18:00, but the Department of Documents opening times vary. For further information see www.iwm.org.uk or ring 020 7415 5320.

The Postal Museum and Archive

The Postal Museum and Archives, Freeling House, Phoenix Place, London WC1X 0DL
For further information see www.postalheritage.org.uk or ring 020 7239 2570.

ACKNOWLEDGEMENTS

Many people have been involved in the creation of this guide and without them I would probably still be accumulating paper. My thanks go to:

Catherine Bradley for allowing me the time to continue researching and writing beyond the initially agreed point of completion, and much more.

Paul Baillie, Tony and Judith Farrington, David Lloyd, Keith Steward, John Sly and James Young for advice, encouragement and material for some of the images.

Pierce and Forbes Noonan at Dix, Noonan and Webb for the images of Henry Cooper vc and Thomas Bryan vc.

Hugh Alexander, Brian Carter and Paul Johnson for the photography of TNA documents and many of the medals.

Ken Wilson at point918 and Briony Hartley at Goldust Design for an elegant and practical design.

My colleagues at the National Archives for all of the documents I have requested and consulted.

The staff at the British Library responsible for the India Office Collection.

Major General Michael Tillotson for agreeing to write a Foreword.

Finally, as always, my special thanks go to Kate, Lucy and Alice for allowing me to spend more time hiding in the office, stuck on the computer, than is healthy.

I would also like to thank my CD collection for keeping me in music and to Marston's Pedigree for the relaxation qualities of beer!

WJGS

September 2008

PART ONE

Campaign Medals

1 Introduction

Although medals for campaigns prior to 1793 are recorded, they were not given to all participants. The first campaign medal given to all who took part in a campaign or battle was the Waterloo Medal. This medal, instituted in 1816, was awarded to all officers and men who took part in the battle of Waterloo on 18 June 1815 and the two minor actions at Ligny and Quatre Bras on 16 June.

Two medals for campaigns against the French that began in 1793 were instituted in 1848, but they were only awarded to those who survived to that time. The Naval General Service Medal covered the period 1793–1840 and the Military General Service Medal covered 1793–1814. It is therefore from 1793 onwards, and the campaign medals issued from then until 1945, that the following chapters propose to cover.

Due to the global nature of campaign medals and places they represent, the campaign medal chapters start with a chapter on the Naval General Service Medal 1793–1840, the Military General Service Medal 1793–1814 and the Waterloo Medal. A chapter arranged geographically for all campaigns outside of the two World Wars, then a chapter on the First World War and then one on the Second World War follow.

1.1 IDENTIFYING THE MEDAL(S)

By far the most effective way of identifying a campaign medal is to use one of the readily available guides. As long as the medal has not been tampered with and it has the correct ribbon, the combination of design and ribbon colour will enable you to identify the medal and this will in turn lead you to the appropriate archival sources.

The two most effective published sources are *British Battles and*

Medals, published by Spink, and *The Medal Yearbook*, published by Token Publishing.

1.2   CREATING MEDAL ROLLS

In order to understand the medal rolls that you will consult to verify entitlement to a particular campaign medal, it is important to understand how they were created.

Once a decision to grant a campaign medal was made, an announcement was published in Army Circulars, General Orders, Army Orders, Admiralty Week Orders, Defence Council Instructions or equivalent (dependent upon date). The announcement would state for which campaign or battle the medal was being granted, the applicable date or range of dates and, in some cases, it would also state those units that were to submit names of eligible individuals. The Order would usually advise on the format of the roll. Admiralty Fleet Orders are in ADM 182, Army Orders in WO 123 and Air Ministry Orders in AIR 72.

In order to create a roll of eligible individuals, it was necessary to look at the musters for the regiment or ship and extract from it the names of those who met the criteria laid down by the Order. A good example to illustrate how a medal roll was compiled is the muster and pay list of the 16th Light Dragoons (Lancers) for the period 1845–6 in WO 12/1279. Alongside the names of the men for the period between December 1845 and January 1846 are annotations for those eligible for the Sutlej Campaign Medal for Moodkee, Ferozeshuhur, Aliwal and Sobraon. See FIGURE 1.

Once a medal roll was completed, it was usually duplicated and a copy sent to the War Office or medal-issuing authority so that the medals could be named to each individual in accordance with the roll.

1.3   USING MEDAL ROLLS

The following three chapters list, where appropriate, all of the campaign medal rolls for campaigns from 1793 to 1945. There are thousands of medal rolls and their individual arrangement can vary from roll to roll.

Prior to the First World War, most army medal rolls are arranged by unit, in regimental order of precedence (see CHAPTER

3), with each unit arranged by rank and then name. Officers of the same rank are quite often listed by seniority (date of commission in the rank) and other ranks of the same rank are usually listed in alphabetical order.

Medal rolls of naval and marine recipients in ADM 171 are usually arranged by ship, with the crew of ships being in alphabetical order. In some rolls there are separate rolls for the Royal Marine Artillery, Royal Marine Light Infantry and Naval Brigade. This is especially so in the Egypt 1882–9 rolls. Each individual roll in ADM 171 is usually arranged in alphabetical order, with the names of the officers at the beginning of each alphabetical section and the ratings following them.

The medal rolls for the Queen's South Africa (QSA) and King's South Africa (KSA) Medals present different challenges. In many cases, more than one battalion of a given regiment served in the Boer War, and then the senior battalion is usually listed in the medal roll first. There are numerous supplementary rolls in QSA and KSA rolls for each regiment, so it is important to look through the whole roll for a given regiment as the person you seek may be on his own on a separate sheet, rather than being with the rest of his battalion.

The First World War medal rolls in WO 329 are arranged by medal and by officers and other ranks, and then by unit. Don't confuse a 1914 Star roll with a 1914/15 Star roll.

The arrangement of each roll in WO 329 can vary; some are in strict alphabetical order, others are by regimental number. Pay particular attention when converting an Army Medal Office reference into a National Archives WO 329 reference.

Many of the medal rolls do no more than confirm entitlement to a campaign medal, but in many cases they can tell you so much more, such as whether an individual was a casualty, where the medal was sent and if a duplicate medal was issued to replace a lost or stolen medal.

2   Naval General Service (1793–1840), Military General Service and Waterloo Medals

2.1   INTRODUCTION

The Naval General Service Medal 1793–1840 (NGS), Military General Service Medal 1793–1814 (MGS) and Waterloo Medal represent the most significant military campaigns fought by Britain until the First World War. These three medals and the Army of India Medal 1799–1826 are considered by many medal collectors to be classics and good examples are much sought after.

The three medals discussed in this chapter represent different research challenges from most others, simply because of the passage of time between the campaigns that the two general service medals represent and when they were actually instituted. Added to this chapter is information about the Gold Medals and Gold Crosses earned by many officers of the period covered by the NGS and MGS.

2.2   THE NAVAL GENERAL SERVICE MEDAL 1793–1840

ADM 171/1 Medal claims including the following actions: 1 June 1794, St Vincent, Camperdown, Nile, Trafalgar, 4 November 1805, St Domingo, Badere Zaffer, Martinique, Guadeloupe, Banda Neira, Lissa, Java, Algiers, Navarino, Syria

ADM 171/2 Medal claims for actions in which first lieutenants or commanders were promoted. This volume also contains particulars of certain claims for the Algiers, Navarino and Syria clasps.

ADM 171/3 Medal claims for boat actions in which the officer commanding was promoted

ADM 171/4 Medal roll for the Algiers clasp

ADM 171/5 Medal roll for the Navarino clasp

ADM 171/6 List of Officers, Men and Boys who served on HM ships in the Syria and China (1840–2) campaigns

ADM 171/7 List of claims for Medals for Service in Syria and China

ADM 171/8 Nominal roll of surviving Officers and Men entitled to clasps to the Naval General Service Medal for actions between 1793 and 1827

ADM 73/94 List of Men (Greenwich Hospital Pensioners) who have received

No. entitled to higher Pay from length of Service, after 17 years	Regimental Number	† Privates.	Muster for the Month, ended the 31 of January 1845		REMARKS, explanatory of the Rewards and Duration of Absence, and Causes of broken Periods; also specifying the precise Dates of Inlistment of Recruits, and the Date on which each Man ceased to be effective as belonging to the Corps.
			Effective and belonging to the Corps Periods		
			From	To	
54	395	Robinson Thomas	1 Jan	31 Jan	Invalid at Calcutta
1-1	297	Rose James	"	"	1 Corp. Good Conduct Pay
1-1	298	Rose Thomas	"	"	
	209	Renshaw John	"	"	1 Corp. Good Conduct Pay
1-1	315	1503 Roberts William	"	"	
1-1	316	1777 Rosbotten William	"	"	
1-1	317	484 Roaife Matthew	"	"	
1-1	318	1570 Shepherd John	"	"	
1-1	320	1274 Smith William	"	"	
1-1	321	1509 Smith Samuel	"	"	Hospital
0-0	322	865 Steer David	"	"	Good Conduct Pay Genl Hospital Loodianah
1-1	323	482 Swan Charles	"	"	
		1690 Salt Elijah	"	"	At Meerut
		309 Slendenen Henry	"	"	At Meerut
1-1		Salmon Israel	"	"	
1-1		542 Swan William	"	"	
1-0	337	1430 Tatton Charles	"	28 "	Killed in action at Alliwal
1-1	338	787 Self Christr	"	31 "	
1-1	339	1452 Sell George	"	"	
1-1	340	1330 Sergeant William	"	"	
1-0		1188 Shepland William	"	"	Genl Hospital Loodianah
1-1		555 Simpson George	"	"	
		1336 Snook George	"	"	Lance Corporal
1-1	349	1357 Salmon Samuel	"	"	
1-1	350	762 Soyer John	"	"	
1-1	351	1171 Scott Edward	"	"	Good Conduct Pay 1 Corp
0-0	352	555 Shoesmith William	"	"	Genl Hospital Loodianah
1-1	353	1001 Spencer William	"	"	Good Conduct Pay 1 Corp
1-1	354	1215 Steele Isaac	"	"	Good Conduct Pay
1-1	355	1465 Stevenson Thomas	"	"	
1-0	356	1362 St George William	"	28 "	Killed in action at Alliwal
1-1	357	1269 Stone Thomas	"	31 "	
1-0		377 Spencer Owen	"	"	Genl Hospital Loodianah
1-1		488 Seanor George	"	"	Farrier
1-1	324	1226 Shaw Samuel	"	"	

* In the case of every Soldier received as a Transfer from another Regiment, his Number in that Regiment

† The words "Good Conduct Pay" to be inserted in the Column of Remarks against the Names of such as are in receipt of Good Conduct Pay.

1400. Sept. 1844.   C. B.—Repeated Sheet.

Medals 1848–9. This roll gives the clasp(s) a pensioner received and their hospital number.

Many of the other records in ADM 73 concerning pensioners are annotated with their NGS entitlements.

Naval General Service Medal Rolls 1793–1840 by K.J. Douglas Morris (1982)
Alphabetical Naval General Service Medal 1793–1840 by C.S. Message (1995)

2.3   THE MILITARY GENERAL SERVICE MEDAL 1793–1814

WO 100/1 Officers: Staff and regimental including Royal Navy
WO 100/2 Officers: Staff and regimental
WO 100/3 NCOs and Men: Royal Horse Guards and Cavalry of the Line
WO 100/4 NCOs and Men: Royal Artillery, Sappers and Miners
WO 100/5 NCOs and Men: 1st and 3rd Foot Guards, 1st–15th Foot
WO 100/6 NCOs and Men: 20th–43rd Foot
WO 100/7 NCOs and Men: 44th–74th Foot
WO 100/8 NCOs and Men: 76th–97th Foot
WO 100/9 NCOs and Men: Infantry A–Y. This volume is arranged by name and appears to contain those missed off earlier rolls.
WO 100/10 NCOs and Men: Royal York Rangers, Upper and Lower Militia, King's German Legion, Wagon Train, etc.
WO 100/11 NCOs and Men: Various Corps
WO 100/12 EGYPT (clasp): Cavalry and Foot Regiments in numerical order, The Queen's German Regiment of Foot, Ancient Irish Regiment of Fencibles, Regiment of Maltese Pioneers
WO 7/40 This file is just described as Medals (1847–8), but it actually contains correspondence concerning appeals relating to the Military General Service Medal.
WO 162/94 Board of General Officers on Claims for Medals: minutes of proceedings 1847–57. Concerning applications for the Military General Service Medals and others
WO 4/751 Medals 1849–51. This file contains Board of General Officers Out Letters concerning the Military General Service Medal. Most of the letters are to the next of kin of the applicant, who died during the application process, or letters to army pensioners about the medal.

FIG 1. (facing) *Muster and Pay List of the 16th Light Dragoons (Lancers) for January–March 1846. This muster is interesting because it has been used to compile the medal roll for those present at the battles of Aliwal and Sobraon as recorded at the extreme left hand side* [WO 12/1279].

The Military General Service Medal 1793–1814 by Col O. N. Kingsley Foster
(1947)
The Military General Service Medal 1793–1814 by A. L. T. Mullen (1990)

2.4   THE WATERLOO MEDAL

WO 100/14 General Staff, 1st and 2nd Life Guards, Royal Horse Guards, 1st
Dragoon Guards, 1st, 2nd, 7th, 10th–13th, 15th, 16th, 18th and 23rd
Dragoons and Hussars, Royal Waggon Train, Royal Horse Artillery, Royal
Artillery, Artillery Drivers, 1st, 2nd and 3rd Foot Guards.

WO 100/15/1 3/1, 4, 3/14, 23, 2/25, 1/27, 2/27, 28 and 2/30 Regiments of Foot

WO 100/15/2 4, 5, 2/59, 2/69, 71, 2/73, 2/78, 79, 91, 92, 1/95, 2/95, 3/95 1st
Rifle Brigade, 2nd Rifle Brigade, 3rd Rifle Brigade, Royal Staff Corps, King's
German Legion – 1st and 2nd Light Dragoons, 1st and 3rd Hussars, 1st and
2nd Light Infantry, 1st–5th and 8th Line Battalions, Artillery.

WO 100/372 List of German Officers and Soldiers and Sailors who fought for
the British prior to and at Waterloo

MINT 16/112 Royal Mint Waterloo Medal roll

WO 1/206 Whilst being described as 'Medal Rolls, regimental', this piece of
WO 1 actually contains lists of all the British Army officers who were
present at Waterloo. It appears very much that this volume was used to
create the Waterloo Roll by Dalton.

Waterloo Medal Roll (Naval and Military Press, 1992)

2.5   GOLD MEDALS

Many of the actions for which a clasp was created for the Naval
General Service Medal were only created because an officer earned
either a Large or Small Naval Gold Medal. These actions were
known as 'Gold Medal' actions and this term is used in the catalogue of ADM 171.

Officers of the Army were not to be left out; some received
Large or Small Army Gold Medals. A small number of officers
earned an Army Gold Cross.

It is easy to find the recipients of Gold Medals and Crosses, as
they are usually annotated as such in the Army List or Navy List.
However, there are a number of sources that will provide you with
the reasons why an individual received a Gold Medal.

A roll of Army Gold Crosses and Medals can be found in WO
100/16, but further information is available. If you look at List
and Index Society Volume LIII (53), *War Office and Associated*

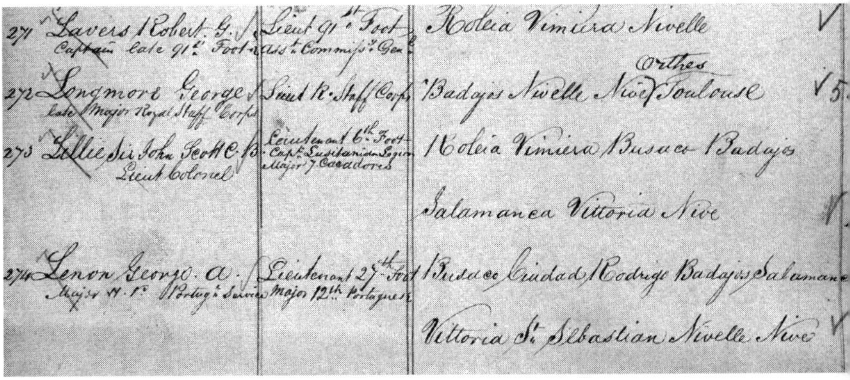
271 Lavers Robert G. Captain late 91st Foot | Lieut 91st Foot Ass.t Commiss.y Gen. | Roleia Vimiera Nivelle
272 Longmore George late Major Royal Staff Corps | Lieut R. Staff Corps | Badajos Nivelle Nive Orthes Toulouse
273 Lillie Sir John Scott C.B. Lieut Colonel | Lieutenant 6th Foot Capt. Lusitanian Legion Major 7 Caçadores | Roleia Vimiera Busaco Badajos Salamanca Vittoria Nive
274 Lenon George A. Major H.P. Portug.e Service | Lieutenant 27th Foot Major 12th Portuguese | Busaco Ciudad Rodrigo Badajos Salamanca Vittoria St Sebastian Nivelle Nive

Fig 2. *The Military General Service Medal roll entry for Sir John Scott Lillie* [WO 100/2]

Records, pages 165–6 under the heading 'Medals: Peninsular War: Talavera, grant of, and list of officers', you will find references to WO 1/254 folio 515, 527. This is the first list of officers who received Gold Medals, and the WO 1, WO 3 and WO 6 references are full of information.

Details of Naval Gold Medal recipients require research using ADM 12 and ADM 1. See CHAPTER 25 on Research Techniques for a full explanation of how to use ADM 12.

2.6 CASE STUDY
John Scott Lillie

Sir John Scott Lillie initially saw service in the Peninsular War with the 6th Foot, including the actions at Roleia and Vimeria in 1808. Returning to action at Busaco in 1810, Sir John was to see action in a number of different battles and engagements in Spain and southern France between 1810 and 1814, not only with the British Army, but also with our Portuguese allies with the 6th Cacaadores and the Lusitanian Legion.

According to his obituary in *The Times*, Sir John Lillie also served at Albuhera, although this is not confirmed on his medal roll entry in WO 100/2 folio 52. The medal roll entry does confirm clasps for *BADAJOZ*, *SALAMANCA*, *VITTORIA* and *NIVE*. See

FIGURE 2. For his service in the Peninsular War, Sir John also received a Peninsular Gold Cross and this was confirmed in his entry in the Army List of 1851.

Sir John Scott Lillie died in 1868. A Military General Service Medal 1793–1814 with the same seven clasps as Sir John's can be seen in PLATE 1.

3 Campaign Medals by Operational Theatre

3.1 INTRODUCTION

Millions of campaign medals have been awarded for service all over the world. Many individuals saw service in more than one continent and many years apart. When you look at a group of medals belonging to one recipient, it is possible to see where in the world that individual has been. Some served all over the world, some predominantly in Africa, some predominantly in India.

To aid research, all the information relating to the campaign medals rolls earned in one continent or geographical region is grouped together. What follows are the appropriate references to each campaign medal. The medals are arranged in chronological order in order of the campaign. Some of the general service medals for service in India or Africa covered wide date ranges and, in many cases, other campaign medals were instituted between the first and last dates of a general service medal. For example the Indian General Service Medal 1845–95 actually covered campaigns between 1849 and 1895, between which the Indian Mutiny Medal 1857–8 and the Second Afghan Medal 1878–80 were also awarded, many men receiving all three or a combination of two of the three.

3.2 AFRICA
South Africa Medal 1834–53
ADM 171/18 Naval and Marine personnel of HM ships *Castor*, *Dee*, *Hermes*, *Rhadamanthus* and *Styx*

WO 100/17 7th Dragoons, 12th Lancers, Royal Artillery, Royal Engineers,
    Cape Mounted Rifles, 2nd Foot, 6th Foot, 12th Foot, 27th Foot, 43rd Foot,
    45th Foot, 60th Foot, 72nd –75th Foot, 90th Foot, 91st Foot, Rifle Brigade
    and Miscellaneous Corps.
    This medal roll is not complete and it is suggested that you consult *The
    South Africa 1853 Medal Roll* by Gordon Everson (Samson, 1978).

Abyssinia Medal 1867–8

ADM 171/36 Naval and Marine personnel
WO 100/19 A Royal Artillery roll for this medal can be found on pages 3–90.
WO 100/43 Staff, Intelligence, Guards, Royal Artillery, Royal Engineers,
    Infantry, Corps, Foreign Officers, India Office returns and Miscellaneous
L/MIL/5/108–109 Indian Army

Ashantee Medal 1873–4

ADM 171/37 contains the roll of the Naval Brigade who served ashore and
    qualified for the clasp Coomassie and the roll for HMS ships that were on
    the coast.
CO 96/115 contains the medal roll for the Armed Forces Police.
WO 100/19 A Royal Artillery roll for this medal can be found on pages
    363–8.
WO 100/42 Royal Artillery
WO 100/44 Staff, Special Service, Royal Artillery, Royal Engineers, 2nd/23rd
    Foot, 42nd Foot, 2nd Rifle Brigade, 1st and 2nd West India Regiments,
    Medical Department, Army Service Corps, Armourer Sergeants, Russell's
    Regiment, Officers of Wood's Regiment and Naval Brigade

South Africa Medal 1877–9

ADM 171/40 Roll of the Naval Brigade who served in the Basuto and Zulu
    Wars
WO 100/19 A Royal Artillery roll for this medal can be found on pages
    353–62 and 389–449.
WO 100/46 General Officers and Staff, 2nd Dragoon Guards, 17th Lancers,
    Royal Artillery, Royal Engineers, 3rd Foot, 4th Foot, 13th Foot, 21st Foot
    and 24th Foot
WO 100/47 57th Foot, 58th Foot, 60th Foot, 80th Foot, 88th Foot, 90th
    Foot, 91st Foot, 94th Foot, 99th Foot and Miscellaneous Corps and
    Regiments
WO 100/48 Colonial Corps
WO 100/49 Colonial Corps
WO 100/50 Medal Rolls, Returned Lists, Colonial Corps (A–W)

WO 100/54 Royal Artillery

Casualty Roll for the Zulu and Basuto War South Africa 1877–79 by I.T.
    Tavender (Hayward, 1985)

South African War Medal 1877–8–9: The Medal Roll by D. R. Forsyth

*The Noble 24th, Biographical Records of the 24th Regiment in the Zulu
    War and the South African Campaigns 1877–79* by N. Holme
    (Savannah, 2000)

Egypt Medal 1882–9

The Egypt Medal comes with two different reverses. Medals earned in
1882 have the year below the Sphinx (Dated Reverse), those earned in
1884 or later do not (Undated Reverse). When researching an Egypt
Medal, it is important to note the reverse variety as this will enable you
start your research in the most appropriate place. There are also a
number of rules regarding which clasps must appear in combination
with another and which clasps should only appear with a Dated
Reverse medal.

ADM 116/40 This Admiralty case file contains information concerning
    a number of civilians under Naval authority who were awarded the Egypt
    Medal 1882. The file also has information about a small number
    of Undated Reverse Egypt Medals for service in 1884 awarded to civilians.

——Egypt 1882 Campaign

ADM 171/41 contains the medal roll for all Royal Navy Vessels that took part
    in the Egyptian War of 1882. The roll is in alphabetical order by name of
    ship. There are also separate rolls for the Royal Marine Light Infantry and
    Royal Marine Artillery. Entries with the letter 'S' on them denote that the
    individual also received a Khedive's Star.

   The rolls of the ships that took part in the bombardment of Alexandria
on 11 July 1882 are annotated with the entitlement to the ALEXANDRIA 11TH
JULY clasp. The ships that took part were HM ships *Alexandra*, *Beacon*,
Bittern, *Condor*, *Cygnet*, *Decoy*, *Hecla*, *Helicon*, *Inflexible*, *Invincible*,
Monarch, *Penelope*, *Sultan*, *Superb* and *Temeraire*.

   Those officers and men of the Royal Navy, Royal Marine Light Infantry
and Royal Marine Artillery who took part in the battle of Tel-el-Kebir on 13
September 1882 were entitled to the clasp TEL-EL-KEBIR, and the rolls are
annotated with details of entitlement to this clasp.

   This medal roll also contains the names of those Masters of a number of
merchant vessels used to move materiel and men to Egypt. There is also a
roll of a number of civilians who were awarded the medal for service in
support of operations between 11 July and 13 September 1882.

L/MIL/7/9981 Grant of Egypt 1882 Medal to Officers and Men of the
Amberwitch and *Tenasserin*

WO 100/42 Royal Artillery

WO 100/54 Royal Artillery

WO 100/55 Staff, Cavalry, Guards and Miscellaneous

WO 100/56 Royal Artillery and Royal Engineers

WO 100/57 2nd Grenadier Guards, 2nd Coldstream Guards, 1st Scots
Guards, 2nd Royal Irish Regiment, 2nd Duke of Cornwall's Light Infantry,
1st Royal Sussex Regiment and 1st South Staffordshire Regiment

WO 100/58 1st Royal Highlanders, 2nd Derbyshire Regiment, 1st Berkshire
Regiment, 1st Royal West Kent Regiment, 1st Shropshire Light Infantry, 3rd
King's Royal Rifle Corps and 1st Manchester Regiment

WO 100/59 2nd Manchester Regiment, 2nd York and Lancaster Regiment, 1st
and 2nd Battalions Seaforth Highlanders, 1st Gordon Highlanders, 1st
Cameron Highlanders, 1st Royal Irish Fusiliers and Miscellaneous

WO 100/60 Mounted Infantry, Commissariat and Transport Corps including
Staff and 2nd, 5th, 8th, 12th, 15th and 17th Companies, Miscellaneous,
Army Veterinary Department, Army Pay Department, Ordnance, Military
Police and Army Post Office

WO 100/61 Signallers, Army Medical Department, Army Hospital Corps,
Chaplains, Scripture Readers, India Contingent, Malta Transport,
Miscellaneous, Clergymen, Civilians and Servants to officers

L/MIL/5/125 Indian Army

——Sudan Campaigns 1884–9

Many men who saw service in Egypt in 1882 went on to see further
service between 1884 and 1889, and earned additional clasps to their
medal awarded for service in 1882. Some men qualified for an Egypt
Medal in 1884 or 1885 and they too could have gone on to earn
additional clasps at a later date. The medal at this time may also be
called the Sudan or Soudan Medal and this frequently appears on
service records.

The following War Office medal rolls are for those men who received an
Undated medal with or without clasps or clasps to Dated medals for the
following operations: SUAKIN 1884, EL TEB, TAMAAI, EL TEB TAMAAI, THE NILE
1884–85, ABU KLEA, KIRBEKAN, SUAKIN 1885, TOFREK, GEMAIZAH 1888, TOSKI
1889. The Catalogue of each of the Admiralty medal roll shows which
specific clasps they record.

ADM 171/42 Medal roll of Naval and Marine personnel who qualified for no-
clasp medals and also for the clasps SUAKIN 1884, EL TEB, TAMAAI and EL TEB
TAMAAI

The clasp SUAKIN 1884 should only be found on a Dated Reverse Egypt Medal.

The arrangement of this roll is such that a man already in possession of a Dated Reverse Egypt Medal will be marked with either a line indicating a no-clasp medal from the 1882 campaign, an A indicating an individual who received an *ALEXANDRIA 11TH JULY* clasp to an 1882 medal or T indicating an individual who received the clasp *TEL-EL-KEBIR*. Men receiving a medal for the first time are denoted as such by having a medal number.

WO 100/42 A Royal Artillery roll for campaigns in 1884 showing entitlement to the clasps *SUAKIN 1884*, *EL TEB*, *TAMAAI* and *EL TEB TAMAAI* can be found on pages 2–10.

WO 100/62 Staff, 1st and 2nd Life Guards, Royal Horse Guards, 2nd–5th and 7th Dragoon Guards, 1st and 2nd Dragoons, 3rd and 4th Hussars, 5th Lancers, 7th, 8th, 10th–11th Hussars, 12th Lancers, 14th and 15th Hussars, 16th and 17th Lancers, 18th and 21st Hussars, Miscellaneous

WO 100/63 G/B Royal Horse Artillery, Royal Artillery Staff, 1/2 and 7/1 London Division, 1/1 Southern Division, 6/1 Scottish Division, 2/1 South Irish Division, North Irish Division

WO 100/64 8, 10, 11, 17, 24, 26 Companies Royal Engineers, including Field Park, Balloon Detachment, Telegraph Section, Miscellaneous

ADM 171/43 Medal roll of Naval and Marine recipients of the clasps *THE NILE 1884–85*, *ABU KLEA*, *KIRBEKAN*, *SUAKIN 1885* and *TOFREK*

This is the first Admiralty medal roll that shows a man's service number, which makes tracing a service record so much easier. Once again, this roll has certain characteristics that require explanation. Men receiving the medal for the first time have a medal number, those already in possession of a no-bar medal have a line and those in possession of an earlier medal with a clasp have a letter code denoting the clasp. There is however some inconsistency about which letter was used. Sometimes it was that for the earliest clasp, sometimes for the most recent. The letters found include A for *ALEXANDRIA 11TH JULY*, T for *TEL-EL-KEBIR*, S84 for *SUAKIN 1884*, E or ET for *EL TEB*, ETT for *EL TEB TAMAAI*, S85 for *SUAKIN 1885*.

The clasp *ABU KLEA* or *KIRBEKAN* must always be accompanied by the *NILE 1884–85* clasp. The clasp *TOFREK* must always be accompanied by the *SUAKIN 1885* clasp.

WO 100/42 A Royal Artillery roll for campaigns in 1884–5 showing entitlement to the clasps *NILE 1884–85*, *ABU KLEA*, *KIRBEKAN*, *SUAKIN 1885* and *TOFREK* can be found on pages 12–42.

Many of the following regiments did not take part in the campaigns as whole units, but they provided small detachments or odd men to supplement the forces taking part.

WO 100/65 Staff, 20th Hussars, 24th Coy RE, 3rd Grenadier Guards, Coldstream Guards, Scots Guards, East Kent R, Royal Lancaster R, Royal Warwicks, Northumberland Fusiliers, Royal Fusiliers, Liverpool R, Norfolk

R, Suffolk R, Somerset Light Infantry, West Yorkshire R, East Yorkshire R, Leicester R, Royal Irish R, Yorkshire R, Lancashire Fusiliers, Royal Scots Fusiliers, Cheshire R, Royal Welsh Fusiliers, King's Own Scottish Borderers, Scottish Rifles, Royal Inniskilling Fusiliers, Gloucester R, Worcester R, East Surrey R, Duke of Cornwall's Light Infantry, West Riding R, Border R, Royal Sussex R, Hampshire R, South Staffordshire Regiment, South Lancashire R, Welsh R

WO 100/66 Royal Highlanders, 2nd Oxfordshire Light Infantry, 2nd Essex R, Derby R, Loyal North Lancashire R, Royal Berkshire R, Royal West Kent R, Shropshire Light Infantry, 2nd Middlesex R, 1st–3rd King's Royal Rifle Corps, Manchester R, North Staffordshire R, York and Lancaster R, 2nd Durham Light Infantry, 1st–2nd Gordon Highlanders, Cameron Highlanders, 2nd Royal Irish Rifles, 2nd Royal Irish Fusiliers, 2nd Argyll and Sutherland Highlanders, Leinster R, Royal Munster Fusiliers, 2nd Royal Dublin Fusiliers, 4th Rifle Brigade.

WO 100/67 Mounted Infantry, Army Signallers, Commissariat and Transport Corps, Medical Staff Corps, Army Hospital Corps, Army Medical Department, National Aid Society, Ordnance Store Corps, Veterinary Department, Army Pay Department, Chaplains, Interpreters, Military Police, Army Post Office, Royal Malta Fencible Artillery

WO 100/68 Indian Contingent (European Officers and Men), Volunteer Rifle Corps and Transport Department, New South Wales Contingent, Canadian Voyageur Contingent, Bashi Bazookz, Kroomen, Shaggichs, Lucas and Aird's employees, Railway and Postal Staff, River Transport employees, Civil Engineers, Servants, Camel and Mule Drivers, List of Egyptian unclaimed medals

WO 100/71 Egyptian Army (including attached British Army personnel), Staff, Cavalry, Artillery, 1st–5th Egyptian Battalions

WO 100/72 Egyptian Army (including attached British Army personnel), 6–8 Egyptian Battalions, 9th–13th Sudanese Battalions, Camel Corps, Artillery, Cavalry, Haifa District Staff (Europeans), HQ Staff (Europeans)

The Abu Klea Medal Rolls by J. V. Webb (privately published, 1981)

ADM 171/49 Naval and Marine personnel of HM ships *Racer* and *Starling* who received the GEMAIZAH 1888 clasp

As with the medal rolls in ADM 171/42 and 43, those men who received a medal for an earlier campaign are annotated as appropriate.

Khedive's Stars 1882–91

By default all those men and women who received an Egypt Medal for campaigns between 1882 and 1889 would have received an appropriately dated Bronze Khedive's Star. Sometimes the preceding Egypt Medal rolls are annotated to the effect that the roll is for both the Egypt

Medal and the Khedive's Star. This is especially so for the Army. The Admiralty rolls frequently have the word Star, or S, and 'sent' annotated in the margins.

ADM 171/50 This is the Admiralty medal roll for those recipients of the Khedive's Star for 1891 and those who also received the *TOKAR* clasp.

East and West Africa Medal 1887–1900

The East and West Africa Medal is frequently called the Ashanti Medal 1887–1900. Whilst the design of the medal and ribbon are identical, the medal was for campaigns in various parts of the African continent.

Many of the following medal rolls cover more than one clasp. In the case of the War Office rolls, WO 100/76 appears more than once. The medal rolls are listed here with the Admiralty and War Office rolls for the same campaigns together.

ADM 171/45 Medal roll for Naval and Marine personnel employed or engaged in various operations for which the following clasps were awarded: *1887–8, 1891–2* and *1892*

WO 100/76 Medal roll for the following clasps issued by the War Office: *1887–8, 1891–2* and *1892*, to the following units:

1st West Indies Regiment, Lagos Hausa Force, Gambia Police, 2nd West India Regiment, Gold Coast Constabulary, Sierra Leone Steamer *Countess of Derby*. Personnel of the following units can also be found in this roll; Royal Artillery, Royal Engineers, 15th and 21st Hussars, Grenadier Guards, Lancashire Fusiliers, Royal Scots Fusiliers, Northamptonshire R, East Yorkshire R, Royal Irish Fusiliers, Scottish Rifles, Army Ordnance Corps, Army Service Corps, 7th King's Royal Rifle Corps, Medical Staff, Commissariat, Civil Police, Political Department, Government Officials, Interpreters, Messengers

ADM 171/46 Medal roll for Naval and Marine personnel employed in operations for which the following clasps or the M'Wele inscription were granted: *WITU 1890, LIWONDI 1893, WITU AUGUST 1893, JUBA RIVER 1893, LAKE NYASSA 1893, GAMBIA 1894, BENIN RIVER 1894, BRASS RIVER 1895, M'WELE 1895–6, BENIN 1897, 1897–98*

FO 83/1795 contains correspondence from personnel employed in East and West Africa who were missed off the War Office medal rolls.

ADM 171/47 Is a further roll for *M'WELE 1895–6* for the 24th Bombay Native Infantry and additional Army and Naval personnel.

FO 83/1798 This Foreign Office file contains applications and correspondence for the East and West Africa Medal with the clasps *BRASS RIVER 1895* and *BENIN 1897* to some FO employees who were missed by the War Office.

WO 100/76 contains a short list of those Army personnel who were entitled to *BENIN 1894, BRASS RIVER 1895, M'WELE 1895–6* and *BENIN 1897*, which came under Admiralty authority.

WO 100/76 War Office medal roll for clasp NIGER 1897 to the following: Royal Niger Constabulary and miscellaneous claims from Coldstream Guards, Scots Guards, Royal Horse Artillery, 3rd Hussars, Royal Artillery, Norfolk R, Royal Fusiliers, South Wales Borderers, Derby R, Essex R, Royal West Surrey R, Bedford R, Leicester R, Loyal North Lancashire R, Seaforth Highlanders, Royal Irish Rifles, Leinster R, 4th Lincoln R, 3rd Middlesex R, Royal Muster Fusiliers, East Yorkshire R, Pembroke Artillery

WO 100/76 War Office roll for DAWKITA 1897

WO 100/83 War Office medal roll for the clasps 1896–98, 1897–98, 1898, 1899 to Royal Artillery, Royal Engineers, Miscellaneous British infantry, Army Service Corps, Army Medical Department, West India Regiment, West African Frontier Force, Niger Battalion, Northern Nigeria Regiment, Gold Coast Regiment, Gold Coast Constabulary, Lagos Hausa Force

ADM 171/48 Medal roll for Naval and Marine personnel for HM ships *Alecto*, *Blonde* and *Fox* who received the clasp SIERRA LEONE 1898–99

WO 100/92 War Office medal roll for the clasp SIERRA LEONE 1898–99 to Staff, Royal Artillery, Royal Engineers, 1st, 3rd and 4th West India Regiment, West Africa Regiment, Sierra Leone and Waterloo Volunteers, Sierra Leone Frontier Police, Miscellaneous British Infantry, Naval Contingent, Army Service Corps, Army Ordnance Corps, Army Medical Department

WO 100/92 War Office roll for the clasp 1900 to the Northern Nigeria Regiment and some applications from the Royal Horse Artillery

WO 100/388 contains a roll of returned medals of the 1st–3rd West India Regiment for the period 1887–1900.

British South Africa Company Medal 1890–7

WO 100/42 Royal Artillery rolls for Matabeleland and Mashonaland can be found on pages 180–1.

WO 100/77 contains another War Office roll for the campaigns in Matabeleland 1893, Rhodesia 1896 and Mashonaland 1897.

British South Africa Company Co Medal 1890–97 by D. R. Forsyth

Central Africa Medal 1891–8

FO 83/1797 A Foreign Office file concerning applications for the above medal

WO 100/42 contains a roll for members of the Royal Artillery who received this medal.

WO 100/76 contains the War Office medal roll for recipients of this medal from the Indian Staff Corps, Royal Artillery, Royal Engineers, Royal Horse Guards, 11th Bengal Lancers, 1st–3rd Lancers Hyderabad Contingent, Grenadier Guards, Coldstream Guards, Scots Guards, Lancashire Fusiliers, Worcester R, Manchester R, Derby R, Oxford Light Infantry, King's Royal

Rifle Corps, Royal Welsh Fusiliers, North Staffordshire R, West Yorkshire R, Rifle Brigade, 4th Middlesex R, Connaught Rangers, Leinster R, King's Own R, 1st, 21st, 22nd, 24th, 26th, 30th–32nd Punjab Infantry, 14th, 15th, 19th, 23rd, 25th–29th Bengal Infantry, 1st, 4th, 15th, 35th, 36th, 45th Sikh Infantry, Indian Medical Department, 1st–2nd British Central Africa Rifles, Uganda Rifles, Civilian Volunteers, Uganda Chiefs, Royal Navy personnel.

Ashanti Star 1896

WO 100/42 Royal Artillery medal roll on page 149 only

WO 100/79 Medal roll created by the War Office for recipients of the Ashanti Star 1896 from the following units: Staff, Royal Horse Artillery, Royal Artillery, Royal Engineers, 5th Lancers, 13th, 15th and 21st Hussars, Grenadier Guards, Coldstream Guards, Scots Guards, Northumberland Fusiliers, 2nd Devon R, King's Own Yorkshire Light Infantry, 2nd West Yorkshire R, 2nd South Staffordshire R, 2nd Shropshire Light Infantry, 3rd–4th King's Royal Rifle Corps, 2nd Royal Irish Fusiliers, Leinster R, Royal Munster Fusiliers, 2nd Rifle Brigade, Army Pay Department, Army Service Corps, Army Medical Department, Nursing Sisters, Army Ordnance Corps, 2nd West India R, Hausa Force, Gold Coast Constabulary, Clerks, Chaplains, Public Works

Ashanti 1895–96 by Ian McInnes and Mark Fraser (Picton Publishing, 1987)

Queen's Sudan Medal 1896–8

WO 100/42 A Royal Artillery roll showing entitlement to both the Queen's and Khedive's Sudan Medal can be found on pages 183–7.

WO 100/80 Royal Navy, Royal Marine Artillery, Staff, 21st Lancers, Royal Artillery, Royal Engineers, Grenadier Guards, Northumberland Fusiliers, Royal Warwickshire Regiment and the Lincoln Regiment

WO 100/81 Lancashire Fusiliers, North Staffordshire Regiment, Seaforth Highlanders, Cameron Highlanders, Royal Irish Fusiliers, 2nd Rifle Brigade, Army Service Corps, Royal Army Medical Corps, Veterinary Department, Army Ordnance Corps, Army Pay Corps, Chaplains and Interpreters

WO 100/82 Indian Contingent and Miscellaneous Corps

WO 100/389 Medals returned from the Northumberland Fusiliers

Khedive's Sudan Medal 1896–1908

ADM 171/51 Admiralty medal roll of Naval and Marine recipients covering the clasps HAFIR, SUDAN 1897, THE ATBARA, KHARTOUM, SUDAN 1899, BAHR-EL-GHAZAL 1900–02

WO 100/406 War Office roll for the clasps TALODI, NYIMA and KATIFA

East and Central Africa Medal 1897–9

FO 83/2001–2004 These Foreign Office files contain applications and
correspondence concerning the above medal.

WO 100/90 War Office medal roll of the medal including those with clasps
LUBWAS, UGANDA 1897–98, 1898 and *UGANDA 1899*. The majority of the
recipients were Indian or African troops, but with European officers. The
roll also includes local officials and a number of women and clergy.

Ashanti Medal 1900

WO 100/93 War Office roll including the clasp *KUMASSI* for recipients from
Special Service Officers, Governor and Staff, Royal Artillery, Royal
Engineers, Miscellaneous British Infantry, West India Regiment, Indian
Army Units, Gold Coast Regiment and Constabulary, King's African Rifles,
Central Africa Regiment, West Africa Regiment, Northern and Southern
Nigeria Regiments, Lagos Battalion, Sierra Leone Frontier Police, Medical
Staff, Civilians and Miscellaneous Claims, Native Kings and Chiefs

Queen's Mediterranean Medal 1899–1902

WO 100/368 contains the medal roll for those militia units who served at
Gibraltar, on Malta and in Egypt between 1899 and 1902 to relieve the
regular units so that they may proceed to the war in South Africa. Units
include the Northumberland Fusiliers, Loyal North Lancashire Regiment,
West Yorkshire Regiment, Royal West Kent Regiment, King's Own
Yorkshire Light Infantry, Seaforth Highlanders and Royal Munster Fusiliers.

Queen's South Africa Medal 1899–1902

ADM 171/53 contains the rolls of Royal Navy ships that served in South
African waters, together with rolls for the Natal Naval Volunteers,
Transport Staff, Harbour Board Officials, Cape Hospital, Cape Victualling
Yard, Marines who served with the Army, RIMS *Clive*, RIMS *Canning*

ADM 171/54 contains the rolls of those naval officers and ratings who served
ashore

The Queen's South Africa Medal to the Royal Navy and Royal Marines by W.
H. Fevyer and J. W. Wilson (Spink and Son, 1983)

Although the specific clasp entitlement of each individual cannot
be guaranteed without looking at the following medal rolls or any
surviving record of service, pages 155–8 of *The Medal Collector* by
Stanley Johnson (London, 1921) contain a useful breakdown of
the individual clasps qualified for by each cavalry and infantry regiment of the British Army.

WO 100/112 Cavalry: 1st and 2nd Life Guards, Royal Horse Guards, 1st–3rd Dragoon Guards
WO 100/113 Cavalry: 4th–7th Dragoon Guards
WO 100/114 Cavalry: 1st and 2nd Dragoons, 3rd and 4th Hussars
WO 100/115 Cavalry: 5th Lancers, 6th Dragoons, 7th and 8th Hussars
WO 100/116 Cavalry: 9th Lancers, 10th and 11th Hussars
WO 100/117 Cavalry: 13th Lancers, 13th–15th Hussars
WO 100/118 Cavalry: 16th and 17th Lancers, 18th Hussars
WO 100/119 Cavalry: 19th and 20th Hussars, 21st Lancers

In order to know in which battalion a member of the Imperial Yeomanry (IY) served, it is necessary to know his company and if at all possible his service number. By far the easiest way to do this is to consult Kevin Asplin's excellent alphabetical index to the Imperial Yeomanry, copies of which can be found in the library and behind the staff desk in the Research Enquiries Room at the National Archives. The index will give you name, number and IY unit(s) and medal entitlement. Once you have the company you can look at the appropriate medal roll in wo 100/120–136.

WO 100/120 Imperial Yeomanry: 1st and 2nd Battalions [1]
WO 100/121 Imperial Yeomanry: 3rd and 4th Battalions
WO 100/122 Imperial Yeomanry: 5th and 6th Battalions
WO 100/123 Imperial Yeomanry: 7th and 8th Battalions
WO 100/124 Imperial Yeomanry: 9th and 10th Battalions
WO 100/125 Imperial Yeomanry: 11th and 12th Battalions
WO 100/126 Imperial Yeomanry: 13th–15th Battalions
WO 100/127 Imperial Yeomanry: 16th–18th Battalions
WO 100/128 Imperial Yeomanry: 19th–22nd Battalions
WO 100/129 Imperial Yeomanry: 23rd–30th Battalions
WO 100/130 Imperial Yeomanry: 31st and 32nd Battalions, Lovat's Scouts, Staffs, Base Depots, Unposted, Hospital Staffs

Many members of the Imperial Yeomanry moved from one company to another and were missed off the medal rolls. What follows are the individual claims submitted by these individuals.

WO 100/131 Imperial Yeomanry: Individual Claims, Officers
WO 100/132 Imperial Yeomanry: Individual Claims, NCOs and Men A–D
WO 100/133 Imperial Yeomanry: Individual Claims, NCOS and Men E–J

WO 100/134 Imperial Yeomanry: Individual Claims, NCOS and Men K–O
WO 100/135 Imperial Yeomanry: Individual Claims, NCOs and Men P–S
WO 100/136 Imperial Yeomanry: Individual Claims, NCOs and Men T–Z

The majority of the Queen's South Africa Medal rolls are arranged by unit, with the cavalry and infantry regiments being easily identified.

However, the medal rolls for the Royal Artillery are arranged by battery and unless you know the battery in which an individual served, a search of the medal rolls will be lengthy. There is, however, a way of finding the appropriate battery. WO 100/137 and 138 are described as 'Nominal Rolls of issue of medals to Officers and Men of the Royal Artillery', and they are, in fact, indexes to the remaining rolls in WO 100/139–146. WO 100/137 and 138 are nominal lists of officers and men, arranged in alphabetical order, providing name, rank, number and Royal Artillery unit (RA), Royal Field Artillery (RFA) and Royal Garrison Artillery (RGA). Once you have found a man within these rolls, you can then look at the medal roll specifically for that unit.

WO 100/139 RA: Staff, A, G, J, L–U, X–Z, AA and BB Batteries, Riding
    Establishment, A and B Depots and Miscellaneous RHA
WO 100/140 RFA: Staff, 2, 4, 5, 7–10, 13, 14 and 17 Batteries
WO 100/141 RFA: 18–21, 26, 28, 37–39, 42–44 Batteries
WO 100/142 RFA: 48, 53, 60–69 and 73 Batteries
WO 100/143 RFA: 74–79, 81–86 Batteries
WO 100/144 RFA: 87–89, 94, 96, 99, 101, 104–107, 110, 115, 117, 119,
    120, 129, 131, 135, 141, 142, 145, 149–151 Batteries, Maxim (Pom-Poms),
    Ammunition Columns and Park, Depots, Mounted Rifles and
    Miscellaneous
WO 100/145 RGA: Maxim Battery, 31, 56, 57, 62, 63, 66, 68, 84, 85, 91, 92,
    97–100 Companies – with Index
WO 100/146 RGA: 101–103 Companies, 4, 6 and 10 Batteries Mountain
    Division, Staff Depots, New Zealand Battery, Militia Volunteers and
    Miscellaneous

In 1902, the last year of the Boer War, the Royal Garrison Artillery (RGA) was reorganized and this caused the RGA medal rolls to be arranged by the new designation, but with the old unit designation. The following is a key of new to old.

Many officers and men of the Royal Artillery had to submit individual claims for their Queen's South Africa Medals.

WO 100/147 RA: Individual Claims, Officers
WO 100/148 RA: Individual Claims, NCOs and Men A–B
WO 100/149 RA: individual Claims, NCOs and Men C–D
WO 100/150 RA: Individual Claims, NCOs and Men E–H
WO 100/151 RA: Individual Claims, NCOs and Men I–L
WO 100/152 RA: Individual Claims, NCOs and Men M–Q
WO 100/153 RA: Individual Claims, NCOs and Men R–S
WO 100/154 RA: Individual Claims, NCOs and Men T–Z
WO 100/155 Royal Engineers (RE): Staff, 5–7 Field Companies
WO 100/156 RE: 8–12 and 17 Field Companies
WO 100/157 RE: 20, 23, 26, 29, 31, 33 and 37 Field Companies
WO 100/158 RE: 38, 39, 42, 45–47, 54 and 55 Field Companies
WO 100/159 RE: Telegraph Division Battalion
WO 100/160 RE: Pontoon and Bridging Troop, Field Troops and Park,
  Searchlight Section, 1 and 2 Balloon Sections and Balloon Repairing Factory
WO 100/161 RE: Base Details, Survey Companies, Tay Section, Mauritius,
  Natal, St Helena, Royal Anglesey, Royal Monmouth
WO 100/162 RE: Volunteer Companies (By Counties) and Electrical Engineers
WO 100/163 Grenadier Guards
WO 100/164 Coldstream Guards
WO 100/165 Scots and Irish Guards
WO 100/166 The Royal Scots and Royal West Surrey Regiments
WO 100/167 East Kent Regiment
WO 100/168 Royal Lancaster Regiment
WO 100/169 Northumberland Fusiliers
WO 100/170 Royal Warwickshire Regiment
WO 100/171 1st–7th Battalions Royal Fusiliers
WO 100/172 Liverpool Regiment
WO 100/173 Norfolk and Lincolnshire Regiments
WO 100/174 Devonshire and Suffolk Regiments
WO 100/175 Somerset Light Infantry and West Yorkshire Regiment
WO 100/176 East Yorkshire and Bedfordshire Regiments
WO 100/177 Leicestershire and Royal Irish Regiments
WO 100/178 Yorkshire Regiment
WO 100/179 Lancashire Fusiliers
WO 100/180 Royal Scots Fusiliers and Cheshire Regiment
WO 100/181 Royal Welsh Fusiliers and South Wales Borderers
WO 100/182 King's Own Scottish Borderers and Scottish Rifles
WO 100/183 Royal Inniskilling Fusiliers and Gloucestershire Regiment

WO 100/184 Worcestershire and East Lancashire Regiments

WO 100/185 East Surrey Regiment and Duke of Cornwall's Light Infantry

WO 100/186 West Riding and Border Regiments

WO 100/187 Royal Sussex and Hampshire Regiments

WO 100/188 South Staffordshire Regiments

WO 100/189 Dorsetshire and South Lancashire Regiments

WO 100/190 Welsh Regiment and Royal Highlanders

WO 100/191 Oxfordshire and Buckinghamshire Light Infantry and Essex Regiment

WO 100/192 Nottinghamshire and Derbyshire Regiment and Loyal North Lancashire Regiment

WO 100/193 Northamptonshire and Royal Berkshire Regiments

WO 100/194 Royal West Kent Regiment, King's Own Yorkshire Light Infantry and Shropshire Light Infantry

WO 100/195 Middlesex Regiment

WO 100/196 1st–4th Battalions, King's Royal Rifle Corps

WO 100/197 9th Battalion King's Royal Rifle Corps, Volunteer Service Companies and Wiltshire Regiment

WO 100/198 Manchester Regiment

WO 100/199 North Staffordshire Regiment

WO 100/200 York and Lancaster Regiment

WO 100/201 Durham Light Infantry

WO 100/202 Highland Light Infantry

WO 100/203 Seaforth Highlanders and Gordon Highlanders

WO 100/204 Queen's Own Cameron Highlanders and Royal Irish Rifles

WO 100/205 Royal Irish Fusiliers and Connaught Rangers

WO 100/206 Argyll and Sutherland Highlanders

WO 100/207 Prince of Wales's Leinster Regiment

WO 100/208 Royal Munster Fusiliers

WO 100/209 Royal Dublin Fusiliers

WO 100/210 1st, 2nd and 4th Battalions Rifle Brigade

WO 100/211 5th and 7th Battalions Rifle Brigade, Natal Field Force, Mounted Infantry with attachments of Ceylon Contingent, Royal Malta Regiment and Burma Mounted Infantry

WO 100/212 Army Service Corps (ASC): Officers, NCOs and Men, Drivers etc. attached to RHA and RFA, St Helena Roll and Miscellaneous

WO 100/213 ASC: 1–37 Companies

WO 100/214 ASC: 38 (or B Supply Company) – 46, 48, 50–56, 58–62, 64–66, 71, 81–91, A Supply, B Remount, C, D and E Supply Companies

WO 100/215 ASC: Individual Claims, NCOs and Men

WO 100/216 ASC: Civilians attached to Companies, Crosbies and Julius Weil's Transports

WO 100/217 ASC: Civilian Individuals, A–K
WO 100/218 ASC: Civilian Individuals, L–Z
WO 100/219 Royal Army Medical Corps (RAMC): Officers, NCOs and Men
WO 100/220 RAMC: Individuals A–K
WO 100/221 RAMC: Individuals L–Z
WO 100/222 RAMC: General Hospitals
WO 100/223 RAMC: Stationary, Brigade and Field Hospitals, Bearer
Companies, Hospital Train and Refuge Camps
WO 100/224 RAMC: Militia Volunteers, Rhodesian Field Force and
Miscellaneous Civilians
WO 100/225 St John's Ambulance, Red Cross Society, Irish, Scottish, Welsh
and Donative Hospitals, Hospital Ships
WO 100/226 Civil Surgeons
WO 100/227 Civil Surgeons: Individual Claims, A–K
WO 100/228 Civil Surgeons: Individual Claims, L–Z
WO 100/229 Nurses
WO 100/230 Army Pay Department, Army Post Office Corps, Army
Veterinary Department, Army Schoolmasters
WO 100/231 Royal Navy, City of London Imperial Volunteers (CIV)
WO 100/232 HMS *Orphir* – Presentation Lists
WO 200/233 Army Ordnance Department
WO 100/234 Remount Department, Military Police
WO 100/235 Chaplains – Church Army, Mission to Soldiers, Salvation Army,
Soldiers Christian Association, Young Men's Christian Association,
Individuals

——South African Colonial Corps (South African Local Forces)

WO 100/236 Ashburner's Light Horse, Bechuanaland Rifles, Bethune's
Mounted Infantry, Border Horse, Border Scouts
WO 100/237 Brabent's Horse
WO 100/238 British South Africa Police, Bushmen and Borderers
WO 100/239 Cape Colony Cyclists Corps, Cape Colonial Forces (Cape
Defence Force) Tembuland and East Griqualand Filed Forces, Clarke's Light
Horse, Cape Colony Ordnance and Defence Departments
WO 100/240 Cape Garrison Artillery, Cape Medical Staff Corps, Cape
Mounted and Special Police
WO 100/241 Cape Mounted Riflemen, Cape Town Highlanders, Cattle
Rangers
WO 100/242 Colonial Light Horse (2nd Battalion Duke of Edinburgh's Own
Volunteer Rifles), Colonial Scouts
WO 100/243 Commander-in-Chief's Body Guard, Composite Cyclists,
Cullinan's Horse, Cyclist Despatch Riders

WO 100/244 Damant's Horse (Late Rimmington's Guides), Dennison's Scouts
WO 100/245 Dordrecht District Volunteer Guard, Driscoll's Scouts
WO 100/246 Duke of Edinburgh's Own Volunteer Rifles
WO 100/247 Eastern Province Horse, East Griqualand Field Force, Farmer's
    Guard, French's Scouts, Frontier Light Horse, Frontier Mounted Rifles
WO 100/248 Gorringe's Flying Column, City of Grahamstown Volunteers,
    Hannay's Scouts, Herschel Native Police
WO 100/249 Imperial Bearer Corps, Imperial Hospital Corps, Imperial
    Irregular Corps
WO 100/250 1st Imperial Light Horse
WO 100/251 2nd Imperial Light Horse
WO 100/252 Imperial Light Infantry, Imperial Military Railways, Imperial
    Yeomanry Scouts
WO 100/253 Johannesburg – Mounted Rifles and District Military Police
WO 100/254 Kaffarian Rifles
WO 100/255 Kimberley Light Horse, Diamond Fields Artillery, Kimberley
    Volunteer Regiment
WO 100/256 Kitchener's Horse, 1st Kitchener's Fighting Scouts
WO 100/257 2nd Kitchener's Fighting Scouts
WO 100/258 Kuruman Scouts, Loch's Horse and Ross Gun Section,
    Lydenburg Mounted Police, Maratrani Mounted Rifles, Marshall's Horse,
    Menne's Scouts
WO 100/259 Midland Mounted Rifles, Montmorency Scouts, Murray's
    Horse, Namaqualand British Scouts
WO 100/260 Natal Volunteer Corps, Border Mounted Rifles, Durban Light
    Infantry, Umvoti Mounted Rifles
WO 100/261 Natal Volunteer Corps and Police
WO 100/262 National (Waldon's) Scouts and Orange River Colony
    Volunteers, Nesbitt's Horse
WO 100/263 New England Mounted Rifles, Neylan's Horse or Orange River
    Scouts, Orange River Colony, Province Mounted Police, Orpen's Light
    Horse, Peninsula Horse, Pietersburgh Light Horse (Late Bushveldt
    Carabineers), Port Alfred Imperial Mounted Rifles, Protectorate Regiment
WO 100/264 Prince Alfred's Guards Mounted Infantry, Prince Alfred's Own
    Cape Artillery, Prince Alfred's Volunteer Guard, Prince of Wales Light
    Horse, Queenstown Rifle Volunteers and Mounted Infantry
WO 100/265 Railway Pioneer Regiments
WO 100/266 Rand Rifles, Rhodesian Field Force, Rhodesia Regiments
WO 100/267 Rhodesia (Southern) Volunteers, Rhodesian Coronation
    Contingent, Robert's Horse, Rundle's Scouts
WO 100/268 1st Scottish Horse, Scottish Cyclists Company
WO 100/269 2nd Scottish Horse

WO 100/270 Scott's Railway Guards, Settle's Scouts
WO 100/271 South African Constabulary (SAC): Headquarters Depot,
Reserve Division, A Division
WO 100/272 SAC: B and C Divisions
WO 100/273 SAC: E Division and Miscellaneous
WO 100/274 South African Light Horse I
WO 100/275 South African Light Horse II
WO 100/276 South African Mounted Irregular Forces, Standerton Mounted
Police, Steindecker's Horse, Struben's Scouts, Tembuland Mounted Rifles
WO 100/277 Thorneycroft's Mounted Infantry, Transkei, Mounted Rifles,
Transvaal Constabulary, Tucker's Scouts, Uitenhage Volunteer Rifles
WO 100/278 Warren's Mounted Infantry, Warren's Scouts, Warwick's Scouts,
Western Light Horse, Western Province Mounted Rifles, Xalanga Mounted
Rifles

——South African District Mounted Troops and Town Guards (DMT and TG)

The following rolls are arranged in alphabetical order by place name.
WO 100/280 DMT and TG: A–C
WO 100/281 DMT and TG: D–J
WO 100/282 DMT and TG: Kimberley
WO 100/283 DMT and TG: K–M
WO 100/284 DMT and TG: N–P
WO 100/285 DMT and TG: Q–T
WO 100/285 DMT and TG: U–Z

——Overseas Colonial Contingents

Australia, Canada and New Zealand all sent troops to South Africa.
The West India Regiment rolls are also included under the above heading,
but they were in fact an established regiment of the British Army.
WO 100/287 Canada and Canadian Scouts, West India Regiment
WO 100/288 New South Wales I
WO 100/289 New South Wales II
WO 100/290 Queensland
WO 100/291 Victoria
WO 100/292 South and West Australia
WO 100/293 Australian Commonwealth Horse, Australian Army Medical
Corps, Doyle's Scouts, Tasmania
WO 100/294 New Zealand Artillery and Contingents 1–6
WO 100/295 New Zealand Contingents 7–10

——Indian Army (IA)

WO 100/296 IA: Staff, British Officers, Cavalry, Artillery and Infantry
WO 100/297 IA: Supply and Transport Corps (arranged according to district),
Indian Mule Pack Train, Private Servants to Officers
WO 100/298 IA: Ordnance, Military Accounts, Medical and Veterinary
Departments, followers attached to British Units and Miscellaneous
Followers (arranged according to districts)
WO 100/299 Headquarters and General Staff
WO 100/300 African Natives
WO 100/301 Field Intelligence Department

A number of miscellaneous medal rolls for the Queen's South
Africa Medal can be found after the main sequence of rolls for the
King's South Africa Medal.

WO 100/371 Burgher Camps Department, Criminal Investigation
Department, Johannesburg Fire Brigade, War Correspondents, Civilians
Grooms and Servants, Civilians employed in Field Canteens, South
Metropolitan Gas Company Reservists and Chinese Regiment of Infantry
WO 100/377 Cape Boy and Fingo Native Contingents at the siege of
Mafeking, and for Natives attached to 1st Royal Irish Regiment,
Stemaicher's Horse, 9 Field Company, Royal Engineers, 3rd Dragoon
Guards and 12 Company Army Service Corps
WO 100/378 Army Post Office Corps: supplementary rolls for NCOs and
Men
WO 100/380 Army Service Corps: Civilian Clerks and Typists: Medal Roll
WO 100/381 Marshall's Horse, nominal list of applicants who served with the
corps
WO 100/382 Brabant's Horse, nominal list of applicants who served with the
corps
WO 100/383 Kitchener's Horse, nominal list of applicants who served with
the corps

A number of miscellaneous individual applications for the QSA
and a list of unclaimed medals can be found in WO 100/379, 384
and 387. WO 100/389 contains the rolls of returned medals that
were forfeited by the recipients.

King's South Africa Medal 1901–2

WO 100/302 Cavalry: 1st and 2nd Life Guards, Royal Horse Guards, 1st–3rd,
5th–7th Dragoon Guards, 1st and 2nd Dragoons
WO 100/303 Cavalry: 3rd and 4 thHussars, 5th Lancers, 6th Dragoons, 7th

and 8th Hussars, 9th Lancers

WO 100/304 Cavalry: 10th and 11th Hussars, 12th Lancers, 13th Hussars

WO 100/305 Cavalry: 14th and 15th Hussars, 16th and 17th Lancers, 18th–20th Hussars, 21st Lancers

WO 100/306 Royal Artillery (RA): G, J, O, P, R, T, V and AA Batteries, Royal Horse Artillery, A and B Depots, Miscellaneous

WO 100/307 RA: 2,4, 5, 7–9, 11, 17, 19–21, 28, 37–39, 42–44, 53, 61, 63–66 and 68 Batteries Royal Field Artillery

WO 100/308 RA: 73, 74, 76–79, 81–88 Batteries Royal Field Artillery, Staffs, Maxims, Pom-Poms, Ammunition Columns, Depots and Miscellaneous

WO 100/309 5, 26, 31, 41, 56, 57, 63, 68, 92, 97, 99–102 companies, 4 and 10 batteries Mountain Division Royal Garrison Artillery, No 3 Depot, District Establishment and Miscellaneous

WO 100/309 RA: Individual Claims, Officers

WO 100/310 RA: Individual Claims, NCOs and Men, A–C

WO 100/311 RA: Individual Claims, NCOs and Men, D–M

WO 100/312 RA: Individual Claims, NCOs and Men, N–Z

WO 100/313 Royal Engineers (RE): Staff, 5–12 Field Companies

WO 100/314 RE: 17, 20, 23, 26, 29, 31, 37, 38, 42, 45–47 and 60 Field Companies

WO 100/315 RE: G and M Companies, Telegraph and Bridging Battalions, 1st–4 Field Troops, Searchlight Section Survey Company, Base Details

WO 100/316 RE: Individuals (alphabetical order)

WO 100/317 Grenadier Guards

WO 100/318 Coldstream, Scots and Irish Guards

WO 100/319 The Royal Scots, Royal West Surrey and East Kent Regiments

WO 100/320 Royal Lancaster Regiment, Northumberland Fusiliers and Royal Warwickshire Regiment

WO 100/321 Royal Fusiliers, Liverpool and Norfolk Regiments

WO 100/322 Lincolnshire and Devonshire Regiments

WO 100/323 Suffolk Regiment and Somerset Light Infantry

WO 100/324 West and East Yorkshire Regiments

WO 100/325 Bedfordshire and Leicestershire Regiments

WO 100/326 Royal Irish and Yorkshire Regiments and Lancashire Fusiliers

WO 100/327 Royal Scots Fusiliers, Cheshire Regiment, Royal Welsh Fusiliers

WO 100/328 South Wales Borderers and King's Own Scottish Borderers

WO 100/329 Scottish Rifles, Royal Inniskilling Fusiliers, Gloucestershire Regiment

WO 100/330 Worcestershire and East Lancashire Regiments

WO 100/331 East Surrey Regiment, Duke of Cornwall's Light Infantry and West Riding Regiment

WO 100/332 Border, Royal Sussex and Hampshire Regiments

WO 100/333 South Staffordshire, Dorsetshire and South Lancashire
Regiments
WO 100/334 Welsh Regiment and Royal Highlanders
WO 100/335 Oxfordshire Light Infantry and Essex Regiment
WO 100/336 Nottinghamshire and Derbyshire and Loyal North Lancashire
Regiments
WO 100/337 Northamptonshire and Royal Berkshire Regiments
WO 100/338 Royal West Kent Regiment, King's Own Yorkshire Light
Infantry and Shropshire Light Infantry
WO 100/339 Middlesex Regiment and King's Royal Rifle Corps
WO 100/340 Wiltshire and Manchester Regiments
WO 100/341 North Staffordshire and York and Lancaster Regiments
WO 100/342 Durham Light Infantry and Highland Light Infantry
WO 100/343 Seaforth Highlanders and Gordon Highlanders
WO 100/344 Queen's Own Cameron Highlanders and Royal Irish Rifles
WO 100/345 Royal Irish Fusiliers, Connaught Rangers and Royal Inniskilling
Fusiliers
WO 100/346 Argyll and Sutherland Highlanders and Prince of Wales's
Leinster Regiment
WO 100/347 Royal Munster Fusiliers and Royal Dublin Fusiliers
WO 100/348 Rifle Brigade and Mounted Infantry
WO 100/349 Army Service Corps (ASC): Officers, NCOs and Men, A–E
Supply Companies, A Remount Company and Attachments to Royal
Artillery
WO 100/350 ASC: 1st–38, 40–45, 47, 48, 50–56, 58, 59, 61–67, 72–74
Companies, Conductors and Civilians
WO 100/351 Royal Army Medical Corps (RAMC): Officers, NCOs and Men
WO 100/352 RAMC: Militia, St John's Ambulance, Civil Surgeons,
Miscellaneous, Individuals
WO 100/353 Nurses
WO 100/354 Field Intelligence Department, Remount and Army Chaplains
Departments and Army Schoolmasters
WO 100/355 Headquarters and General Staff, Army Ordnance and Army Pay
Departments, Army Post Office Corps, Army Veterinary Department and
Military Police
WO 100/356 Imperial Yeomanry I
WO 100/357 Imperial Yeomanry II

——South African Colonial Corps (South African Local Forces)
The following rolls are arranged in alphabetical ranges by name of unit.
WO 100/358 Ashburner's Light Horse – Cape Colonial Forces
WO 100/359 Cape Garrison Artillery – Cape Mounted Rifles

WO 100/360 Cape Town Highlanders – Frontier Light Horse
WO 100/361 Gorringe's Flying Column – Imperial Light Infantry
WO 100/362 Johannesburg Mounted Rifles – Kitchener's Fighting Scouts
WO 100/363 Marshall's Horse – Oudtshoorn Volunteer Rifles
WO 100/364 Peninsula Horse – Scottish Horse
WO 100/365 Scott's Railway Guards – Steinaecker's Horse
WO 100/366 South African Constabulary
WO 100/367 Tembuland Mounted Rifles – Western Province Mounted Rifles, Miscellaneous
WO 100/369 Indian Army
WO 100/370 Overseas Colonial Contingents
WO 129/12 is a nominal roll of Imperial Yeomanry Officers and it also annotates those who received the King's South Africa Medal.

Transport Medal 1899–1902

Awarded to Masters and certain other officers of merchant ships used to move men and material to South Africa and China. Granted with the clasps S. AFRICA 1899–1902 and CHINA 1900

ADM 171/52 Admiralty Medal roll of Claims by Officers of the Mercantile Marine

Africa General Service Medal 1902–56

ADM 171/56 Medal rolls of Naval and Marine personnel who qualified for the clasps JUBALAND, GAMBIA, ARO 1901–1902, SOMALILAND 1902–04 and SOMALILAND 1908–10

Each roll is arranged in alphabetical order by name of ship.

FO 83/2170 and 2171 These two files contain applications for Africa General Service Medal with the clasps GAMBIA, JUBALAND, ARO 1901–1902 and LANGO to those missed off the War Office rolls.

WO 100/91 War Office Medal rolls for the clasps UGANDA 1900, B.C.A 1899–1900, JUBALAND and GAMBIA to the following: Officers of British Regiments, Government Officials, Indian troops, East African Rifles, West India Regiment, civilian volunteers, Central Africa Regiment, Gambia Police, Royal Navy (including some Royal Naval Reservists), Miscellaneous claims, Uganda Rifles and other Africa units

• The following War Office rolls contain the clasps SOMALILAND 1901, SOMALILAND 1902–04 and JIDBALI.

WO 100/100 Staff, Cavalry, Royal Artillery, Royal Engineers, Infantry, Army Service Corps. Army Ordnance Department, Veterinary Department, Chaplains and Boer Contingent

WO 100/101 Indian Army: Cavalry and Camel Corps and Sappers and Miners

WO 100/102 Indian Army: Artillery and Infantry

WO 100/103 Medical Corps British and Indian Armies and Royal Indian
Marine
WO 100/104 Indian Army: Supply and Transport Corps, Ordnance
Department and Miscellaneous
WO 100/105 King's African Rifles, Somali Levies and Miscellaneous

WO 100/390 contains medal rolls for the clasps:
  ARO 1901–1902 to Staff, Lagos Battalion, Northern Nigeria Regiment,
  Southern Nigeria Regiment, Royal Navy, Civilians
  LANGO 1901 to 4th King's African Rifles
  KISSI 1905 to Sierra Leone Battalion West African Frontier Force
  NANDI 1905–06 to 1st and 3rd King's African Rifles, Indian Contingent, 4th
  King's African Rifles, East Africa Protectorate Police, Kisumu Police, Nandi
  Police, Ravine Police, Kericho Police.
WO 100/391 contains medal rolls for the clasps:
  NORTHERN NIGERIA to Northern Nigeria Regiment
  NORTHERN NIGERIA 1902 to Northern Nigeria Regiment
  NORTHERN NIGERIA 1903 to Northern Nigeria Regiment, Southern Nigeria
  Regiment, Lagos Battalion.
WO 100/392 contains medal rolls for the clasps:
  NORTHERN NIGERIA 1903 to Northern Nigeria Regiment
  NORTHERN NIGERIA 1903–1904 to Northern Nigeria Regiment, Northern
  Nigeria Constabulary
  NORTHERN NIGERIA 1904 to Northern Nigeria Regiment.
  NORTHERN NIGERIA 1906 to Northern Nigeria Regiment, Northern Nigeria
  Constabulary.
WO 100/393 contains medal rolls for the clasps: *SOUTHERN NIGERIA, SOUTHERN
  NIGERIA 1902, SOUTHERN NIGERIA 1902–03, SOUTHERN NIGERIA 1904, SOUTHERN
  NIGERIA 1904–5, SOUTHERN NIGERIA 1905, SOUTHERN NIGERIA 1905–6* to
  Southern Nigeria Regiment.
WO 100/394 contains medal rolls for the clasps:
  EAST AFRICA 1902, EAST AFRICA 1904, EAST AFRICA 1905, EAST AFRICA 1906 to
  King's African Rifles, East African Police
  WEST AFRICA 1906 to Native Staff, Northern Nigeria Regiment
  WEST AFRICA 1908, WEST AFRICA 1909–1910 to Southern Nigeria Regiment.
WO 100/396 contains the medal roll for the clasp *SOMALILAND 1908–10* to
  Royal Engineers, Norfolk Regiment, Army Service Corps, Army Pay Corps,
  Army Ordnance Corps, 113th Infantry Indian Army, 127th Baluchistan
  Light Infantry, Indian Subordinate Medical Department, 1st, 3rd, 4th and
  6th King's Africa Rifles, Royal Indian Marine Ship *Hardinge.*
WO 100/408 contains medal rolls for the clasps: *EAST AFRICA 1913, EAST AFRICA
  1914, EAST AFRICA 1913–14, SHIMBER BERRIS 1915* and *NYASALAND 1915*

WO 100/409 contains medal rolls for the clasps: *JUBALAND 1917–1918* and
NIGERIA 1918.

WO 100/410 contains medal rolls for the clasps: *EAST AFRICA 1918* and
SOMALILAND 1910.

ADM 171/64 Medal roll for Naval and Marine personnel of HM ships *Ark
Royal*, *Clio* and *Odin* who received the clasp *SOMALILAND 1920*

AIR 2/2267–2270 These Air Ministry files contain the medal roll for those
Royal Air Force personnel who received the clasp *SOMALILAND 1920* for
service with Z Unit.

Another medal roll for RAF personnel will be placed in the series AIR 81
when it is accessioned.

The Africa General Service Medal to the Royal Navy and Royal Marines by
W.H. Fevyer and J.W. Wilson (London Stamp Exchange 1990)

Khedive's Sudan Medal 1910–25

WO 100/407 contains the medal roll with the clasps: *ATWOT, SOUTHERN
KORDOFAN 1910, SUDAN 1912, MANDAL, MIRI, ZERAF 1913–1914, MONGALLA
1915–1916, DARFUR 1916, FASHER, LAU-NUER, NYIMA 1917–1918, ATWOT 1918,
GARJAK NUER, ALIAB DINKA, NAYALA AND DARFUR 1921*

3.3 CASE STUDY
Ali Wadi Songoro

At the auctioneers Spink a few years ago, an Africa General Service
Medal (AGS) with the clasps *NANDI 1905–06* and *EAST AFRICA
1904* to Bugler Ali Wadi Songoro, King's African Rifles (KAR)
caught my eye. The medal was nothing special, although the clasp
EAST AFRICA 1904 is quite rare, with only 493 being issued.
What made me remember the name was a book I had read recently called *Kenya Diary* by Richard Meinertzhagen, which was all
about his time with 3rd King's African Rifles.

I checked Ali Wadi Songoro's medal in WO 100/390 for the
NANDI 1905–06 clasp and WO 100/394 for the *EAST AFRICA
1904* clasp. I make a habit of looking quite closely at all multiple
clasp AGS Medals that appear at auction, as some are quite often
entitled to clasps which were either never issued, or issued much
later than the medal and were subsequently lost. Such was the case
with Ali Wadi Songoro, since he was also entitled to the *EAST
AFRICA 1913–14* clasp.

A medal over 100 years old becomes more interesting with a

photograph of the recipient – why Meinertzhagen's *Kenya Diary* was so important!

Ali Wadi Songoro and his medal can be seen in PLATES 2 and 3.

3.4   INDIA, AFGHANISTAN, BURMA AND SOUTH EAST ASIA

A significant number of the following medal rolls are held in the India Office collection at the British Library, in the series L/MIL/5.

Army of India Medal 1799–1826

ADM 171/11 List of Naval Claimants for the clasp AVA

L/MIL/5/42 Miscellaneous Correspondence, extracts from Military Letters, Memoranda and List of Claimants

L/MIL/5/43 Index of Claimants in above

L/MIL/5/44 Receipts for 1500 medals with the names of the recipients

WO 100/13 Rolls for the following regiments: 8th, 11th, 16th, 19th, 22nd, 27th and 29th Dragoons, 1st, 13th, 14, 17th, 22nd, 24th, 38th, 41st, 44th, 45th, 47th, 53rd, 54th, 59th, 65th, 66th, 67th, 74th, 76th, 87th, 89th and 94th Regiments of Foot, Staff Officers India

The Army of India Medal Roll by R. J. Gould and K. J. Douglas Morris (Hayward, 1974)

Jellalabad Medal 1842 (First Afghan War 1841–2)

L/MIL/5/68 Surviving medal roll

Scinde Medal 1843

L/MIL/5/69 22nd Regiment of Foot and East India Company Forces

Sutlej Medal 1845–6

L/MIL/5/70 3rd Light Dragoons, 9th and 16th Lancers, 9th, 10th, 29th, 31st, 50th, 53rd, 62nd and 80th Regiments of Foot, Bengal Horse Artillery, 1st, 3rd, 4th, 5th, 7th and 8th Bengal Light Cavalry, 2nd, 3rd, 4th, 8th, 9th and 11th Bengal Irregular Cavalry, 1st and 2nd Bengal European Regiments, 2nd, 3rd, 7th, 11th, 12th, 14th, 16th, 24th, 26th, 27th, 30th, 33rd, 36th, 38th, 41st, 42nd, 43rd, 45th, 47th, 48th, 54th, 55th, 59th, 63rd, 68th and 73rd Bengal Native Infantry, Nusseeree Battalion, Sirmoor Battalion, Shekawatte Brigade, Bengal Engineers, Bengal Sappers and Miners and Medical Subordinates

The Army of the Sutlej 1845–46 Casualty Roll

Punjab Medal 1848–9

L/MIL/5/71 British Army
L/MIL/5/72 East India Company Forces
WO 100/13 10th, 24th, 32nd and 61st Regiments of Foot only
Punjab Campaign 1848–9 Casualty Roll

Indian General Service Medal 1854–95

ADM 171/17 PEGU Naval personnel who qualified for this clasp between 28 March 1853 and 30 June 1853

ADM 171/39 PERAK Medal roll of the Naval Brigade personnel who served with the expedition to the Malay Peninsular between 2 November 1875 and 20 June 1876

ADM 171/44 BURMA 1885–87 Medal roll of personnel who served in the Third Burmese War 14 November 1885–30 April 1887

L/MIL/5/52 PEGU All Army Units

L/MIL/5/53 PEGU Bengal ships: *Damodali, Fire Queen, India, Lord William Bentinck, Luckia, Mahanuddy, Nemesis, Nerbuddah, Phlegethon, Pluto, Prosperine, Soane, Sutledge, Tenasserim*

L/MIL/5/54 PEGU Bombay ships: *Berenice, Feroze, Medusa, Moozuffer, Sesostris*

L/MIL/5/55 PERSIA All Army Units

L/MIL5/56 PERSIA Bombay ships: *Ajdahe, Assaye, Assyria, Berenice, Clive, Comet, Euphrates, Falkland, Feroze, Hugh Lindsay, Lady Falkland, Napier, Nitseris, Planet, Punjaub, Semiramis, Victoria*

L/MIL/5/46 NORTH WEST FRONTIER and UMBEYLA British Army: Cavalry, Royal Artillery, Royal Engineers, 7th–32nd Regiments

L/MIL/5/47 NORTH WEST FRONTIER and UMBEYLA British Army: 53rd Regiment – 3rd Rifle Brigade

L/MIL/5/48 NORTH WEST FRONTIER and UMBEYLA British Army: Draft rolls

L/MIL/5/49 NORTH WEST FRONTIER and UMBEYLA Indian Army

L/MIL/5/50 NORTH WEST FRONTIER and UMBEYLA Indian Army supplementary rolls

L/MIL/5/51 NORTH WEST FRONTIER and UMBEYLA Indian Army numerical returns

L/MIL/5/57 BHOOTAN and NORTH WEST FRONTIER (for Hazara 1868) British Army

L/MIL/5/58 BHOOTAN and NORTH WEST FRONTIER (for Hazara 1868) Copy of above

L/MIL/5/59 BHOOTAN and NORTH WEST FRONTIER (for Hazara 1868) Indian Army

L/MIL/5/60 BHOOTAN and NORTH WEST FRONTIER (for Hazara 1868) Indian Army: Native Troops

L/MIL/5/61 LOOSHAI Europeans

L/MIL/5/62 *LOOSHAI* Indians

L/MIL/5/63 *JOWAKI 1877–8* All Units

L/MIL/5/64 *NAGA 1879–80* All Units

L/MIL/5/65 *BURMA 1885–7* Civilians only

L/MIL/7/10896 *BURMA 1885–7* Naval and Marine personnel

WO 100/19 *NORTH WEST FRONTIER* A Royal Artillery roll can be found on pages 101–50.

WO 100/20 *NORTH WEST FRONTIER* 7th Hussars, Royal Artillery, Royal Engineers, 1st/6th Foot, 1st/7th Foot, 1st/19th Foot, 1st/22nd Foot, 2nd/22nd Foot, 32nd Foot, 53rd Foot, 1st/60th foot, 61st Foot, 71st Foot, 79th Foot, 81st Foot, 87th Foot, 93rd Foot, 98th Foot, 101st Foot, 3rd Rifle Brigade, Staff and Miscellaneous Corps

WO 100/21A *NORTH WEST FRONTIER, BHOOTAN* and *UMBEYLA* This medal roll is in alphabetical order by name of recipient. It shows name, rank and unit, and whether the individual is entitled to one of the three clasps mentioned above. Most of the units mentioned in WO 100/20 can also be found here.

7th Hussars, Royal Artillery, 1st/6th Foot, 1st/7th Foot, 22nd Foot, 32nd Foot, 51st Foot, 53rd Foot, 55th Foot, 61st Foot, 77th Foot, 80th Foot, 81st Foot, 93rd Foot, 98th Foot, 101st Foot and 3rd Rifle Brigade

WO 100/20 *BHOOTAN* 55th Foot and 80th Foot

WO 100/19 *PERAK* and *JOWAKI 1877–78* Royal Artillery only, on pages 195–210 and 371–84 respectively

WO 100/45 *PERAK* and *JOWAKI 1877–78* Two medal rolls are incorporated into WO 100/45. The rolls are arranged in alphabetical order, with each letter of the alphabet then arranged by unit. In each section of the roll it starts with *PERAK* and is followed by that for *JOWAKI 1877–78*.

PERAK: Royal Artillery, Royal Engineers, 3rd Foot, 10th Foot, 80th Foot and Miscellaneous

JOWAKI 1877–78: Royal Artillery, 51st Foot, 4th Rifle Brigade and Miscellaneous

WO 100/19 *NAGA 1879–80* Page 194 contains the roll for 3 officers and 1 other ranks of the Royal Artillery who received this clasp.

WO 100/42 *BURMA 1885–87* A Royal Artillery roll can be found on pages 43–102.

WO 100/69 *BURMA 1885–87* Staff, Royal Artillery, Royal Engineers, 2nd Royal West Surreys, 2nd Liverpools, 2nd Somerset Light Infantry and 2nd Royal Scots Fusiliers

WO 100/70 *BURMA 1885–87* 1st Royal Welch Fusiliers, 2nd South Wales Borderers, 2nd Hampshire, 1st King's Own Yorkshire Light Infantry, 2nd Munster Fusiliers, 1st Rifle Brigade, Medical, Commissariat and Miscellaneous

WO 100/42 *BURMA 1887–89* A Royal Artillery roll can be found on pages
103–15.

WO 100/73 *BURMA 1887–89* Staff, Artillery, Engineers, Infantry, Rifle Brigade,
Medical Staff and Miscellaneous

WO 100/42 *HAZARA 1888, SIKKIM 1888* and *CHIN LUSHAI 1889–90* Royal
Artillery rolls for the above-mentioned clasps can be found on pages
117–25, 128–31 and 132 respectively.

WO 100/74 *HAZARA 1888, SIKKIM 1888* and *CHIN LUSHAI 1888–90* A detailed
breakdown of this roll can be found in the WO 100 paper catalogue.

WO 100/42 *SAMANA 1891, HAZARA 1891, HUNZA 1891, N E FRONTIER 1891,
BURMA 1889–92, LUSHAI 1889–92* and *WAZIRISTAN 1894–5* Royal Artillery
rolls for the above-mentioned clasps can be found on pages 133–6, 125,
144, 148, 146–7 (*BURMA 1889–92* and *LUSHAI 1889–92* together) and 161
respectively.

WO 100/75 *SAMANA 1891, HAZARA 1891, N E FRONTIER 1891, BURMA 1889–92,
LUSHAI 1889–92* and *WAZIRISTAN 1894–95* Such is the complicated nature of
this medal roll, it is recommended that you consult the detailed analysis of it
in the WO 100 paper catalogue.

WO 100/21B *CHIN HILLS 1892–93* and *KACHIN HILLS 1892–93* Royal Artillery,
Royal Garrison Artillery, Royal Engineers, 1st Norfolk, 2nd Yorkshires,
Indian Army, Supply and Transport Corps and Miscellaneous

Indian Mutiny Medal 1857–8

ADM 171/29 Medal roll of the Naval Brigade personnel from HM ships
Shannon and *Pearl* who served ashore between 10 May 1857 and 30
December 1858

L/MIL/5/66 Naval personnel

L/MIL/5/73 British Army: Cavalry, Medical, Staff, Royal Artillery, Royal
Engineers

L/MIL/5/74 British Army: Cavalry

L/MIL/5/75 British Army: 4th–56th Regiments

L/MIL/5/76 British Army: 60th Regiment – Camel Corps

L/MIL/5/77 Bengal Army: Cavalry, Native Infantry, Medical, Staff, Miscellaneous

L/MIL/5/78 Partial Index of Cavalry in above

L/MIL/5/79 Bengal Army: Artillery, Engineers, Commissariat, Invalids

L/MIL/5/80 Bengal Army: European Infantry, Original Garrison of Lucknow,
Staff and Pupils of La Martinière School

L/MIL/5/82 Madras Army

L/MIL/5/83 Bombay Army

L/MIL/5/85 HM ships *Shannon* and *Pearl* Naval Brigades, Royal Marine
Artillery, Royal Marine Light Infantry

L/MIL/5/86 Civilians, Police and Militia Levies

L/MIL/5/87–103 Supplementary rolls.

A separate index for these rolls is available at the British Library.

WO 54/745 This file is described as Medal Book 1857–60, but in fact contain receipts for Indian Mutiny awarded to the Royal Engineers.

WO 100/35 Cavalry, Medical Staff, Military Train, Miscellaneous

WO 100/36 1st/4th Foot, 1st/5th Foot, 1st/6th Foot, 8th Foot, 1st/10th Foot, 1st/13th Foot, 1st/20th Foot, 1st/23rd Foot, 1st/24th Foot, 27th Foot and 29th Foot

WO 100/37 32nd–60th Foot

WO 100/38 2nd/60th Foot–81st Foot

WO 100/39 82nd–97th Foot, 2nd and 3rd Rifle Brigade

WO 100/405 75th Foot

Casualty Roll for the Indian Mutiny 1857–59 by I.T. Tavender (Hayward, 1983)

Indian Mutiny: Alphabetical Roll of British Units by K.J. Asplin (1998)

Second Afghan War Medal 1878–80

L/MIL/5/110 British Army: Cavalry

L/MIL/5/111 British Army: Engineers

L/MIL/5/112 British Army: Artillery

L/MIL/5/113 British Army: 1st–14th Regiments

L/MIL/5/114 British Army: 15th–65th Regiments

L/MIL/5/115 British Army: 66th Regiment – 4th Rifle Brigade

L/MIL/5/116 British Army: Staff, Miscellaneous, Medical, Veterinary, Transports and Signalling

L/MIL/5/117–120 Bengal and Bombay Armies

L/MIL/5/121 Madras Army

L/MIL/5/124 Indian Army

WO 100/51 General Staff, 6th Dragoon Guards, 8th Hussars, 9th Lancers, 10th Hussars, 15th Hussars, E battery 3rd Brigade Royal Artillery, Royal Engineers,
5th–9th, 11th, 12th and 14th Regiments of Foot

WO 100/52/1 15th, 17th, 18th, 34th, 35th, 51st, 59th, 60th, 63rd, 65th–67th, 70th and 72nd Regiments of Foot

WO 100/52/2 67th Regiment of Foot

WO 100/53 78th, 81st, 85th and 92nd Regiments of Foot, 3rd Rifle Brigade, Army Signallers, Army Medical Department, Army Veterinary Department, Miscellaneous

WO 100/54 Royal Artillery only

The Second Afghan War 1878–1880 Casualty Roll by A. Farrington (London Stamp Exchange, 1986)

Kabul to Kandahar Star 1880

L/MIL/5/122 British Army
L/MIL/5/123–124. Indian Army

India Medal 1895–1902

WO 100/42 Royal Artillery rolls for the RELIEF OF CHITRAL 1895 and PUNJAB FRONTIER 1897–98 and TIRAH 1897–98 can be found on pages 151–5 and 157–60 and 163–79.

WO 100/78 RELIEF OF CHITRAL 1895

East Kent, Suffolk, Devon, Somerset Light Infantry, Bedford, 2nd Royal Scots Fusiliers, Royal Welsh Fusiliers, 2nd King's Own Scottish Borderers, East Lancashire, East Surrey Regiments, 1st King's Royal Rifle Corps.

Other regiments present in the roll: Staff, Cavalry, Royal Artillery, Royal Engineers, Norfolk Regiment, Gordon Highlanders, Seaforth Highlanders, Ordnance Corps, Army Medical Department, Army Veterinary Department, Commissariat, Transport Department, Telegraph Department

- Rolls for the following clasps: PUNJAB FRONTIER 1897–8, MALAKAND 1897, SAMANA 1897, TIRAH 1897–8 and WAZIRISTAN 1901–02

WO 100/84 Staff, 4th Dragoon Guards, 11th Hussars, Royal Engineers, Medical Staff Corps, Army Ordnance Corps, Commissariat and Transport Department, Army Veterinary Department, Government Telegraph Department

WO 100/85 F and K Batteries Royal Horse Artillery, 3rd, 9th, 10th, 51st and 57th Field Batteries Royal Artillery, 1st, 3rd, 7th, 8th and 9th Mountain Batteries Royal Artillery, 5th Company Western Division Royal Artillery, Miscellaneous Royal Artillery

WO 100/86 Royal West Surrey Regiment, East Kent Regiment, Devonshire Regiment, Somerset Light Infantry, 2nd Royal Irish Regiment

WO 100/87 2nd Yorkshire Regiment, Royal Scots Fusiliers, 2nd King's Own Scottish Borderers, 2nd Royal Inniskilling Fusiliers, Duke of Cornwall's Light Infantry, 2nd Royal Sussex Regiment

WO 100/88 Dorset Regiment, 2nd Oxford Light Infantry, Northamptonshire Regiment, Royal West Kent Regiment

WO 100/89 2nd Yorkshire Light Infantry, 2nd Highland Light Infantry, Gordon Highlanders, 2nd Argyll and Sutherland Highlanders, 3rd Rifle Brigade, Miscellaneous

WO 100/75 WAZIRISTAN 1901–2

Europeans Only – Indian Staff Corps, Chaplains, Royal Artillery, Royal Engineers, Cheshire Regiment, Dorset Regiment, Middlesex Regiment, 2nd Suffolk Regiment, Border Regiment, Wiltshire Regiment, Yorkshire Regiment, 1st and 5th Punjab Cavalry, 1st, 2nd, 28th, 29th Punjab Infantry,

3rd, 4th, 35th, 45th and 53rd Sikh Infantry, 9th, 17th, 23rd Bombay
Infantry, 23rd Pioneers, 11th and 13th Rajputs, 38th Dogras, 123rd
Outram's Rifles, 1/2nd, 1/3rd, 1/5th and 2/5th Gurkhas, 43rd and 44th
Gurkha Rifles, Zhob Levy, Indian Medical Service, Supply and Transport
Corps, Civilians, Postal Department, Mule Corps
Indian General Service Medal 1895 Casualty Roll by A. Farrington (London
Stamp Exchange, 1987)

Tibet Medal 1903–4
WO 100/395 Staff and Miscellaneous Units of the British and Indian Armies

Indian General Service Medal 1908–35
The RAF rolls when transferred will be in the series AIR 81
L/MIL/7/4052 Grant of IGS for *WAZIRISTAN 1919–21* and *MAHSUD* to the RAF
L/MIL/7/4056 Grant of IGS for *WAZIRISTAN 1921–24* to the RAF

• Clasps: *NORTH WEST FRONTIER 1908* and *ABOR 1911–1912*
WO 100/397 Staff and Miscellaneous Units of the British and Indian Armies.

• Clasps: *AFGHAN NWF 1919, WAZIRISTAN 1919–21* and *MAHSUD
1919–20* (Other Ranks Rolls)
WO 100/467 King's Dragoon Guards, Corps of Dragoons, Corps of Hussars,
Corps of Lancers, Royal Artillery
WO 100/468 Royal Field Artillery
WO 100/469 Royal Field Artillery, Royal Horse Artillery, Royal Engineers,
Royal Signals
WO 100/470 Grenadier Guards, Scots Guards, Royal Scots, Queen's
Regiment, East Kent Regiment, Royal Lancaster Regiment,
Northumberland Fusiliers, Royal Warwickshire Regiment, Royal Fusiliers
WO 100/471 Liverpool Regiment, Norfolk Regiment, Lincolnshire Regiment
WO 100/472 Devon Regiment, Suffolk Regiment, Somerset Light Infantry,
West Yorkshire Regiment
WO 100/473 East Yorkshire Regiment, Bedfordshire and Hertfordshire
Regiment, Leicestershire Regiment, Royal Irish Regiment, Yorkshire
Regiment, Lancashire Fusiliers, Royal Scots Fusiliers, Cheshire Regiment,
Royal Welsh Fusiliers
WO 100/474 South Wales Borderers, King's Own Scottish Borderers, Scottish
Rifles, Royal Inniskilling Fusiliers, Gloucestershire Regiment,
Worcestershire Regiment, East Lancashire Regiment, East Surrey Regiment,
Duke of Cornwall's Light Infantry, West Riding Regiment, Border Regiment
WO100/475 Royal Sussex Regiment, Hampshire Regiment, South
Staffordshire Regiment

WO 100/476 Dorset Regiment, South Lancashire Regiment, Welsh Regiment, Royal Highlanders, Oxfordshire and Buckinghamshire Light Infantry, Essex Regiment, Notts and Derby Regiment, Loyal North Lancashire Regiment, Northamptonshire Regiment, Royal Berkshire Regiment

WO 100/477 Royal West Kent Regiment

WO 100/478 King's Own Yorkshire Light Infantry, Middlesex Regiment, King's Royal Rifle Corps, Wiltshire Regiment, Manchester Regiment, North Staffordshire Regiment, York and Lancaster Regiment, Durham Light Infantry

WO 100/479 Highland Light Infantry, Seaforth Highlanders, Gordon Highlanders, Cameron Highlanders, Royal Irish Rifles, Connaught Rangers, Argyll and Sutherland Highlanders, Royal Dublin Fusiliers, Rifle Brigade, 14th London Regiment, 25th London Regiment, Army Cyclist Corps, Royal Tank Regiment

WO 100/480 Machine Gun Corps

WO 100/481 Royal Army Service Corps, Royal Army Medical Corps

WO 100/482 Royal Army Ordnance Corps, Royal Army Veterinary Corps, Royal Army Pay Corps, Military Mounted Police, Military Foot Police, Military Provost Staff Corps, Army Education Corps, Miscellaneous

WO 100/483 Issues from India (Refs I 184, I 20, I 46, I 65)

• Clasps: *AFGHAN NWF 1919, WAZIRISTAN 1919–21, MAHSUD 1919–20* (Officers Rolls)

WO 100/484 Staff – Duke of Cornwall's Light Infantry

WO 100/485 West Riding Regiment – Corps, including Indian Army Reserve of Officers, Nurses and Miscellaneous

• Clasp: *MALABAR 1921–22*

WO 100/487 Staff, 2nd Dragoon Guards, Corps of Hussars, Royal Field Artillery, Royal Garrison Artillery, Royal Signals, Suffolk Regiment, Dorset Regiment, Leinster Regiment, Royal Tank Corps, Royal Army Service Corps, Royal Army Medical Corps, Royal Army Ordnance Corps, Miscellaneous

• Clasp: *WAZIRISTAN 1921–24*

WO 100/488 3/6th Dragoon Guards, Cavalry, Royal Garrison Artillery, Royal Horse Artillery, Royal Field Artillery, Royal Engineers

WO 100/489 Royal Signals, Royal Scots, Queen's Regiment

WO 100/490 King's Own Royal Regiment, Northumberland Fusiliers, Royal Warwickshire Regiment, Royal Fusiliers, Norfolk Regiment, Devon Regiment, Suffolk Regiment, Somerset Light Infantry, West Yorkshire Regiment, Bedfordshire and Hertfordshire Regiment, Green Howards, Lancashire Fusiliers, Royal Scots Fusiliers, Cheshire Regiment, Royal Welsh Fusiliers, Royal Inniskilling Fusiliers, Gloucestershire Regiment,

Worcestershire Regiment

WO 100/491   Border Regiment, Dorset Regiment, South Lancashire Regiment, Welsh Regiment, Black Watch, Oxfordshire and Buckinghamshire Light Infantry, Essex Regiment, Sherwood Foresters, Loyal Regiment, Northamptonshire Regiment, Royal Berkshire Regiment, Royal West Kent Regiment, King's Own Yorkshire Light Infantry, King's Royal Rifle Corps, York and Lancaster Regiment, Cameron Highlanders, Rifle Brigade

WO 100/492   Machine Gun Corps, Royal Tanks Corps, Royal Army Service Corps, Royal Army Medical Corps, Royal Army Ordnance Corps, Army Education Corps

WO 100/492   Miscellaneous (Rank and File), Officers of the Staff, Royal Artillery, Royal Signals, Royal Army Service Corps, Royal Army Medical Corps, Royal Army Veterinary Corps, Miscellaneous

- Clasps: *NORTH WEST FRONTIER 1930–31, BURMA 1930–32* and *NORTH WEST FRONTIER 1935*
  The Rolls for the above three clasps will be added to WO 100, probably being WO 100/495–497.

Indian General Service Medal 1936–9

L/MIL/7/4084–4085   Issue of the clasp *NORTH WEST FRONTIER 1937–39* to the RAF

WO 100   The medal rolls for the clasps *NORTH WEST FRONTIER 1936–37* and *NORTH WEST FRONTIER 1937–39* will be added to WO 100 when they are accessioned.

British North Borneo Company's General Service Medal 1937–41

CO 874/678 and 679   contain information concerning qualification for the award, together with list of names of recipients of the medal. Many of the names were subsequently published in the *North Borneo Gazette* in CO 855.

General Service Medal 1918–62

- Clasp: *S.E ASIA 1945–46*
  The medal roll for members of the Army who received this clasp will shortly be added to WO 100.

3.5   CASE STUDIES

John Buxton

Indian Mutiny Medals are not particularly rare, but they can be awkward to research because, like many medal rolls for campaigns in India, the rolls can be complex, incomplete and split between the India Office collection at the British Library and the National Archives at Kew.

John Buxton was born in Montreal, Canada, in 1838. He joined the 34th Regiment of Foot in Nottingham in 1855, the regiment having recently returned from the Crimea.

Along with the whole regiment, John Buxton soon found himself out in India taking part in operations to suppress the mutiny. For his service in India between 1857 and 1858, John Buxton received the Indian Mutiny Medal with the clasp LUCKNOW. The medal is confirmed in L/MIL/5/75 and WO 100/37. See FIGURE 3

After serving with the 34th Foot, John transferred to the 45th Foot in 1867, probably, like many men at the time, so that he could stay in India. Eventually discharged from the 45th as a sergeant in 1877, John Buxton returned to England and settled in Nottingham. If you look for him on the 1881 census, he can be found quite easily with his wife and two children, both of whom were born in India.

The record of service of John Buxton from WO 97/1905 recording his Indian Mutiny Medal, can be seen in FIGURE 4. The medal itself can be seen in PLATE 4.

Michael Dowling

The story of 1569 Sergeant M. Dowling, 70th Foot, deserves more pages than can be spared, but it does reinforce the point about using all available sources. The problem of researching many campaign medals awarded to soldiers of the British Army between 1870 and 1890 is that the records of service of most men who were not discharged with a pension in this period, no longer exist. Amongst this category must be placed the men who only saw limited service without pension and men who died in service.

Many limited service men earned South Africa Medals 1877–9,

FIG 3. (facing top) *Indian Mutiny medal roll for the 34th Regiment, showing John Buxton and his entitlement to the clasp* LUCKNOW [WO 100/37]

FIG 4. (facing below) *The record of John Buxton, 45th Regiment, late 34th Regiment, showing him in possession of the Indian Mutiny Medal* [WO 97/1905]

W. O. Form 83.

HER MAJESTY'S *Forty Fifth* REG. OF *Infantry*

Whereof *Lieutenant General Henry Cooper* is Colonel.

48649 [Place and Date] *Bangalore 15 December* 187 *6*.

PROCEEDINGS OF A REGIMENTAL BOARD, held this day, in conformity to the Articles of War, for the purpose of verifying and recording the Services, Conduct, Character, and cause of Discharge of No. 54/4139 3/1506 *Serjeant John Buxton*. of the Regiment above-mentioned.

President.
Major L. Adams 45 Regt

Members.
Captain N. H. Fillon 45 Regt   *Captain J. E. Barnes 45 Regt*

THE BOARD having examined and compared the Regimental Records, the Soldier's Book, and such other Documents as appeared to them to be necessary, report that after making every deduction required by Her Majesty's Regulations, the Service up to this day, which he is entitled to reckon, amounts to *20* years, *263* days, as shown by the detailed Statement on the 2nd page; during which period he served abroad *15 277/365* years, viz.:

at *East Indies* — *15 277/365* years,
in — years;

and further, that his DISCHARGE is proposed in consequence of *his being claimed it on termination of his second period of limited Engagement.*

[Here state whether—Completion of period, at his own request, or as unfit for further Service. Or any other cause.]

With regard to the CHARACTER and CONDUCT of *No. 54/4139 3/1506. Serjeant John Buxton*, the Board have to report, that upon reference to the Defaulter's Book, and by the Parole testimony that has been given, it appears that *his*

[Insert opposite—the man's Character, the number of Good Conduct Badges in his possession, and all Badges of Merit, or gallant conduct in the Field, conferred upon him, and if in possession of a School Certificate, record it and state the class.]

Conduct has been Good He was when promoted in the possession of two good conduct badges and would had he not been promoted have been now in possession of four good Conduct Badges. He is in possession of a 4th Class Certificate of Education also the India Mutiny Medal

[Insert the number of times his Name appears in the Regimental Defaulters' Book, and that he has been tried by Court Martial.

The charge, finding, and sentence,]

He has been three times entered in the Regimental defaulters' Book He has been twice tried by Courts martial.

Indian General Service Medals 1854–95, Egypt Medals 1882–9 and Second Afghan War Medals 1878–80 .

Verifying the medal to 1569 Sergeant Dowling in WO 100/52/1 revealed nothing unusual, so the next step was to find a record of service (FIGURE 5).

As the medal was named to a sergeant, it was good indication of a career soldier. The records of service of soldiers discharged to pension between 1760 and 1913 are at the National Archives in the series WO 97. As Dowling's medal was for a campaign between 1878 and 1880, I searched the 1873–82 section of WO 97 for Infantry Regiments and the box covering his name.

I found a set of papers for a Sergeant Michael Dowling of the 70th Foot who was invalided out of the army with pension in April 1882, but crucially the service number was 1678 and not 1569. Was the medal roll wrong and the medal named incorrectly? Consultation of the Second Afghan Medal roll at the British Library in L/MIL/5/114 agreed with the roll in WO 100/52/1, so it was necessary to look further.

There were a number of things that could be done, such as looking at the muster and pay lists for the 70th Foot in WO 12 and WO 16, looking more closely at the record of service from 1678 Michael Dowling and at the Disability Discharge Registers in WO 116. As the record of service of 1678 Michael Dowling gave his cause of discharge as invaliding and the date of April 1882, a consultation of WO 116 was done first and this confirmed that 1678 Sergeant Michael Dowling 70th had been invalided as insane and sent to the Kilkenny County Asylum.

Now that the end of Michael Dowling's career was confirmed, it was a case of working backwards, using the Muster and Pay Lists in WO 16 first and then, if necessary, the records in WO 12.

The Muster and Pay List for the first four months of 1882 proved very revealing. In the Sergeant's section of the list were listed 1569 Michael Dowling (as per the medal) and 1678 Michael Dowling (as per the record of service). Crucially both names were bracketed together 'Embarked for England Insane'! See PLATE 5.

By using the Muster and Pay Lists in WO 12 and WO 16, it transpired that 1569 joined the 70th in December 1869. He subsequently

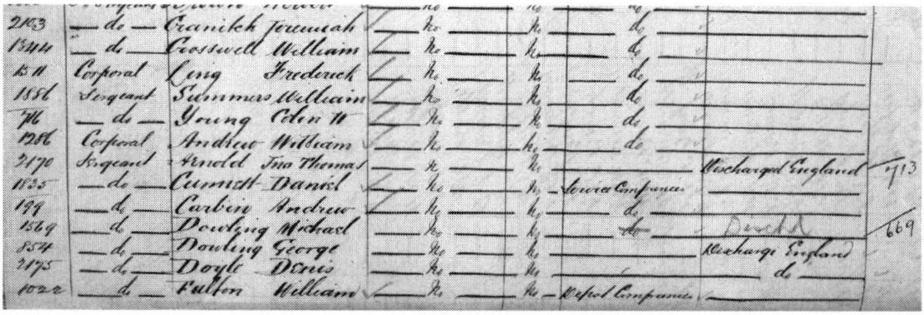

2143	— do —	Cranitch Jeremiah	no	no	do		
1344	— do —	Cresswell William	no	no	do		
1511	Corporal	Long Frederick	no	no	do		
1886	Sergeant	Summers William	no	no	do		
716	— do —	Young Colin W	no	no	do		
1286	Corporal	Andrew William	no	no	do		
2170	Sergeant	Arnold Jno Thomas	no	no		Discharged England	713
1835	— do —	Cumnatt Daniel	no	no	Service Companies		
199	— do —	Carbin Andrew	no	no	do		
1569	— do —	Dowling Michael	no	no	do	Dead	669
854	— do —	Dowling George	no	no		Discharge England	
2175	— do —	Doyle Denis	no	no		do	
1022	— do —	Fulton William	no	no	Depot Companies		

FIG 5. *Second Afghan War 1878–80 medal roll, showing the entry for 1569 Sgt M. Dowling, 70th Foot* [WO 100/52/1]

deserted in August 1870. 1678, by contrast, joined the 70th in September 1870. The 70th left Ireland for service in India in 1871.

1678 Michael Dowling gave his occupation on enlistment as 'clerk' and he was soon working in the regimental office, probably working on the Muster and Pay lists of the regiment. 1569 Michael Dowling makes a re-appearance in the pay list in 1872, as he is listed amongst the new arrivals. Both 1678 and 1569 appear constantly in the pay lists until they are invalided in 1882.

For the Second Afghan War period, both men were initially left at Regimental HQ in Mooltan when the rest of the regiment went into Afghanistan. However, during the last three months that the 70th were in Afghanistan, 1569 is shown as being with them on operations, so qualifying for the Second Afghan War Medal 1878–80.

As the final muster has both 1569 and 1678 bracketed together, and there is only one set of papers in WO 97 and one entry in WO 116, I am led to believe that 1569 Michael Dowling and 1678 Michael Dowling were one and the same man, who was very good with figures! I have entitled a talk about this medal 'I paid once but the Army paid twice!'

The Second Afghan Medal 1878–80 to Michael Dowling can be seen in PLATE 6.

James Moore

The Indian General Service Medal 1854–95, with the clasps *CHIN-LUSHAI 1889–90* and *N E FRONTIER 1891*, to 4258 Sergeant

James Moore, Commissariat and Transport Department, appears quite correct. The naming style is correct and the medal has not been tampered with. However, it does not appear on any medal roll.

The record of service of James Moore makes no mention of his medal, but does confirm his service with the Rifle Brigade before transferring to the Indian Unattached List to serve with the Commissariat and Transport Department. There is nothing on James Moore's medical sheet or conduct sheet to connect him with the two campaigns his medal represents.

As James Moore was on the Unattached Lists in Bengal, a check of the list was called for. The Unattached Lists usually give a one-line entry per man, stating when they joined the list, their parent unit and how they were currently employed. The 1890 Bengal Unattached List in L/MIL/10/276 revealed James Moore to be currently on the Chin-Lushai Expedition, thereby confirming his entitlement to his medal!

James Moore's Indian General Service Medal 1854–1985 with the clasps *CHIN-LUSHAI 1889–90* and *NE FRONTIER 1891* can be seen in PLATE 7.

3.6 CHINA

Forces of the British Army, the the East India Company and the Indian Army fought a number of wars in China. Three campaign medals were awarded for what became known as the First China (or Opium) War, the Second China (or Arrow) War and the Third China (Boxer Rebellion) War.

China Medal 1840–2

The problem with the medal for the First China War is that a number of medal rolls, most notably for the British Army, do not exist.

ADM 171/6 List of Officers, Men and Boys who served in HM ships in the Syria and China campaigns

ADM 171/7 List of claims for Medals for Service in Syria and China

ADM 171/12 Naval Officers and Ratings

ADM 171/13 Supplementary roll noting those noted as dead on above roll

L/MIL/5/67 Staff, Bengal volunteers, Madras Ordnance Department, Madras Artillery, Madras Medical Department, Madras Field Engineers, 2nd, 6th, 14th, 36th, 37th and 41st Madras Native Infantry

Plate 1 A Military General Service Medal 1793–1814 identical to that earned by Sir John Scott Lillie

Plate 2 (*top*) Bugler Ali Wadi Songoro, 3rd King's African Rifles

Plate 3 (*right*) Ali Wadi Songoro's Africa General Service Medal with three clasps

Plate 4 The Indian Mutiny
Medal with *Lucknow* clasp
earned by John Buxton,
34th Regiment

Plate 5 (*top*) The Muster and Pay List of 2nd East Surrey Regiment recording the departure of Sgt Michael Dowling
WO 16/1644

Plate 6 (*right*) The Second Afghan War Medal 1878–80 earned by Sgt Michael Dowling, 70th Regiment (later 2nd East Surrey Regiment)

Plate 7 (*right*) The Indian General Service Medal 1854–95 with clasps *CHIN LUSHAI 1889–90* and *NORTH EAST FRONTIER 1891* earned by Sgt James Moore, Commissariat and Transport Department

Plate 8 (*right*)
Lt A.W.S. Reeve RNR,
British War Medal

Plate 9 (*facing page, top*)
The Merchant Navy record
(front) of Stanley Berry
BT 372/526

Plate 10 (*facing page, below*)
The Merchant Navy record
(back) of Stanley Berry
BT 372/526

2 **Particulars**

(1) Surname...... BERRY
        (BLOCK CAPITALS)
(2) Christian or First Names...... Stanley
(3) Date of Birth...... 2.3.1924
(4) Place of Birth...... Bolton
(5) Colour of (a) eyes...... Blue (b) hair...... Lt. Blue
(6) Complexion...... Fresh
(7) Height ...... 5 ft. 11 ins.
(8) Distinguishing Marks ...... none
(9) Nationality—see Panel 7. British

C.R.S.53

M.M.O.
Embossing
Stamp

U.S.-43

R 271313

Signature of Holder......

LEFT-HAND FINGERPRINTS
(Plain impressions of four fingers)

M. OFFICE
15 JAN 1946
31
CORNHILL LIVERPOOL

THUMBS—PLAIN IMPRESSIONS
LEFT   RIGHT

Surplus to Requirements

M. OFFICE
JAN 1946
31
CORNHILL, LIVERPOOL

6
Endorsements

Ration Cards and Books issued, etc.

RB12S   22/3   10.1.45
11/59/9.   24.1.45
                  29.4.45
RB12S. 29/9/48   9.7.45
9/9. 4/1/44   27/9..
    11/1/44.
    25/1/44   25 NOV 1945
8.2.44:   9.12.45
18/9/44.   23/12/45
                 6.1.46
                 20.1.46

Clothing Coupon Books issued, etc.

(43) 10/5/43
27. 26/8/43
(9) 2/9/43
15.%. 10
7 3/1
1.2. 4.
20.4.45

M. OFFICE
15 JAN 1946
31
CORNHILL, LIVERPOOL

Spare 1   1939–43 Star
           Ribbon issued.

Spare 2

Spare 3

DECLARATION

I Declare (i) that the person to whom this Identity Card relates has satisfied me that he (she) is a seaman, and (ii) that the photograph within bearing my official stamp is a true likeness of that person, that the signature within is his (her) true signature, that the fingerprints within are his (hers), that he (she) possesses the physical characteristics entered within and has stated to me the date and place of his (her) birth as entered within.

Signature of Supt. of Mercantile Marine Office—

Date...... 22.3.1943

This form of Identity Card is issued to those seamen only, who satisfy the Superintendent of the Mercantile Marine Office that they are British subjects.

Plate 11 Stanley Berry's
1939–45 Star, Atlantic Star
and War Medal 1939–45

L/MIL/5/66   Naval Forces
WO 55/1240   Royal Artillery

Second China War Medal 1857–60

ADM 171/30   Marine Brigade personnel
ADM 171/31   Naval Officers and Ratings arranged in alphabetical order by ship: A–D
ADM 171/32   Naval Officers and Ratings arranged in alphabetical order by ship: E–J
ADM 171/33   Naval Officers and Ratings arranged in alphabetical order by ship: K–R
ADM 171/34   Naval Officers and Ratings arranged in alphabetical order by ship: S–Z
L/MIL/5/106   East India Company forces
L/MIL/5/107   Indian Navy ships: *Auckland, Berenice, Coromandel, Feroze, Prince Arthur, Victoria* and *Zenobia*
L/MIL/5/66   Naval personnel
WO 100/40   Staff, 1st Dragoons, Royal Artillery, Royal Engineers, Military Train, Commissariat, Military Store Department, Medical Staff, Army Hospital Corps and Civilians
WO 100/41   2/1st Foot, 1/2nd Foot, 1/3rd Foot, 31st Foot, 44th Foot, 59th Foot, 2/60th Foot, 67th Foot and 99th Foot
China Medal Roll 1856–1860 by K.J. Asplin (Savannah, 2004)

Third China War Medal 1900

ADM 171/55   Medal roll of naval and marine personnel who were landed in China during the Boxer Rebellion and who were eligible for the clasps
    Relief of Pekin, Taku Forts 1900 or *Defence of Legations*
WO 100/94   Staff, Cavalry, Royal Horse Artillery, Royal Field Artillery and Royal Garrison Artillery
WO 100/95   Royal Engineers, Infantry, Army Service Corps and Army Ordnance Corps
WO 100/96   Royal Army Medical Corps, Indian Medical Staff, Army Pay Department and Army Veterinary Department
WO 100/97   Chinese Regiments and Volunteers, Interpreters, War Correspondents and Civilians
WO 100/98   Sappers and Miners, Supply and Transport Corps, Indian Ordnance (British) Miscellaneous and Miscellaneous Natives
WO 100/99   Indian Army: Cavalry and Infantry
The China War Medal 1900 to the Royal Navy and Royal Marines by W.H. Fevyer and J. W. Wilson (Spink, 1985)

Transport Medal 1899–1902

Awarded to Masters and certain other officers of merchant ships used to move men and material to South Africa and China. Granted with the clasps S. AFRICA 1899–1902 and CHINA 1900.

ADM 171/52 Admiralty medal roll of claims by Officers of the Mercantile Marine.

3.7 NEW ZEALAND

New Zealand Medal 1845–7 and 1860–6

ADM 171/16 Medal roll for the First and Second Maori Wars, 1845–47 and March 1860– July 1866

WO 100/18 Royal Artillery, Royal Engineers, 1st/12th Foot, 2/14th Foot, 2/18th Foot, 40th Foot, 43rd Foot, 50th Foot, 57th Foot, 58th Foot, 65th Foot, 70th Foot, 99th Foot, Army Hospital Corps, Commissariat, Staff Corps, Military Train, Local Forces

WO 100/19 A Royal Artillery roll for this medal can be found on pages 1st, 2 and 255–346.

The New Zealand Medal to Colonials: Detailed Medal Rolls for the New Zealand Wars 1845–1872 by R. Stowers (1999)

3.8 BALTIC AND CRIMEA

Baltic Medal 1854–6

ADM 171/19 List of Naval Claimants arranged in alphabetical order: A–D

ADM 171/20 List of Naval Claimants arranged in alphabetical order: E–J

ADM 171/21 List of Naval Claimants arranged in alphabetical order: K–R

ADM 171/22 List of Naval Claimants arranged in alphabetical order: S–Z

Crimean War Medal 1854–6

ADM 171/23 Medal roll of the Marine Brigade personnel who qualified for the clasps SEBASTOPOL, BALAKLAVA and INKERMAN

ADM 171/24 Medal roll of the Naval Brigade personnel who qualified for the clasps SEBASTOPOL and INKERMAN

ADM 171/25 Medal roll of the Naval and Marine personnel who qualified for the clasp AZOFF

The Azoff Campaign by P. Duckers and N. Mitchell (1997)

WO 100/22 Royal Artillery (RA, RHA up to the 6th Battalion)

WO 100/23 Royal Artillery (7th–12th Battalions), Royal Engineers

WO 100/24 General and Line Cavalry

WO 100/25 Foot Guards

WO 100/26 1st Foot, 3rd Foot, 4th Foot, 7th Foot and 9th Foot

WO 100/27 13th Foot, 14th Foot, 17th–21st Foot

WO 100/28 23rd Foot, 28th Foot, 30th Foot, 31st Foot, 33rd Foot and 34th

Foot

WO 100/29   38th Foot, 39th Foot, 41st Foot, 42nd Foot, 44th Foot and 46th
   Foot

WO 100/30   47th–50th Foot, 55th Foot and 56th Foot

WO 100/31   57th Foot, 62nd Foot, 63rd Foot, 68th Foot, 71st Foot and 72nd
   Foot

WO 100/32   77th Foot, 79th Foot, 82nd Foot, 88th Foot, 89th Foot and 90th
   Foot

WO 100/33   93rd Foot, 95th Foot, 97th Foot, 1st and 2nd Rifle Brigade

WO 100/34   Medical Corps, Turkish Contingent, Sardinian Contingent, Land
   Transport Corps, Ordnance Corps and Chaplains

WO 100/364   Presentation of Medals for Service in the Crimea, 18 May 1855:
   List of Recipients.

Presented by The Queen: the Crimea Medal Ward Ceremony 18 May 1855 by
   P. Duckers and N. Mitchell (1996)

Turkish Crimea Medal

The Admiralty rolls for the Turkish Crimea Medal are very useful as the
entries of most individuals are annotated with their clasp entitlement
for the British Crimea Medal. The annotations are I for Inkerman, B for
Balaclava, S for Sebastopol and Az for Azoff. The rolls are arranged by
name of ship.

ADM 171/26   Ships A–F

ADM 171/27   Ships G–Q

ADM 171/28   Ships R–Z

WO 100/373   Distribution of Turkish Medals: lost medals 1857–62

Casualty Roll for the Crimea 1854–55 by F. and A. Cook (Hayward, 1976)

3.9   CANADA

Canada General ServiceMedal 1866–70

ADM 171/35   Medal roll for Naval personnel serving in Canada between 1866
   and 1870 and qualifying for the clasps FENIAN RAID 1866, RED RIVER 1870 or
   FENIAN RAID 1870

WO 100/110   Army medal roll for the Fenian Raid and Red River Expedition

3.10   MIDDLE EAST

The Indian General Service Medal 1854–95 with the clasp PERSIA
is listed in 3.4 above.

Naval General Service Medal 1915–62

ADM 171/62   Medal roll for Naval and Marine recipients of the clasps PERSIAN

GULF 1909–1914, IRAQ 1919–1920 and *N W PERSIA 1920*

ADM 1/8680/103 contains late applications for the *IRAQ 1919–20* clasp.

The Naval General Service Medal 1915–1962 to the Royal Navy and Royal Marines by W.H. Fevyer and J.W. Wilson (Naval and Military Press, 1995)

General Service Medal 1918–62

The Campaign Medal Record Cards of RAF personnel noting recipients of General Service Medals will be in AIR 81 when accessioned.

- Clasps: *IRAQ, S PERSIA, N W PERSIA, KURDISTAN, SOUTHERN DESERT IRAQ* (British Army)

Medal rolls for the above clasps (unless otherwise stated) for both the British and Indian Armies are in WO 100/411–466 as follows:

WO 100/411 Other Ranks 1st Dragoon Guards, 7th Dragoon Guards, Corps of Dragoons, 8th Hussars, Corps of Hussars, Corps of Lancers, Duke of Lancaster's Own Yeomanry, Shropshire Yeomanry, North Somerset Yeomanry, Royal Gloucester Hussars Yeomanry, Royal Horse Artillery and Royal Field Artillery

WO 100/412 Other Ranks Royal Horse Artillery and Royal Field Artillery, Royal Garrison Artillery

WO 100/413 Other Ranks Royal Engineers, Royal Signals, Grenadier Guards, Coldstream Guards, Scots Guards, Irish Guards, Royal Scots, Queen's, East Kent, Royal Lancaster, Northumberland Fusiliers, Royal Warwickshire, Royal Fusiliers

WO 100/414 Other Ranks Liverpool, Norfolk, Lincolnshire, Devon, Suffolk, Somerset Light Infantry, West Yorkshire, East Yorkshire, Bedfordshire and Hertfordshire, Leicestershire, Royal Irish, Yorkshire, Lancashire Fusiliers, Royal Scots Fusiliers, Cheshire, Royal Welsh Fusiliers, South Wales Borderers, King's Own Scottish Borderers, Cameronians, Royal Inniskilling Fusiliers, Glocestershire, Worcestershire, East Lancashire, East Surrey, Duke of Cornwall's Light Infantry, Duke of Wellington's, Border, Royal Sussex

WO 100/415 Other Ranks Hampshire, South Staffordshire, Dorset, South Lancashire, Welch, Royal Highlanders, Oxfordshire and Buckinghamshire Light Infantry, Essex, Notts and Derby, Loyal North Lancashire, Northamptonshire, Royal Berkshire, Royal West Kent, King's Own Yorkshire Light Infantry

WO 100/416 Other Ranks King's Shropshire Light Infantry, Middlesex, King's Royal Rifle Corps, Wiltshire, Manchester, North Staffordshire, York and Lancaster, Durham Light Infantry, Highland Light Infantry, Seaforth Highlanders, Gordon Highlanders, Cameron Highlanders

WO 100/417 Other Ranks Royal Ulster Rifles, Royal Irish Rifles, Royal Irish Fusiliers, Connaught Rangers, Argyll and Sutherland Highlanders, Leinster, Rifle Brigade

WO 100/418 Other Ranks Machine Gun Corps, Royal Tank Corps, 19th London, 23rd London, 25th London, RASC

WO 100/419 Other Ranks RAMC, RAOC, RAVC, RAPC, Army Education Corps, Military Mounted Police, Military Foot Police, Military Provost Staff Corps, Military Pioneer Corps, Corps of Military Accountants, RAF, Australian Wireless Signal Squadron, Australian Nurses, Mauritius Labour Battalion

WO 100/420 Officers Staff, 1st Dragoon Guards, 4th Dragoon Guards, 5th Dragoon Guards, 7th Dragoon Guards, 7th Hussars, 8th Hussars, 9th Lancers, 13th Hussars, 14th Hussars, 18 Hussars, Reserve Regiment of Cavalry, Northants Yeomanry, Lovat's Scouts, Royal Artillery, Royal Horse Artillery, Royal Field Artillery, Royal Garrison Artillery, Royal Engineers, Coldstream Guards, Queen's, East Kent, Royal Lancaster, Northumberland Fusiliers, Royal Warwickshire, Royal Fusiliers, Liverpool, Norfolk, Devon, Somerset Light Infantry, West Yorkshire, East Yorkshire, Bedford, Leicestershire, Royal Irish, Yorkshire, Cheshire, Royal Welsh Fusiliers, South Wales Borderers, King's Own Scottish Borderers, Cameronians, Royal Inniskilling Fusiliers, Gloucestershire, Worcestershire, East Lancashire, East Surrey, Duke of Cornwall's Light Infantry, Duke of Wellington's, Royal Sussex, Hampshire, South Staffordshire, Dorset, South Lancashire, Welch, Royal Highlanders, Oxfordshire and Buckinghamshire Light Infantry, Essex, Notts and Derby, Loyal North Lancashire, Northamptonshire, Royal Berkshire, Royal West Kent

WO 100/421 Officers King's Own Yorkshire Light Infantry, King's Shropshire Light Infantry, Middlesex, King's Royal Rifle Corps, Wiltshire, Manchester, North Staffordshire, York and Lancaster, Durham Light Infantry, Highland Light Infantry, Seaforth Highlanders, Gordon Highlanders, Cameron Highlanders, Royal Ulster Rifles, Royal Irish Fusiliers, Connaught Rangers, Argyll and Sutherland Highlanders, Leinster, Royal Munster Fusiliers, Royal Dublin Fusiliers, Rifle Brigade, Army Cyclist Corps, Machine Gun Corps, Royal Tank Corps, Labour Corps, Monmouth, 2nd London, 4th London, 14th London, 15th London, RASC, RAMC, RAOC, RAVC, Royal Army Chaplains Department, RAPC, Army Education Corps, Corps of Military Accountants, School of Equitation, General List, Extra Regimentally Employed, RAF, Indian Army, Financial Advisers, Queen Alexandra's Imperial Military Nursing Service and Reserve, Territorial Force Nursing Service, Miscellaneous

- Clasp: *NORTHERN KURDISTAN* only
WO 100/421 Miscellaneous

- Clasps: *IRAQ, S PERSIA, N W PERSIA, KURDISTAN* (Indian Army, unless otherwise stated)

WO 100/422 Corps of Military Staff Clerks, Staff, Indian Medical Department

WO 100/423 Indian Medical Department, Indian Unattached List, Indian Miscellaneous List, Indian Army Ordnance Corps

WO 100/425–431 Indian Army Service Corps

WO 100/432 Indian Army Reserve of Officers, Military Works Service, Indian Remount Department, Corps of Guides, 1st Punjab, 2nd Punjab, 8th Punjab

WO 100/433 10/14th Punjab (late 71st Punjabis), 15th Punjab, 2/15th Punjab (late 2/26th Punjabis), 3/4th Bombay Grenadiers (late 108th Infantry)

WO 100/434 10/4th Bombay Grenadiers (late 1/113th Infantry), 2/113th Infantry, 1/3rd Gurkha

WO 100/435 Gurkha, 7th Gurkha, 8th Gurkha, 2/10th Baluch (late 126th Baluch Light Infantry)

WO 100/436 5/2nd Punjab, 35th Scinde Horse, 5/5th Mahratta Light Infantry

WO 100/437 2/1st Madras Pioneers, 13th Frontier Force Coke's Rifles, 10/5th Maharatta Light Infantry (late 114 Mahrattas, including their roll for Southern Desert Iraq)

WO 100/438 1/10th Gurkha, 3/6th Rajputana Rifles (late 122nd Rajputana Infantry), 2/19th Hyderabad (late 2/96th Infantry), 10/19th Hyderabad (late 2/94th Russell's Infantry)

WO 100/439 1/19th Hyderabad (late 1/94th Russell's Infantry), 5/19th Hyderabad (late 99th Infantry), 6th Rajputana Rifles (late 13th Rajput)

WO 100/440 5/6th Rajputana Rifles (late 125th Napiers), 2/6th Rajputana Rifles (late 120th Rajputana Infantry 4/7th Rajput (late 8th Rajputs), 10/7th Rajput (late 16th Rajputs)

WO 100/441 Indian Army Veterinary Corps, 1st Duke of York's (Skinner's Horse) (late 3rd Skinner's Horse and 1st Lancers), 2/12th Frontier Force (late 52nd Sikhs), 6/13th RR (late 59th Scinde Rifles), 1/19th Royal Garhwal Rifles (late 1/39th Garhwal Rifles), 2/39th Royal Garhwal Rifles

WO 100/442–446 Royal Artillery (Indian Other Ranks)

WO 100/447 1/4th Hazara Pioneers (Late 106th Pioneers) 20th Lancers (late 15th Lancers), Aden Motor Transport Section, Dairy Farms, Followers

WO 100/448 8th King George's Own Light Cavalry (late 36th Light Cavalry and 30th Lancers), 4/10th Baluch (late 2/129th Baluch), 2nd Gurkha Rifles, 1/11th Gurkha Rifles, 4/16th Punjab (late 3/9th Bhopal)

WO 100/449 3/16th Punjab, 2/6th Royal Jat Light Infantry, Indian Labour Corps

WO 100/450 10/3rd Madras (late 86th Carnatic Infantry), 4th Gurkha Rifles, Military Accounts Department, 2/11th Sikhs, 3/11th Sikhs (late 45th Sikhs)

WO 100/451 1/11th Sikhs, 2/11th Sikhs, 3rd Cavalry (late 5th and 8th Cavalry), 4/2nd Bombay Pioneers (late 48th Pioneers)

WO 100/452 3/2nd Bombay Pioneers (late 128th Pioneers), 63rd Palamcottah Light Infantry, 2/10th Gurkha Rifles, 37th Lancers (late 1/81st Pioneers), 10/1st Madras Pioneers, 32nd Lancers,

WO 100/453   3/10th Baluch (late 1/127th Baluch Light Infantry), 16th Light
  Cavalry (late 27th Light Cavalry), 20th Burma Rifles (late 3/70th and 85th
  Burma Rifles), 10/1st Punjab (late 2/1st Brahmans)

WO 100/454   1st Brahmans, South Persia Rifles, 4th Duke of Cambridge's
  Own Hodson's Horse late 9th Horse and 10th Lancers), 11th King
  Edward's Own Lancers, 12th Pioneers

WO 100/455   12th Pioneers (returned medals from above roll), Indian Signals
  Corps

WO 100/456   3/3rd Madras (late 79th Carnatic Infantry), 4/3rd Madras (late
  83rd Wallajahbad Light Infantry), 2/123rd Outram's Rifles, Bengal Sappers
  and Miners

WO 100/457   Miscellaneous, Royal Engineers, Overseas Depot, Kirkee,
  2/116th Mahrattas

WO 100/458   80th Carnatic Infantry, Burma Military Police, 3/153rd Rifles,
  10/3rd Sikh Pioneers (late 2/23rd Sikhs), 2/3rd Sikh Pioneers (late 32nd Sikh
  Pioneeers)

WO 100/459   1st/42 Deoli, 2/119th Infantry, Kapurthala-Jagatjit Infantry,
  Assam rifles, 2/11th Gurkha Rifles, 2/9th Delhi

WO 100/460   49 Bengalis, 1/10th Baluch (late 1/124th Infantry), 2/7th
  Rajputs, Madras Sappers and Miners, Royal Bombay Sappers and Miners

WO 100/461   92th Cavalry (late 12th Frontier Force, Sam Browne's Cavalry),
  2/117th Mahrattas, 1/3rd Brahmans, 3/124th Baluchistan Infantry

WO 100/462   Indian Army Hospital and Army Bearer Corps, Survey Party,
  Assyrian Battalion, Indian Machine Gun Corps, Railway Construction
  Companies, Disbanded Madras Infantry, 4/13th Frontier Force Rifles,
  1/12th Frontier Force (late 51st Sikhs)

WO 100/463   Royal Indian Marine, 16th Cavalry, 34th Poona Horse, 17th
  Cavalry, India Office Rolls, Interpreters

WO 100/464 Indian and Iraqi Units   Iraq Miscellaneous, Railway Defence
  Force, Inland Waterways Transport Royal Engineers, Works Companies
  Royal Engineers

WO 100/465 Iraqi Units   Iraq Levies, 2nd Battalion Iraq Levies, 3rd Battalion
  Iraq Levies, 4th Battalion Iraq Levies, Pack Batteries, etc. Iraq Levies, 3rd
  Cavalry Regiment Iraq Levies, Civilians Iraq (Europeans employed in civil
  administration)

WO 100/466 Indian and Iraqi Units   Civilians Iraq (Europeans employed in
  Civil Administration, including Indian Posts and Telegraphs), India
  Miscellaneous

Iraq Active Service Medal 1924–32

AIR 2/2423   Iraq Service Medal, award for military service in the Euphrates
  1937–8

WO 32/4299 and 4300 Award of Iraq Active Service Medal to British Officers
  1926–31
WO 100/403 Nominal roll of British Officers and Other Ranks and
  Correspondence relating to issue of Medals

3.11   ROLLS TO COME

The remaining army medal rolls for the India General Service Medal 1908–35, with clasps. NORTH WEST FRONTIER 1930–1, BURMA 1930–2, MOHMAND 1933 AND NW FRONTIER 1935 should all be available by mid-2007.

Army medal rolls for General Service Medal 1918–62 for clasps PALESTINE, S.E ASIA 1945–46, BOMB AND MINE CLEARANCE 1945–49, BOMB AND MINE CLEARANCE 1945–56 and PALESTINE 1945–48 are currently being prepared for transfer from the Ministry of Defence. As for Royal Navy and RAF records, I can add little to what has been said in other parts of this book.

4   First World War Campaign Medals

4.1   INTRODUCTION

At the end of the First World War, campaign medals were issued in their millions. Some of the medals issued for campaign service between 1914 and 1918 are rarer than others. Statistically the Territorial Force War Medal is the rarest, with only some 34,000 issued. The British War Medal, with over 6,500,000 issued, is the most common. See PLATE 8. However, some 100,000 Bronze British War Medals were also issued in bronze rather than silver, and these are quite rare.

In this chapter all of the key primary sources will be discussed, together with the information they contain, and the strengths and weaknesses of the sources.

4.2   THE ADMIRALTY

The medal rolls for most of the First World War Campaign Medals issued under the authority of the Admiralty are in the records series ADM 171, and are available on microfilm. There are, however, a number of medal rolls in ADM 116 that are not microfilmed and they require ordering via the document-ordering computer.

The medal rolls in ADM 171 follow a standard format and are usually typed rather than handwritten, which makes reading them easier. The rolls are arranged in 6 columns as follows:

COLUMNS 1–3	surname, forename and initial(s), rank/rating, service number
COLUMN 4	medal(s) qualified for
COLUMN 5	to whom the medals were sent
COLUMN 6	remarks

Apart from the information regarding surname, forename and initial(s) being easily understood, the information in columns 4–6 is usually abbreviated or in a code. The following are the most common abbreviations and codes.

FOUND IN COLUMN 4
1914 ST. *1914 Star*
1914 ST.C. *1914 Star with clasp*
ST. *1914/15 Star*
B. *British War Medal*
V. *Victory Medal*

FOUND IN COLUMN 5
S. *Self* (i.e. the recipient)
FR. *Father*
MR. *Mother*
SR. *Sister*
BR. *Brother*
W. *Wife*
Ww. *Widow*
DR. *Daughter*
GODMR. *Godmother*
GODFR. *Godfather*
GRDFR *Grandfather*
UNIV. LEG. *Universal Legatee*
RES. LEG. *Residual Legatee*
LEG. REP. *Legal Representative*

EXECR. *Executor*
EXECX. *Executrix*
ADMINR. *Administrator*
ADMINX. *Administratrix*
A.M. *Issued to the Air Ministry for disposal to recipient*
W.O. *Issued to the War Office for disposal to recipient*
B.o.T. *Issued to the Board of Trade for disposal to recipient*
By A.M. *Issued by the Air Ministry*
By W.O. *Issued by the War Office*
By B.o.T. *Issued by the Board of Trade*
F. *Forfeited*
C.o.P. *Commissioner of Police*
N.O. Wellington *Naval Office, Wellington* (there were also other offices)
D.N.D. Ottawa *Department of National Defence, Ottawa*
Nav. Rep. *Naval Representative, Commonwealth of Australia*
B.N.M. Athens *British Naval Mission to Greece*
D.R.I.M. *Director, Royal Indian Marine*
392000, etc. *Refers to relevant medal issue paper*
Ship name *Still serving at sea at the time of medal(s) issue*

FOUND IN COLUMN 6
R. *Run* i.e. deserted
D. *Discharged with Disgrace*
Dups. *Duplicates issued*
I.C. 1000/1914, etc. *Refers to Naval Law (NL) Issue Certificate number and year.*
    (Wills paper)

The rolls are divided into groups according to branch of Naval service and rank.

Royal Navy, Royal Naval Volunteer Reserve and Royal Naval Air Service: Officers

ADM 171/89   A–Ga
ADM 171/90   Ge–Ode
ADM 171/91   Ode–Z

Royal Marine Light Infantry and Royal Marine Artillery: Officers
ADM 171/92   A–Z

Royal Naval Reserve: Officers
ADM 171/92   A–Mas

ADM 171/93	Mat–Z	Pages 2–262

Miscellaneous: Officers

ADM 171/93	Mercantile Marine Reserve	Pages 263–440
	Nigerian Marine	Pages 441–5
	Nyasaland Volunteer Reserve	Page 446
	Royal Indian Marine	Page 447
	Foreigner (Chinese)	Page 448
	Uganda Volunteer Reserve	Page 448
	South Africa RNVR	Page 449
	Army	Page 449
	Civilians	Page 450
	Fishery Reserve	Page 451

Royal Navy: Ratings

ADM 171/94	A–Ba
ADM 171/95	Bak–Be
ADM 171/96	Bi–Bri
ADM 171/97	Bro–Can
ADM 171/98	Cap–Cog
ADM 171/99	Cog–Cue
ADM 171/100	Cu–Dug
ADM 171/101	Duh–Ff
ADM 171/102	Fi–Gid
ADM 171/103	Gif–Gy
ADM 171/104	H–Hay
ADM 171/105	Haz–Hop
ADM 171/106	Hor–Jol
ADM 171/107	Jon–Lau
ADM 171/108	Lav–Ly
ADM 171/109	M–Mas
ADM 171/110	Mat–My
ADM 171/111	N–Pax
ADM 171/112	Pay–Py
ADM 171/113	Q–Rom
ADM 171/114	Ron–Sib
ADM 171/115	Sic–Sta
ADM 171/116	Ste–Tay
ADM 171/117	Tea–Vy
ADM 171/118	W–Who
ADM 171/119	Whu–Z

Royal Naval Reserve: Ratings

ADM 171/120	A–Cun
ADM 171/121	Cup–Hug
ADM 171/122	Hui–Map
ADM 171/123	Mar–Sey
ADM 171/124	Sha–Z

Royal Naval Volunteer Reserve: Ratings

ADM 171/125	A–Dak
ADM 171/126	Dal–Hip
ADM 171/127	Hir–Mop
ADM 171/128	Mor–Sic
ADM 171/129	Sid–Z

Mercantile Marine Reserve: Ratings

ADM 171/130	A–Fou	
ADM 171/131	Fow–Mea	
ADM 171/132	Meb–War	
ADM 171/133	Wat–Z	Pages 1–118

Miscellaneous

ADM 171/133	Civilians	Pages 119–97
	Australian Naval Forces	Pages 198–200
	Maltese RNR	Pages 201–22
	Newfoundland RNR	Pages 223–300
	Shore Wireless Service	Pages 301–20
	Fishery Reserve	Pages 321–499
	Canteen Staff	Pages 500–66
	Belgian Field Hospital	Page 567
	Belgian Red Cross Ambulance	Page 568
	Royal Naval Nursing Service	Pages 569–76
	British Eastern Auxiliary Hospital, Serbia	Page 577
	Mrs Stobart's Hospital Unit	Page 578
	Voluntary Aid Detachment	Pages 579–580
	Women's Royal Naval Service	Page 581–end

Natives

ADM 171/134 contains rolls for: Chinese, Colombo Minesweeping Service, Egypt Government Service, Interpreters, Lake Nyasa, Lake Victoria and Nigerian Marine

Royal Marine Light Infantry and Royal Marine Artillery: Other Ranks

ADM 171/167	A–Con

ADM 171/168	Coo–Ham
ADM 171/169	Han–Mam
ADM 171/170	Man–Sha
ADM 171/171	She–Z

Royal Indian Marine Service

The medal rolls of the Royal Indian Marine are in the series ADM 116/2154 and 2155, but they are not arranged in any logical order.

1914 Star Issue Roll

ADM 171/139

The 1914 Star to the Royal Navy and Royal Marines by W.H. Fevyer and J. W. Wilson (Naval and Military Press, 1995)

Silver War Badge

There are a number of pieces of ADM 171 concerned with the Silver War Badge as issued by the Admiralty. The records take the form of applications and issues. As the badges are all numbered, the easiest way to research a badge is to find the roll that covers the badge number. This will give you the name, rank or rate, service number and date issued. Once you know who received the badge, you can research that person in the appropriate place.

ADM 171/173	Officers' Applications
ADM 171/174	WRNS Applications
ADM 171/175	Ratings' Applications: A–D
ADM 171/176	Ratings' Applications: E–K
ADM 171/177	Ratings' Applications: L–R
ADM 171/178	Ratings' Applications: S–Z
ADM 171/179	Ratings' Applications: A–D
ADM 171/180	Ratings' Applications: E–K
ADM 171/181	Ratings' Applications: L–R
ADM 171/182	Ratings' Applications: S–Z
ADM 171/183	Issues: Badge Nos 1–10200
ADM 171/184	Issues: Badge Nos 10201–20440
ADM 171/185	Issues: Badge Nos 20441–30580
ADM 171/186	Issues: Badge Nos 30581–45800
ADM 171/187	Issues: Badge Nos 45801–48600 (includes lists of returned badges)

Mentioned in Despatches (MiD): Issue of Oak Leaves

ADM 171/188	Names A–Car
ADM 171/189	Names Cox–D
ADM 171/190	Names E–Hea

ADM 171/191	Names Hea–K
ADM 171/192	Names L–M
ADM 171/193	Names N–R
ADM 171/194	Names S–Z

4.3 THE AIR MINISTRY

Currently there are no First World War Campaign Medal rolls for the Royal Air Force. There is, however, a large collection of campaign medal index cards, which, when accessed, will be in the records series AIR 81. The cards, arranged in alphabetical order, provide name, rank, number and medals earned. The cards cover all campaigns from 1914 to 1948, not including the Second World War.

There are a number of points regarding medal entitlement for those men who served in the two flying services, Royal Flying Corps (RFC) and Royal Naval Air Service (RNAS), which amalgamated on 1 April 1918 to become the Royal Air Force (RAF), and those who qualified for medals after the RAF was formed.

Men of the RNAS who qualified for medals prior to 1 April 1918 will be found amongst the Admiralty medal rolls in ADM 171. Men of the RFC, who saw service overseas prior to 31 December 1915 and who qualified for a 1914 Star or 1914/15 Star, may be found in the War Office medal records in WO 329 and WO 372. Many men, who qualified for their First World War medals with units other than the RFC and who then transferred into the RFC or the RAF, may also be found in the War Office medal records.

If no medal records are found in either ADM 171 or WO 329 and WO 372, the only other source is the records of service in either AIR 76 RAF Officers or AIR 79 RAF Airmen. One of the pages in these records of service should either be stamped 'Services Considered for Grant of War Medals' or the details of the medals earned should be written on the record.

Although quite a few Silver War Badges (SWB) were issued to members of the Royal Air Force, the only surviving roll is a fraction of the total number issued. The RAF SWB roll is in AIR 2/197/C33296.

For more information about the records in AIR 76 and Air 79, see *Air Force Records: A Guide for Family Historians* by

William Spencer, published by the National Archives (2008).

4.4   THE BOARD OF TRADE

The medal roll for the issue of the British War Medal and Mercantile Marine War Medal is in the records series BT 351. This series is available on microfiche and is arranged in alphabetical order and takes the form of a card index.

Many men and women who served in the Mercantile Marine also saw service in the armed forces, either before or after qualifying for medals with the Mercantile Marine. In many cases, these people also qualified for campaign medals for their military service, and their records in BT 351 are usually annotated to the effect that only the Mercantile Marine Medal was being issued by the Board of Trade, the remaining medals being issued by the service in which the individual had served.

A medal card in BT 351 provides the following information: surname, forename, place and year of birth, Certificate of Competency or Discharge 'A' Number, the date when the appropriate ribbon(s) and medal(s) were issued and to where.

The Merchant Navy Silver War Badge rolls can be found in three files:

MT 9/1132 Badges issued to T.L. Boyle, J.F. R. Stanley, G. Brocklebanks, H.G. Biggleston, W. Carson and G.L. Williams
MT 9/1242 Silver War Badge – Awards and conditions
MT 9/ 1404 Silver War Badges – List of recipients

4.5   THE WAR OFFICE
4.5.1 Introduction

The First World War campaign medal records of the War Office take two forms: the Medal Index Cards (MIC) in WO 372 and the Medal Rolls in WO 329. The MICs are available on microfiche (see 4.5.2) and online on the DocumentsOnline section (see 4.5.3) of the National Archives website or **www.ancestry.co.uk**. The records in WO 329 (see 4.5.6) are only available in their original form apart from some of the earliest rolls for the Royal Artillery.

The records in WO 372 and WO 329 contain the names of millions of men and women from the Army and civilian organizations

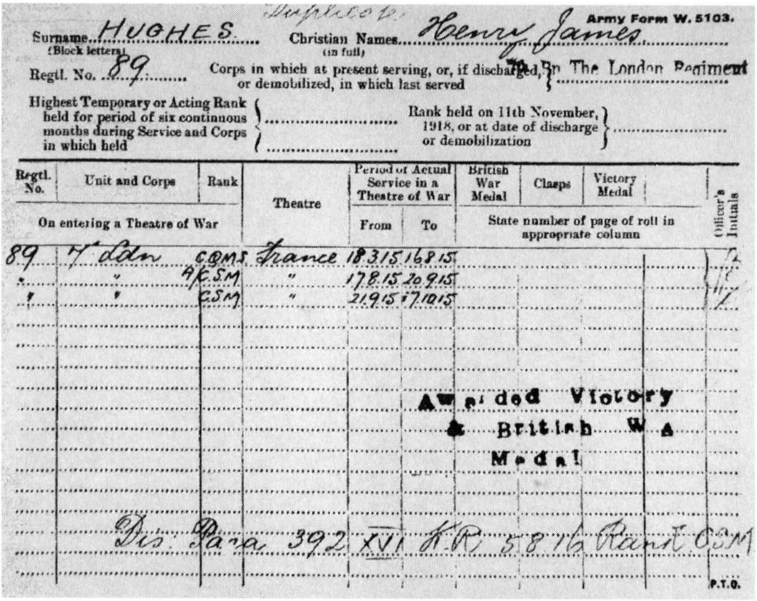

Army Form W. 5103.

Surname (Block letters) HUGHES Christian Names (in full) Henry James

Regtl. No. 89 Corps in which at present serving, or, if discharged, or demobilized, in which last served 4th The London Regiment

Highest Temporary or Acting Rank held for period of six continuous months during Service and Corps in which held ....

Rank held on 11th November, 1918, or at date of discharge or demobilization ....

Regtl. No.	Unit and Corps	Rank	Theatre	Period of Actual Service in a Theatre of War: From	To	British War Medal	Clasps	Victory Medal	Officer's Initials
On entering a Theatre of War						State number of page of roll in appropriate column			
89	4 Ldn	CQMS	France	18.3.15	16.8.15				
"	"	A/CSM	"	17.8.15	20.9.15				
"	"	CSM	"	21.9.15	7.10.15				

Awarded Victory & British War Medal

Dis: Para 392 XVI K.R. 5.8.16 Rank CSM

P.T.O.

FIG 6. *A War Office Medal Record Card for the First World War*

who qualified for one or more of the medals granted for service between 1914 and 1920. The records of those individuals who qualified for a Silver War Badge may also be found in these records.

In order for the Army to create the medal rolls and the Medal Index Cards, it first had to record the personal data of all those men and women who served overseas. Each card recorded the rank(s), unit(s), service number(s), operational theatre(s) and dates relevant to an individual's service overseas. The data could be used to determine the medal entitlement of an individual and what would be put onto the Medal Index Card. An example of one of these cards can be seen in FIGURE 6.

Within the records in WO 372 are many examples of men with the same name. In order for the clerks at the Army Medal Office to locate a specific card, they were arranged in a way that the army would understand. The cards are arranged in what is called the 'Regimental Order of Precedence'. This means that the different regiments and corps are in an order based on when each was founded, so if there are five men of the same name, they will be in the order of date on which the unit they first served in was founded.

Regimental Order of Precedence

1st Life Guards
2nd Life Guards
Royal Horse Guards
Household Battalion
Royal Horse Artillery
1st (The King's) Dragoon Guards
2nd Dragoon Guards (Queen's Bays)
3rd (The Prince of Wales's) Dragoon Guards
4th (Royal Irish) Dragoon Guards
5th (Princess Charlotte of Wales's) Dragoon Guards
6th Dragoon Guards (Carabiniers)
7th (The Princess Royal's) Dragoon Guards
1st (Royal) Dragoons
2nd Dragoons (Royal Scots Greys)
3rd (King's Own) Hussars
4th (The Queen's Own) Hussars
5th (Royal Irish) Lancers
6th (Inniskilling) Dragoons
7th The Queen's Own) Hussars
8th (The King's Royal Irish) Hussars
9th (The Queen's Royal) Lancers
10th (The Prince of Wales's Own Royal) Hussars
11th (Prince Albert's Own) Hussars
12th (The Prince of Wales's Royal) Lancers
13th Hussars
14th (The King's) Hussars
15th (The King's) Hussars
16th (The Queen's) Lancers
17th (the Duke of Cambridge's Own) Lancers
18th (Princess of Wales's) Hussars
19th (Alexandra, Princess of Wales's Own) Hussars
20th Hussars
21st (Empress of India's) Lancers
The Yeomanry Regiments
Royal Artillery
Royal Field Artillery
Royal Engineers

Royal Flying Corps
Grenadier Guards
Coldstream Guards
Scots Guards
Irish Guards
Welsh Guards
Royal Scots (Lothian Regiment)
Queen's (Royal West Surrey) Regiment
Buffs (East Kent Regiment)
King's Own (Royal Lancaster Regiment)
Northumberland Fusiliers
Royal Warwickshire Regiment
Royal Fusiliers (City of London Regiment)
King's (Liverpool Regiment)
Norfolk Regiment
Lincolnshire Regiment
Devonshire Regiment
Suffolk Regiment
Prince Albert's (Somersetshire Light Infantry)
Prince of Wales's Own (West Yorkshire Regiment)
East Yorkshire Regiment
Bedfordshire Regiment
Leicestershire Regiment
Royal Irish Regiment
Alexandra, Princess of Wales's Own (Yorkshire Regiment)
Lancashire Fusiliers
Royal Scots Fusiliers
Cheshire Regiment
Royal Welsh Fusiliers
South Wales Borderers
King's Own Scottish Borderers
Cameronians (Scottish Rifles)
Royal Inniskilling Fusiliers
Gloucestershire Regiment
Worcestershire Regiment
East Lancashire Regiment
East Surrey Regiment
Duke of Cornwall's Light Infantry
Duke of Wellington's (West Riding Regiment)
Border Regiment
Royal Sussex Regiment
Hampshire Regiment

South Staffordshire Regiment
Dorsetshire Regiment
Welsh Regiment
Black Watch (Royal Highlanders)
Oxfordshire and Buckinghamshire Light Infantry
Essex Regiment
Sherwood Forester (Nottinghamshire and Derbyshire Regiment)
Loyal North Lancashire Regiment
Northamptonshire Regiment
Princess Charlotte of Wales's (Royal Berkshire Regiment)
Queen's Own (Royal West Kent Regiment)
King's Own (Yorkshire Light Infantry)
King's (Shropshire Light Infantry)
Duke of Cambridge's Own (Middlesex Regiment)
King's Royal Rifle Corps
Duke of Edinburgh's (Wiltshire Regiment)
Manchester Regiment
Prince of Wales's (North Staffordshire Regiment)
York and Lancaster Regiment
Durham Light Infantry
Highland Light Infantry
Seaforth Highlanders (Ross-shire Buffs, The Duke of Albany's)
Gordon Highlanders
Queen's Own Cameron Highlanders
Royal Irish Rifles
Princess Victoria's (Royal Irish Fusiliers)
Connaught Rangers
Princess Louise's (Argyll and Sutherland Highlanders)
Prince of Wales's Leinster Regiment (Royal Canadians)
Royal Munster Fusiliers
Royal Dublin Fusiliers
Rifle Brigade (Prince Consort's Own)
West India Regiment
Royal Army Chaplains Department
Army Service Corps
Royal Army Medical Corps
Army Ordnance Corps
Army Veterinary Corps
Machine Gun Corps
Royal Tank Corps
Labour Corps
Honourable Artillery Company

Monmouthshire Regiment
Cambridgeshire Regiment
London Regiment
Hertfordshire Regiment
Northern Cyclist Battalion
Highland Cyclist Battalion
Kent Cyclist Battalion
Huntingdon Cyclist Battalion

This order of precedence contains most of the key units of the British Army. However, there are a variety of units to be found with the Medal Index Cards that appear after the British Army and are more easily found by using the MICs in DocumentsOnline.

4.5.2 Medal Index Cards on Microfiche

Available on microfiche in the Microfilm Reading Room, the Medal Index Cards (MIC) are arranged in alphabetical order, with each range of names in regimental order of precedence. One card contains all the information for one person.

Each sheet contains a maximum of 360 cards. The first card is in the top left hand corner, and the last in the bottom right hand corner. When the original cards were put on microfiche, they were done of groups of six.

A sheet of microfiche is arranged thus.

1	4	7	10		67	70
2	5	8	11	◄ 12 BLOCKS OF 6 ACROSS ►	68	71
3	6	9	12		69	72
73	76					
74	77					
75	78					

↑
5 BLOCKS OF 6
DOWN
↓

355	358
356	359
357	360

4.5.3 Medal Index Cards on DocumentsOnline

Although many people visiting the National Archives still use the microfiche copies of the Medal Index Cards (MIC), they have been digitized and are now available on the DocumentsOnline section of the National Archives website **www.nationalarchives.gov.uk/documentsonline/**. It is now possible to download an MIC from any computer that can access the internet from anywhere in the world.

Unlike using the microfiche, where you start by looking for the sheet of fiche covering the name, the digitized version is searchable by name, rank(s), number(s) or unit(s). As many men saw service in more than one unit, it is quite possible for there to be up to five different sets of details beyond the individual's name.

In many cases by using the digitized version, it is possible to find an MIC quicker than by the manual method, especially when you have the information taken from the medal with which to search the database.

If you print an MIC away from the National Archives, you may still wish to convert the original Army Medal Office references into WO 329 references. This can only be done at the National Archives.

Please note that all of the microfiched index cards for the First World War, the cards for the campaign medals and the Distinguished Conduct Medal, Military Medal, Meritorious Service Medal, Territorial Force Efficiency Medal and the Mentions in Despatches have all been digitized and consequently any search may produce more than one card for the same man.

Information about all of the First World War Medals and all of the WO 372 document references that appear on the database, are explained on the DocumentsOnline website **www.nationalarchives.gov.uk/documentsonline/**.

4.5.4 Interpreting a Medal Index Card

There are at least four different styles of Medal Index Card (MIC); an example can be seen in FIGURE 7. All should contain the name, rank, number (if appropriate) and unit of individual in the top half. Down the left-hand side are the names of the medals an individual qualified for and alongside these should be the original Army Medal Office references.

After the names of the medals, information may be found concerning the Silver War Badge, if appropriate. The annotation will be something like 'SWB list' and an alpha-numeric reference that can be traced using WO 329/1.

On an MIC with details of a Silver War Badge, reference is frequently made to either Army Orders or King's Regulations as the reason for an individual's discharge. Army Orders are available in WO 123 and King's Regulations are available on the open shelves of the Microfilm Reading Room. The most frequently referred to paragraph of King's Regulations is Para. 392, with article XVI ('no longer physically fit for war service') appearing very often.

Below the names of the medals, there should be the term 'Theatre of War first served in'. Alongside this, there may be a numerical code or the name of operational theatre where the individual first served. Below this, the card should say 'Date of entry therein'. This is the date of arrival in the operational theatre. If the theatre and date sections are blank, it usually denotes first operational service in France from 1916 onwards.

The bottom right-hand corner of the MIC is given over for remarks. In this area of the card it may be possible to find the date an individual was killed or died, if they were a prisoner of war, if they were commissioned or if the medals were returned or forfeited.

If the individual was a recipient of a 1914 Star, it is possible that they qualified for a clasp to the medal. If so, the MIC will be annotated with either 'Clasp and Roses' or 'C and R'.

If an individual had a Mention in Despatches (MiD), the MIC may have the annotation, 'emblems' at the bottom of the card or in the remarks box. This refers to the oakleaf emblems denoting an MiD that would be worn on the ribbon of the Victory Medal.

On some Medal Index Cards, there may be mention of entitlement campaign medals for campaigns after the end of the First World War. In many cases, the medals mentioned will be the General Service Medal for service in the Middle East, e.g. Iraq or Persia, or the Indian General Service Medal 1908–35 for service in Afghanistan or Waziristan. In both cases, the medal rolls for these medals are now in WO 100.

Some MICs are annotated with information regarding the issue of post-First World War Regular Army Long Service and Good Conduct medals. In most cases, the Army Order number and year are given. This information can be used with the Army Orders in WO 123 or the medal rolls in WO 102.

In the remarks section of the MIC, information about the return of a medal may also be recorded. Frequently, reference will be made to an article from King's Regulations. King's Regulations for 1914 are available on the open shelves in the Microfilm Reading Room.

4.5.5 *Operational Theatre Alpha-numeric Codes*
The operational theatre codes and the applicable dates were announced in two Army Orders. For those personnel who first saw operational service at any time up to 31 December 1915 and who received a 1914 Star or 1914/15 Star, the codes differ slightly from those who only saw their first operational service from 1 January 1916 onwards. The codes are usually found on the Medal Index Cards, but they sometimes appear on the medal rolls in WO 329.

In the list below, use the left-hand column if a person received a 1914 or 1914/15 Star; if the person received only a British War Medal and Victory Medal, use the right-hand column. Please be aware that there are always exceptions and so take this as a guide.

To 31 December 1915	From 1 January 1916	
1	1	WESTERN EUROPE
		a France and Belgium
		b Italy
2	2	BALKANS
		a Greek Macedonia, Serbia, Bulgaria and European Turkey
		b Gallipoli (Dardanelles)
	3	RUSSIA (4/5 August 1914–1/2 July 1920)
3	4	EGYPT
		a 4/5 November 1914–18/19 March

1916
b   18/19 March 1916–31 October/1
November 1918

4   5   AFRICA
a   East Africa, Nyasaland and Northern
Rhodesia
b   South West Africa
c   Cameroon
d   Nigeria
e   Togoland

5   6   ASIA
a   Hedjaz
b   Mesopotamia
c   Persia
d   Trans Caspia
e   South West Arabia
f   Aden
g   Frontier Regions in India
h   Tsingtau

6   7   AUSTRALASIA
a   New Britain
b   New Ireland
c   Kaiser Wilhelmland
d   Admiralty Islands
e   Nauru
f   German Samoa

4.5.6 Medal Rolls in WO 329

Once you have located the Medal Index Card (MIC) for the individual you seek, you may wish to convert the Army Medal Office references into National Archives WO 329 references and then order the appropriate medal roll on the document-ordering computer.

It is necessary to consult two books before you order the appropriate medal roll. The first book, *Key to the Medal Roll Index*, will enable you to find the correct roll in the second book, WO 329/1. The Key is arranged by medal type and by 'Other Rank' or 'Officer', and lists all of the different alpha-numeric Army Medal

Office references and on which page of WO 329/1 they can be found. The British War Medal and Victory Medal are usually to be found on the same medal roll.

Arrangement of the *Key to the Medal Roll Index*

MEDAL	PAGE
BWM and VM O/Rs	1–6
BWM and VM Off	7–13
1914 Star O/Rs	13–15
1914 Star Off	15–21
1914/15 Star O/Rs	21–4
1914/15 Star Off	24–30
TFWM O/Rs	30–3
TFWM Off	33–6
SWB All ranks	37–9

4.5.7 New Records
Two small but significant collections of First World War Medal records will be transferred to the National Archives, having been recovered from the Army Medal Office, at the beginning of 2006. The Medal Index Cards for the Indian Defence Force and a number of other organisations that came under the Indian Army will be added to WO 372.

A number of medal rolls known as 'Third Echelon Rolls' will be added to WO 329.

4.6   CASE STUDY
Thomas Bryan
A 1914/15 Star named to 22040 Pte T Bryan, Northumberland Fusiliers, can be researched in one of two ways: by using the microfiche or by using DocumentsOnline.

Using the microfiche copies of the Medal Index Cards, first you will need to find the fiche that covers the name. If there is more than one fiche, you will need to find the one that covers the surname and initial. According to the regimental order of precedence, the Northumberland Fusiliers are quite high, so if there are a number of people named T Bryan, the one you need should appear quite early in the card sequence.

FIG 7. (top) *The Medal Index Card of 22040 Private Thomas Bryan* VC
FIG 8. (inset) *Thomas Bryan being presented with his Victoria Cross*
FIG 9. (bottom) *The Medal Index Card of Taffy IV, the regimental mascot of the 2nd Welsh Regiment*

Using DocumentsOnline for the same case, you could search by surname, number and regiment. By putting all of this into the database, there is only one result.

The Medal Index Card of 22040 Pte T Bryan, Northumberland Fusiliers is illustrated opposite (FIGURE 7).

What can be seen from this MIC is that 22040 Private Thomas Bryan, Northumberland Fusiliers was awarded the Victoria Cross and this was gazetted on 8 June 1917. The MIC also confirms entitlement to the British War and Victory Medals and the Silver War Badge. The card is also annotated with Bryan's date of enlistment and his date of discharge.

A more unusual MIC is that for Taffy IV, the regimental mascot of the Royal Welsh Fusiliers (FIGURE 9).

By far the best book about researching medals of the First World War is *The Collector and Researchers Guide to the Great War* by Howard Williamson (privately published, 2003).

5   Second World War Campaign Medals

5.1   INTRODUCTION

For service in the Second World War, eight stars represent service in various parts of the world and two medals were instituted for service between 3 September 1939 and 2 September 1945. A number of dominions also instituted their own medals to be awarded in addition to those instituted in Britain.

The majority of records relating to the issue of stars and medals awarded for service in the Second World War are still maintained by the Ministry of Defence and a number of other government departments. There are numerous files about the creation of the

Medal index card for Bryan, Thomas.

Name.		Corps.	Rank.	Regtl. No.
VC		Raoth'd Fus	Pte	22040
BRYAN.		—"—	L/Cpl	—"—
Thomas				

Medal.	Roll.	Page.		Remarks.
VICTORY	O/1/105	58	3897	Award of V.C.
BRITISH				Date of Gazette
15 STAR	O/1/24 B	1206		8-6-17
5/186	B/44485			EN 11-3-15
SWB List O/2325/1				BS 4-9-18
Theatre of War first served in	(1) FRANCE			PARA 372/2(V1)(c.R
Date of entry therein	22-12-15			R.1362

Medal index card for Taffy the IV, regimental goat.

Name.		Corps.	Rank.	Regtl. No.
TAFFY		2 Welsh R	The	
THE IV			REGIMENTAL GOAT.	

Medal.	Roll.	Page.	Remarks.
VICTORY	F/4104 B	24 b	Deleted Authy & being
BRITISH			Died
14 STAR	G/1/2	195	20-1-15
Theatre of War first served in			
Date of entry therein	13·8·14		R.1380.

stars and medals for the period 1939–1945 and many booklets relating to the various qualifications, examples being found in ADM 116/4707–4708, WO 279/378, WO 315/39

What follows is information, where available, about what records are already in the public domain relating to Second World War medal issues and entitlements, together with some details about records still retained by the Ministry of Defence.

5.2   AIR MINISTRY

A single file containing applications for stars and medals by civilian aircrew of 45 Group can be found in AIR 2/11915. The majority of applications concern flights made across the Atlantic and flights around Europe and North Africa.

5.3   BOARD OF TRADE

By far the most complete set of records concerning Second World War medal issues is that relating to service in the Merchant Navy. The records in BT 395 are only available on DocumentsOnline.

It is possible to search BT 395 by name of the recipient. When you search for an individual, the results page will provide you with the name of the recipient, their date of birth and the Merchant Navy 'Discharge A' number. To see what medals an individual received, it is necessary to download the entry you are interested in.

Each download produces the page of the medal roll with the person in whom you are interested on it. The page has the names down the left-hand side and the medal entitlement in a table to the right. The medal entitlement table appears thus:

1939	AT	AF	PA	BU	FR	WM
	IT	CL	CL	CL	CL	CL

KEY TO ABBREVIATIONS: 1939 = 1939–45 Star; AT = Atlantic Star; AF = Africa Star; PA = Pacific Star; BU = Burma Star; FR = France and Germany Star; WM = 1939–45 War Medal; IT = Italy Star; CL = Clasp.

Each medal that the individual was awarded would be crossed through on the table. The CL means that the person was awarded a clasp as well. The table would be read in the following way:

If a person received the Atlantic Star with the clasp *FRANCE*

AND GERMANY, then CL below AT would be crossed through.

If a person qualified for the *NORTH AFRICA 1942–43* clasp for the Africa Star, CL below AF would be crossed through.

If the person qualified for a Pacific Star and then a Burma Star, they would receive the Pacific Star with the clasp *BURMA* and the CL below PA would be crossed through.

If a person qualified for Burma Star and then a Pacific Star, they would receive a Burma Star with the clasp *PACIFIC* and CL below BU would be crossed through.

If a person qualified for a France and Germany Star and then an Atlantic Star, they would receive a France and Germany Star with the clasp *ATLANTIC* and CL below FR would be crossed through.

If an entry is annotated OLE, this means Oak Leaf Emblem and this indicates that an individual had a Mention in Despatches.

Two files containing details of stars and medals earned by civilian aircrew of airlines, such as the British Overseas Airways Corporation, can be found in BT 245/321 and 322. These two files are arranged in alphabetical order and contain completed application forms for stars and the 1939–45 War Medal. In many cases, there is more than one application form for each individual. Each application form provides details of the flights each applicant made to qualify for each star or medal.

5.4   COLONIAL OFFICE

A deceptively large amount of information concerning Second World War medal entitlement to men and women who served in the colonies can be found in CO 820. In this series are files listing a number of colonies, and their descriptions appear to relate to the policy regarding entitlement, when in fact they contain the names of people from the given colony and the stars and medals to which they are actually entitled.

CO 820/63/7	Aden: Defence and War Medals
CO 820/63/8	Aden: Defence and War Medals
CO 820/64/1	British Honduras: Defence and War Medals; Campaign Stars
CO 820/64/2	Bahamas: War Medals for the Police
CO 820/64/3	Barbados: Defence and War Medals; Campaign Stars
CO 820/69/1	British Guiana: War Medals for the Police

CO 820/69/2   British Guiana: War Medals
CO 820/71/1   Brunei Volunteer Force: Defence Medals and Campaign Stars
CO 820/64/4   Cyprus: Defence and War Medals
CO 820/64/5   Cyprus: Campaign Stars
CO 820/64/6   Cyprus: Campaign Stars
CO 820/65/1   Falkland Islands: Defence Medals
CO 820/65/2   Falkland Islands: Defence and War Medals
CO 820/65/3   Falkland Islands: Defence and War Medals
CO 820/67/4   Far East volunteers: Defence and War Medals; Campaign Stars
CO 820/67/5   Far East military forces: Defence and War Medals; Campaign
      Stars
CO 820/67/6   Far East military forces: Defence and War Medals; Campaign
      Stars
CO 820/69/4   Far East Awards for Civilian Defence Workers
CO 820/69/5   As above
CO 820/69/6   As above
CO 82069/7   As above
CO 820/76/2   Far Eastern Forces: Defence and War Medals and Campaign Stars
CO 820/76/3   Far East: Civilian Defence Workers: Defence Medals
CO 820/76/4   Far Eastern Forces and Civilian Defence Workers: Defence and
      War Medal and Campaign Stars
CO 820/65/4   Fiji: Defence and War Medals; Campaign Stars
CO 820/65/5   Gambia: War Medals; Campaign Stars
CO 820/69/3   Gambia: War Medals
CO 820/65/6   Gambia: War and Defence Medals; Campaign Stars
CO 820/65/7   Gibraltar: Defence and War Medals
CO 820/65/8   Gibraltar: Defence Medals
CO 820/74/8   Leeward Islands: War Medals
CO 820/74/9   As above
CO 820/74/10 Malta: Defence and War Medals and Campaign Stars
CO 820/75/1   Mauritius: Defence and War Medals and Campaign Stars
CO 820/75/2   As above
CO 820/66/1   Nigeria: Defence and War Medals
CO 820/75/3   As above
CO 820/75/4   As above
CO 820/66/3   Palestine: Defence and War Medals; Campaign Stars
CO 820/70/1   Palestine Police: Award Claims
CO 820/70/2   As above
CO 820/70/3   As above
CO 820/70/4   Palestine Police and Palestine Volunteers: Award Claims
CO 820/75/5   Palestine: Defence Medals
CO 820/75/6   St Helena: Defence Medals

CO 820/66/4   Trinidad: Defence and War Medals; Campaign Stars
CO 820/75/7   As above
CO 820/67/1   Western Pacific: Defence Medals; Campaign Stars
CO 820/67/2   Western Pacific: Defence Medals; Campaign Stars
CO 820/67/3   Western Pacific: Defence Medals; Campaign Stars
CO 820/76/1   As above
CO 820/66/5   Zanzibar: Defence and War Medals; Campaign Stars
CO 820/76/1   Colonial Forces: individual applications: Defence and War
   Medals and Campaign Stars

5.5   FOREIGN OFFICE

Many foreign nationals saw service under the British during the Second World War and they became eligible for the same stars and medals awarded to service personnel. Although there are no consolidated medal rolls for awards granted to foreign nationals, there are a number of files containing the medal entitlement of a number of individuals involved in special operations and intelligence work, and these files can be found in FO 372 and WO 32 (see CHAPTER 19).

5.6   SPECIAL OPERATIONS EXECUTIVE (SOE)

Some information concerning the issue of British Campaign Stars and Medals to members of the Special Operations Executive can be found in HS 8.

5.7   RECORDS STILL RETAINED BY THE MINISTRY OF DEFENCE

5.7.1   *Admiralty (RN and RM)*

The Second World War medal records of Naval Ratings are arranged by service number with the medal entitlement of each individual annotated on a card. The Officers' records are in alphabetical order and provide similar information to the ratings.

5.7.2   *Air Ministry (RAF)*

The Second World War campaign medals concerning RAF personnel take two forms. In the case of Officers, there is a name index noting the entitlement of each individual. The Airmen's records are in the form of issue slips giving name, rank, number and medal entitlement. Unfortunately, they are not in alphabetical or service number order, but by the administrative order in which they were applied for and despatched by the Air Ministry.

5.7.3 War Office (Army)

There are no such things as medal rolls for the Second World War issues to the Army. Although medal record cards CS20s were created for each man or woman entitled to Second World War campaign medals and stars, they do not all survive.

As each individual applied for their campaign medal(s), the applications were checked against the criteria for each award and an entitlement was formulated. Once the entitlement was confirmed, the medals were issued and the medal entitlement was annotated on the record of service. It is therefore the record of service that will have the information about which Second World War campaign stars and medals an individual was entitled to.

5.8   OTHER FILES

There are a number of files concerning the policy of granting Second World War campaign medals and stars. There are a large number of Treasury files concerning the campaign medals in T 300. Most of the files in T 300 are concerned with the qualification for each star or medal, potential numbers and manufacturing costs.

Of all the records series where some information about Second World War medal entitlement may be found, the most important series is WO 32. A number of files that appear as policy files concerning whether or not certain organizations should receive medals, do in fact contain lists of eligible individuals.

5.9   CASE STUDY

Stanley Berry

Stanley Berry was born in 1925 and joined the Merchant Navy as a 3rd Radio Officer in 1943. Further details of his merchant service are rather scant, but for his service he received the 1939–45 Star, Atlantic Star and 1939–45 War Medal. The issue of what was then described as the 1939–43 Star is recorded on his record of service. See PLATES 9 and 10.

After the war, Stanley spent some time in the Royal Army Education Corps, leaving as a Captain, before becoming a teacher in Leicester. He left his medals to me when he died in 1976.

The medals earned by Stanley Berry can be seen in PLATE 11.

Gallantry and Meritorious Service Awards

6   Introduction

The British Honours system and the records associated with it are complicated and therefore require some general guidance. There are many ways to research an award for gallantry or meritorious service: you can research by the award, by the gazette date, the campaign or event, by service, by place and by name. The following chapters attempt to cover all of the key areas where records are likely to be found. There will be omissions as it is impossible to list all the sources in a book of this size.

6.1   THE PROCESS

In order to create a research strategy it is necessary to understand the system by which an individual was recommended for an award and how that fact was publicized.

A deed was performed by an individual, which resulted in a recommendation, either written or verbal. The recommendation was then put in a letter to be circulated to interested parties, thus starting a procedure that might eventually result in an award. There are many files in the National Archives and in the India Office Collection at the British Library concerning such procedures, the majority of which do not mention individuals.

There are six points from deed to investiture, where archival evidence may be found:

Deed
Recommendation
Consideration
Local promulgation
London Gazette or equivalent
Investiture

It is possible to find documentary evidence at any of the above-mentioned points. If you are lucky, you may find something relating to them all. However, of the six points above, the second or fifth are the points where you are most likely to find the information you seek.

6.2   CITATION AND RECOMMENDATION

Throughout the chapters on awards for gallantry and meritorious service, as well as the Coronation and Jubilee Medals, frequent reference is made to recommendations as opposed to citations. Some awards, when announced in the *London Gazette*, are accompanied by a citation, most notably the Victoria Cross. Most awards, when announced in the *London Gazette*, are done so without a citation, good examples being Military Medals.

The dictionary definition of a citation is 'a formal statement of the achievements of a person', yet a published citation actually 'cites' (refers to) part of, or a whole, recommendation for an award. The recommendation is (after the deed) that part of the honours process that initiates a sequence of administrative events, which if successful, results in an award being announced in the *London Gazette* or equivalent.

There are thousands of recommendations for awards at the National Archives and in the India Office Collection at the British Library, and it is these you should look for to find out what an individual did to receive their award.

6.3   THE RECORDS

The best place to start with any award is the *London Gazette*, since from the publication of an award you can obtain so much information relating to who, when, where and why.

Most of the military records concerning honours and awards are described, at least superficially, in the online Catalogue. Many items can be found by keyword searching the online Catalogue, but you can only find something if it is described effectively. Practical knowledge of the records and the departments that created them can be of immense use, but it isn't always necessary.

A list of the most important medal records series at the National Archives and the India Office Collection at the British Library can be found just before the index.

7 The *London Gazette*

7.1 INTRODUCTION

Since 1665, the *London Gazette* has been the official newspaper of the state, publishing announcements relating to military commissions, promotions and appointments, and most importantly, military and civil honours and awards. The *London Gazette* is usually published on a weekly basis. Supplements are also produced in addition to the weekly editions. Supplements were a very frequent occurrence in wartime, to announce military commissions, promotions and appointments, and honours and awards.

When an honour or award is announced in the *London Gazette*, terms used to describe this are the 'gazetting of an award', or 'when the award was gazetted'. In order to pursue information in the *London Gazette* and any source of information relating to an honour or award announced in the newspaper, the question 'When was the award gazetted?' will frequently be asked.

There are a number of different routes to this information, either by using the indexes to the *London Gazette* or published sources relating to specific honours and awards.

The London Gazette is held by the National Archives in the records series ZJ 1. The gazettes for the First and Second World Wars are available on microfilm in the Open Reading Room. All other gazettes need to be ordered on the document-ordering computer. As the *London Gazette* is still in print, the most recent editions are available in the library at the National Archives.

7.2   THE *LONDON GAZETTE* INDEX

Over the life of the *London Gazette*, the index has changed. In order to use the index effectively it is necessary to be aware of these changes. In the past, the index usually appeared quarterly, i.e. every three months: March, June, September and December. In some instances, the indexes appeared half yearly or even yearly.

In the index, alongside each item listed is the page number on which that item appears. Depending on the date coverage of the index, it may require a little further work to locate the specific *London Gazette* containing the announcement. For example, if the index entry is found in a March index, the entry could be in January, February or March; in a June index entry in April, May or June; a September index entry in July, August or September; and a December index entry in October, November or December.

The index should always tell you what date range it covers. In the ZJ 1 paper catalogue, an index volume will always be described as such, with many of the index volumes also marked with an asterisk.

In the case of honours and awards announced during the two World Wars, the page number found in the index can be applied to the paper catalogue. The page number range for any given month of any given year is always shown in the paper catalogue, with the appropriate ZJ 1 piece number being given on the left-hand side of the page.

All awards are announced under the main heading of 'State Intelligence'. Prior to 1942, each specific honour or award could be found under the letter of the alphabet thought most appropriate. For example, the Albert Medal could be found under A, the Most Honourable Order of The Bath under B, the Most Exalted Order of the Indian Empire could be found under I and the Most Exalted Order of the Star of India under S.

In the case of Orders of Chivalry, where there were different classes of the Order, the most senior class was always listed first. If there were Civil and Military Divisions of the same Order, they would also be used in the index as appropriate.

In the case of gallantry awards, where a first or subsequent bar was being announced to the same award, the bar announcements usually appeared after the main list of first awards, for example:

Award of the Military Cross
Award(s) of a First bar to the Military Cross
Award(s) of a Second bar to the Military Cross

Under each heading the names of the recipients would appear in alphabetical order.

Foreign awards announced in the *London Gazette* can also be found in the index. The most usual way they appear in the index is as follows:

1 Alphabetical order by name of country, e.g. Belgium, then France, then Japan.
2 Then, in alphabetical order by name of award, e.g. under Belgium, Croix de Guerre before Order of Leopold.
3 Each Order is listed by class, if appropriate, e.g. Crown of Italy is structured: Grand Cross, Commander, Officer, Cavalier. St Anne of Russia is structured: 1st Class, 2nd Class, 3rd Class. The names of recipients under each class are in alphabetical order.

From January 1942, the arrangement of the index was simplified. Instead of having all of the different awards and then an alphabetical list of the recipients of those awards, two new headings were instituted: 'Honours, Decorations and Medals', and 'Mentions in Despatches and Commendations'. Under each heading, there is an alphabetical list of recipients and the page number where their award is announced, but there is no longer any indication of the type of award. Only consultation of the specific page will reveal that!

The paper catalogues listing honours and awards announced in the First and Second World Wars are available on the open shelves in the Open Reading Room.

7.3   THE *LONDON GAZETTE* ONLINE

The *London Gazette* from 1900 is available online at **www.gazettes-online.co.uk**. It is possible to search the *London Gazette* by name of individual and, where published, read the citation for a given award. The *London Gazette* is currently working on putting the 19th-century material online.

7.3.1 *Using the* London Gazette *Online*

Having entered **www.gazettes-online.co.uk**, it is necessary to select the *London Gazette* and proceed down the following path:

Historians → Search The Archive

You will be taken to a page Headed 'Advanced Search' where to can make a number of different selections and populate a number of boxes with your search term(s).

From the 'Historic Event' drop down menu it is possible to select 'Boer War', 'World War 1' or 'World War 2'. By selecting one of these choices, the date fields further down the 'Advanced Search' page will be populated automatically.

If you are unsure of the dates or have a more specific date range you wish to search, you can select the start and end dates for your search yourself.

Unless you know the Gazette page number, I would leave that part of the search page blank.

The words you wish to use in your search can be placed in one of three boxes:

With all the words:
With the exact phrase:
With at least one of the words:

You can put almost anything in these three boxes but I would recommend using name, rank, number and unit search terms only.

Once you have set your search requirements, click on the search button. Any results that you get will be listed by per cent score, with the closest search to 100 per cent, based upon your search term(s), being listed first. Each individual result gives gazette date, issue number and a précis of where the search term(s) appears. Click on 'See PDF' to view the complete page.

When you view a page of the *London Gazette* in PDF, it is possible to search the page by clicking on the binocular icon. If you use this facility, it will show you exactly where the information you have searched for appears on the page.

It is possible to be more imaginative when searching the *London Gazette* online. For example, you can search using a variety of terms connected with honours and awards:

1 Use the term 'first (or second etc.) clasp to the Efficiency Decoration'.
2 Use place names when looking for despatches outside of the two World Wars.
3 Use the term 'despatch' when looking for despatches.
4 Use the name of the author (if known) when looking for a despatch.

What you are using is a search engine of the *London Gazette*, so use it to its full capability.

8 Colonial, Dominion and Indian Gazettes

8.1 INTRODUCTION

There over a hundred different colonial and dominion gazettes held by the National Archives. Of all the different types of announcement to be found in a gazette, the ones most likely to be sought by anyone researching medals are those relating to awards for gallantry or meritorious service, Long Service and Good Conduct medals or Coronation or Jubilee medals.

The gazettes are arranged in a similar format and most are indexed. It is possible to find the name of a medal recipient in the index, but if not, it may be necessary to look for the following terms:

Awards
Birthday Honours
Decorations

Honours
Long Service Awards
Medals
New Year Honours

Once you have found a given entry in the index, it should, like the *London Gazette*, give you a page number where the appropriate announcement will be found.

8.2 THE NATIONAL ARCHIVES GAZETTE LIST

What follows is a list of the Colonial Office (CO) and Dominions Office (DO) records series where gazettes may be found. The list is in alphabetical order and it also provides the date range of each series. You may notice that many places have two different series: one Colonial Office and one Dominion Office. This illustrates the changed status of a colony to a dominion. Most of the changes relate to Australia, Canada and South Africa. Be aware that there are gaps in some of the series, in many cases due to occupation by an enemy during wartime.

COLONY OR DOMINION	SERIES	DATE RANGE
Aden	CO 853	1932–67
Alberta	CO 556	1905–24
Alberta	DO 14	1925–80
Anguilla	CO 242	1879–89
Antigua	CO 1049	1967–89
Australia, Commonwealth of	CO 559	1901–25
Australia, Commonwealth of	DO 16	1926–87
Bahamas	CO 564	1894–89
Barbados	CO 32	1867–89
Basutoland	DO 145	1961–75
Bechuanaland Protectorate	DO 145	1961–75
Bermuda	CO 647	1902–89
British Bechuanaland	CO 451	1887–95
British Colombia	CO 63	1863–1925
British Colombia	DO 34	1926–75
British Guiana	CO 115	1838–1975
British Honduras (Belize)	CO 127	1861–1975
British Malaya	CO 740	1921–37
British New Guinea (Papua)	CO 453	1888–1921

British North Borneo (Sabah)	CO 855	1883–1980
British South Africa Company	CO 455	1894–1923
Brunei	CO 985	1951–1975
Canada	CO 46	1825–1925
Canada	DO 29	1926–78
Cape Colony	CO 52	1823–1925
Cape of Good Hope	DO 32	1926–61
Ceylon	CO 58	1818–1948
Ceylon (Sri Lanka)	DO 104	1947–75
Cyprus	CO 70	1878–1965
Dominica	CO 75	1865–1975
East Africa and Uganda Protectorate	CO 457	1899–1907
East African Commons Services Organization & East Africa Community	CO 1050	1966–77
East Africa High Commission	CO 921	1948–66
Falkland Islands	CO 458	1891–1990
Federated Malay States	CO 574	1909–48
Federation of Malaya (Malaysia)	CO 930	1948–80
Federation of the West Indies	DO 136	1958–61
Fiji	CO 86	1874–1975
Gambia	CO 460	1883–1974
Ghana	CO 132	1957–75
Gibraltar	CO 94	1839–1965
Gold Coast	CO 99	1872–1957
Griqualand West	CO 109	1876–80
Hong Kong	CO 132	1846–1990
India	DO 105	1948–79
Iraq	CO 813	1921–55
Irish Free State	CO 785	1923–25
Irish Free State (Republic of Ireland)	DO 37	1926–75
Jamaica	CO 141	1794–1968
Johore	CO 653	1911–79
Kedah and Perlis	CO 819	1925–79
Kelantan	CO 928	1948–79
Kenya	CO 542	1908–75
Labuan	CO 573	1890–1906
Lagos	CO 150	1881–1906
Leeward Islands	CO 156	1872–1965
Malacca	CO 929	1948–79

Malta	CO 162	1818–1965
Manitoba	CO 577	1905–25
Manitoba	DO 38	1926–75
Mauritius	CO 171	1823–1975
Natal	CO 1082	1858–1925
Natal	DO 40	1926–61
Nauru	DO 83	1926–65
Negri Sembilan, Sungei Ujong		
and Jelebu	CO 463	1896–1980
New Brunswick	CO 192	1842–1923
New Brunswick	DO 43	1924–68
Newfoundland	CO 198	1844–1923
Newfoundland	DO 42	1924–68
New Guinea		
(former German territory)	CO 667	1914–25
New Guinea	DO 85	1926–75
New Hebrides (Vanuatu)	CO 829	1927–78
New South Wales	CO 205	1832–1925
New South Wales	DO 46	1926–80
New Zealand	CO 212	1841–1925
New Zealand	DO 50	1926– 80
Nigeria	CO 658	1914–76
Norfolk Island	DO 135	1956–60
North-Eastern Rhodesia	CO 669	1903–11
North Rhodesia (Zambia)	CO 670	1911–70
Northern Nigeria	CO 586	1900–13
Northwest Territories	CO 216	1883–1905
Northern Territory (Australia)	DO108	1948–74
Nova Scotia and Cape Breton	CO 593	1905–25
Nova Scotia	DO 52	1926–75
Nyasaland (Malawi)	CO 541	1894–1975
Ontario	CO 595	1905–25
Ontario	DO 52	1926–78
Orange Free State	CO 662	1911–25
Orange Free State	DO 56	1926–61
Orange River Colony	CO 597	1900–10
Pahang	CO 466	1897–1977
Pakistan	DO 106	1948–72
Palestine	CO 742	1919–48
Papua New Guinea	DO 86	1922–49
Penang	CO 933	1948–77
Perak	CO 467	1888–1980

Perlis	CO 931	1948–77
Prince Edward Island	CO 230	1832–1925
Prince Edward Island	DO 87	1926–68
Quebec	CO 602	1905–25
Quebec	DO 59	1926–73
Queensland	CO 237	1859–1925
Queensland	DO 62	1926–89
Rhodesia and Nyasaland	DO 125	1953–63
Sarawak	CO 604	1903–80
Saskatchewan	CO 605	1905–25
Saskatchewan	DO 66	1926–68
Selangor	CO 469	1890–1975
Seychelles	CO 470	1889–1976
Sierra Leone	CO 271	1817–1975
Singapore	CO 932	1945–70
Somaliland	CO 922	1942–60
South Africa High Commission	CO 548	1901–22
South Africa High Commission	DO 91	1923–60
South Africa, Union of	DO 12	1926–78
South Australia	CO 16	1839–1925
South Australia	DO20	1926–80
Southern Nigeria	CO 591	1900–13
Southern Rhodesia	CO 815	1923–25
Southern Rhodesia	DO 65	1926–75
South West Africa	CO 294	1915–25
South West Africa	DO 78	1926–68
St Christopher (St Kitts) and Nevis	CO 242	1879–1989
St Helena	CO 251	1845–1990
St Lucia	CO 257	1857–1975
St Vincent	CO 264	1831–1975
Straits Settlements	CO 276	1867–1942
Sudan	CO 675	1907–17
Sungei Ujong	CO 475	1893 only
Swaziland	DO 145	1961–75
Tanganyika	CO 737	1919–64
Tanzania	DO 146	1946–75
Tasmania	CO 283	1816–1925
Tasmania	DO 70	1926–87
Tobago	CO 289	1872–98
Tonga	CO 676	1905–75
Transvaal	DO 73	1927–7

Trengganu	CO 909	1939–75
Trinidad (later Trinidad and Tobago)	CO 299	1833–1975
Turks and Caicos Islands	CO 681	1907–65
Uganda	CO 612	1908–73
Vancouver Island	CO 308	1864–66
Victoria	CO 312	1851–1925
Victoria	DO 76	1926–90
Wei Hai Wei	CO 744	1908–30
Western Australia	CO 21	1836–1925
Western Australia	DO 24	1926–89
Western Pacific High Commission	CO 692	1914–71
Western Samoa	DO 107	1923–70
Zanzibar	CO 689	1913–65

8.3   INDIA OFFICE (BRITISH LIBRARY) GAZETTE LIST

A number of different gazettes are held within the India Office Collection at the British Library. These gazettes represent not only India, but also its states and provinces. There are also gazettes for Burma.

All of the following gazettes are in the series V/11.

V/11

1–359	India	1864–1944
360–815	Calcutta	1832–1947
816–1047	Assam	1874–1947
1048–1231	Bihar and Orissa	1912–54
1232–1236	Agra	1850–54
1237–1351	North Western Provinces and Oudh	1862–1901
1352–1585	United Provinces	1902–55
1586–2128	Madras (Fort St George)	1832–1947
2129–2605	Bombay	1831–1947
2605–2778	Sind	1869–1947
2779–3082	Punjab	1872–1947
3083–3106	North West Frontier Province	1932–47
3107–3341	Central Provinces	1875–1947
3342–3405	Coorg District	1885–1947
3406–3894	Burma	1875–1952
3895–3899	Andamans and Nicobars	1895–1903
3700–3719	Mysore Residency	1914–47
3720–3735	Rajahmundry and Godavari Districts	1857–76

9   General Advice

The advice and records series discussed in this chapter cover broad areas and unusual ones that would not normally sit anywhere else.

9.1   ORDERS OF CHIVALRY

Prior to the First World War, there were very few appointments to the Orders of Chivalry. It is very easy to find items at the National Archives by keyword searching the online Catalogue using 'order' and 'garter' or 'thistle' or 'patrick' or 'bath'.

There are a number of records series with information concerning Orders of Chivalry. At the National Archives, the most significant is WO 104 the Register of Appointments to the Order of the Bath from 1827–1949.

Records about the Order of St Michael and St George can be found in the following CO records series:

CO 447	Original Correspondence	1836–1932
CO 728	Register of Correspondence	1859–1952
CO 734	Entry Book of Out Letters	1838–1934
CO 844	Original Warrants and Letters Patent	1852–99

In the India Office collection at the British Library, there are numerous files concerning appointments, register, list and correspondence concerning the Most Exalted Order of the Star of India and the most Eminent Order of the Indian Empire in L/PS/13 and L/PS/15.

For more information about the history of, and appointments to, the Orders of Chivalry, please consult the published works listed at the end of the book.

9.2   ADMIRALTY

The vast majority of Admiralty records concerning awards are discussed in later chapters. The basic technique for finding most of them, using ADM 12 as the starting point, is described in CHAPTER 25 on Research Techniques. Of all the 19th-century Admiralty records concerning awards, the most difficult to find yet one of the most rewarding is ADM 7/913.

ADM 7/913 is described as 'Abstract of war services and recommendations for campaign awards, 1854–99'. This file contains the names of nearly all Royal Navy and Royal Marine Officers and Warrant Officers who were Mentioned in Despatches. The details for which the individuals were 'Mentioned' are quite full. The list of 'Mentions' for the Egypt 1882 campaign is printed and includes 'Mentions' for the bombardment of Alexandria on 11th July and the battle of Tel el Kebir on 13th September.

9.3   THE WAR OFFICE

There are a number of key War Office Records series concerning honours and awards, most of which are discussed in later chapters. WO 32 War Office and successors: Registered Files (General Series) from 1845 and still accruing covers a multitude of subjects from Awards to Zulus – and everything and everywhere in between! The series is arranged by code, both numerical and alphabetical. The numerical codes relating to awards are 46 (Operations), 50 (Awards and Medals), 51 (Despatches) and 52 (Orders of Chivalry).

All country codes in WO 32 are prefixed O for Overseas and then each country or region is given an alphabetical country code. You can keyword search WO 32 on the online Catalogue, and the key codes mentioned above should help you understand what you retrieve.

I have placed the War Office records concerning the annuity Meritorious Service Medal (MSM) here because they didn't really sit anywhere else. They could have been discussed in the chapter on Long Service Awards, but it is an award over and above an extra one for long service. The registers of awards for the MSM are in the series WO 101 and the registers currently cover the period 1846–1919. The registers do not include the Immediate MSM, see CHAPTER 12.

The arrangement of the registers in WO 101 varies enormously: some have name indexes, some are by regimental order of precedence. Most of the registers provide not only details about the MSM, they also include potted service histories of the recipients.

The post-First World War MSM registers are currently being transferred to the National Archives and they will enable further

MSM awards to be confirmed. The MSM selection lists from 1950 onwards are also being transferred.

There is a Register of the Most Excellent Order of the British Empire in WO 387; it covers the period 1920–49 and is nothing more than lists of names extracted from the *London Gazette.*

Submissions to the Sovereign for awards of the Distinguished Conduct Medal (DCM) can be found in WO 146, but once again there is very little detail as to the reason why a name was being submitted. See *The Distinguished Conduct Medal 1855–1910* by P. E. Abbott for further guidance about this award.

9.4 POLICE AWARDS

There are many recommendations for police awards at the National Archives, the majority being in HO 45. A large number of recommendations for awards to police officers outside of the United Kingdom can also be found in HO 45, but the Indian Police and the Burma Police had their own awards.

It is possible to find recommendations for the Indian Police Medal (IPM) and the Burma Police Medal at the British Library. Many of the Indian Awards files are in L/PS/13 and L/PS/15. These awards were gazetted; see CHAPTER 8 for further information. A list of IPMs and their citations as published can be found in MSS Eur E 358/2 at the British Library.

9.5 RECOMMENDATIONS FOR AWARDS IN COLONIAL OFFICE, DOMINIONS OFFICE AND FOREIGN OFFICE RECORDS

Finding recommendations for awards in the records of the Colonial Office (CO), Dominions Office (DO) and Foreign Office (FO) records is helped by the wealth of basic sources, but hindered by the routes to them.

The key Foreign Office series concerning awards are discussed in CHAPTER 19. However, other recommendations for awards may be found amongst the records of each country, embassy or consulate. Locating such records can only be done by using the various registers of correspondence and, having found a reference in those, in the appropriate original correspondence series.

Recommendations in the Colonial Office and Dominion Office records can be located in a similar way as the Foreign Office, by using the registers of correspondence for the appropriate colony or dominion, and then the appropriate original correspondence series.

The best place to start when looking for any of the above mentioned records series are the FO Index, the CO Index and the DO Index. Each of these indexes, arranged in alphabetical order, will provide you with the appropriate series for the register of correspondence and then the series for the original correspondence. In many cases, the date coverage of the registers of correspondence and the original correspondence may vary. Many of the surviving items of original correspondence from *c.*1930 are adequately described on the Catalogue and it is therefore not necessary to use the registers.

10   Civilian Awards

10.1   INTRODUCTION

Many of our most notable politicians and statesmen, and many people from ordinary walks of life have been honoured by the state. Finding information about them in any depth would be very time consuming. In the case of the most significant appointees to the oldest orders of chivalry, by far the quickest way to find out about them and their awards is to look at *The Dictionary of National Biography*, *Who Was Who* or *Who's Who*.

For those noblemen and women appointed to the Orders of Chivalry, I would recommend *Burke's Peerage* or *Debretts*. There are a number of very good books about the individual Orders of Chivalry and these are listed in APPENDIX C on Published Sources.

Although this chapter is split into chronological ranges, many of the records series cover almost the most whole period from 1850 to 1970.

10.2 PRE-1914

Of all the awards granted to civilians, excluding politicians and statesmen, most were for acts of bravery, either in the workplace or in situations that occurred around them. As rewards for gallantry are really a 20th-century creation, awards from the 19th century are rare, by type and in numbers. You may also wish to consult CHAPTER 21 on Gallantry (Life Saving).

10.2.1 Records of the Board of Trade

There are two significant record series under the Board of Trade: BT 97 the Albert Medal Records and BT 261 Marine Division: Gallantry at Sea Awards.

The Albert Medal Register in BT 97 consists of only two pieces: BT 97/1 is the register and covers 1866–1913; BT 97/2 is a photograph album of the recipients, but this only covers 1866–79.

The records in BT 261 cover the period 1856–1981 and the majority of the awards covered in the book are Sea Gallantry Medals.

BT 261

1	Lists of persons rewarded by British, Colonial and Foreign Governments	1856–79
2	Mercantile Marine Rewards Register	1865–1914
3	Notes on Rewards for Acts of Gallantry at Sea and Undated related matters, Lists of Awards of Albert Medals	
4	Register of Awards given by HM Government	1876–80
5	As above	1886–1909
6	As above	1910–32
7	As above	1932–81
8	Register of Awards given to British Seamen by Foreign Governments	1909–73
9	Correspondence relating to institution of Mercantile Marine War Medal	1927
10	Cases of Gallantry at Sea considered for Awards: Accounts of actions and subsequent Awards	1935–41
11	As above	1941–3
12	As above	1942–4
13	As above	1944–6
14	Alphabetical Register of Awards given to Seamen	1941–9 and 1968–79

15   Accounts of Cases submitted for consideration   1944–6
      by Honours and Awards Committee

10.2.2 Home Office

Recommendations for the Albert Medal, Edward Medal and King's Police Medal can all be found in the records series HO 45. If you know the name of the recipient, you can search the HO 45 catalogue online, using their name. You can also search the catalogue by the name of the medal awarded. The King's Police Medal is quite often shortened to KPM or Police Medal. HO 45 is full of recommendations for KPMs for both gallantry and meritorious service for the police in the UK and the colonies.

A useful place to start researching an Albert Medal or Edward Medal is to consult *Heroic Endeavour* by D. Henderson. This book gives you all the key information, such as name, date and place of incident, and when the award was announced in the *London Gazette*.

Police Gallantry 1909–1978 by J. Peter Farmery (Australia, 1995) is the best place to start for King's or Queen's Police Medal for gallantry.

10.2.3 Ministry of Transport

A small number of pre-1914 files concerning awards can be found in the series MT 9.

10.2.4 Ministry of Power

A file concerning the Daran Colliery Explosion in 1909 and recommendations for awards can be found in POWE 6/5.

10.3   FIRST WORLD WAR

The First World War saw many thousands of men and women of the British Empire contribute to the war effort in some form, whether it was in the armed forces or in a civil capacity supporting the war effort. Many of these people found themselves in dangerous situations where they performed acts of great bravery. Some were recognized by the State for their unflinching contribution to the war effort. See FIGURE 10.

Nearly all of the awards granted to civilians were announced in the *London Gazette*, but very few of the announcements tell you why the individual got an award. What follows are descriptions of the records concerning civilian awards for gallantry and meritorious service.

The key record series containing information about honours and awards have already been described above. However a number of files of note are:

HO 45/10887/350619 List of Awards in connection with fire and explosion at Morecambe Shell Factory 1917–18

HO 45/11016/377171 War Services of Firemen: British Empire Medal 1919–21

MUN 4/5387 1918–1919 Canada: Recommendations for Honours and Awards

MUN 4/6647 1918–1919 British Empire Order: Recommendations from Aircraft Production Department

MUN 7/400 1917–1919 Award of Edward Medal for bravery shown by Munitions Examiner at an explosion at No 1 Filling Station, Watford, Herts

Sergeant Fred Crepin
"N" Division.

This Special Constable has rendered exceptional service as apart from his regular patrol duties he has driven his own Motor Car under very trying circumstances. He has performed all kinds of transport work while the barrage was at its worst. He showed exceptional courage in arresting a criminal believed to be armed and who struggled desperately with Sgt. Crepin before being secured and taken by him to Stoke Newington Station where he was found to be Paddy Walsh a man wanted for a violent assault, and other burglaries. Crepin was called by a civilian and although off duty he at once proceeded to where the man Walsh had been seen and then found him. Walsh was sentenced to five years penal servitude and the Judge highly commended Sgt. Crepin's action which led to a pest of Society being put away.

S/C. A.B. Holmes
"N" Division.

This man showed great courage in dealing with two men who were breaking into enclosed premises having a van with them to cart away the booty. He obtained the assistance of P.C. 631N and as the men ran away, Holmes, who had a cycle, chased and successively caught both men who were safely lodged in Stoke Newington Police Station and subsequently sentenced to twelve months hard labour and recommended for deportation. The occurrence took place at 6.20 a.m. on March 24th. 1917.

FIG 10. *A typical recommendation for a Medal of the Order of the British Empire* [HO 45/11071/380323]

MUN 7/553 1918–1919 Recommendations for Awards of British Empire Medals to Employees of establishments manufacturing poison gases and explosives

An example of a First World War recommendation can be seen in FIGURE 10.

10.4 BETWEEN THE WARS

Once again, most of the key record series have been described above. However, the odd files outside of the usual government departments include CO 129/513/8 Attacks by Chinese pirates on shipping: awards for bravery 1929.

10.5 SECOND WORLD WAR

The greatest number of awards for gallantry and meritorious service granted to civilians was during the Second World War. From George Crosses for rescues and bomb disposal to appointments to the Most Excellent Order of the British Empire for service towards the war effort, the range of awards and the range of records are almost as diverse.

See CHAPTER 17 for more information about Second World War awards to civilians. Records concerning awards granted in the New Year and Birthday Honours Lists are also discussed in a separate chapter.

10.6 SINCE 1945

Information concerning acts of gallantry or meritorious service is dispersed amongst the records of many different government departments. Unlike the records concerning awards to service personnel, many of the records concerning civilians are closed for 75 years from creation of the files. This is mostly true of files concerning awards announced in the New Year or Birthday Honours Lists. Recommendations for awards announced at other times of the year, especially awards for gallantry, are quite often open.

10.6.1 Board of Trade

The records of the Marine Crews Department of the Board of

Trade, which contain some files concerning honours and awards, are in the records series BT 238. Most of the file descriptions in the series are sufficient for you to locate them by keyword searching on the catalogue. The current date range of the files is from 1953 to 1967.

Not all of BT 238 concerns Honours and Awards. The following piece numbers all relate to awards: BT 238/1–15, 77–93, 95–8, 206–15.

10.6.2 Home Office
Once again most of key series are described above although many of the files concerning awards to civilians are frequently closed. Some Home Office recommendations that are open are in the series HO 286.

10.6.3 Ministry of Agriculture, Fisheries and Food
A collection of files concerning acts of bravery by men employed in the fishing industry are preserved in the series MAF 209. MAF 209/907–909 are three files described as 'Acts of gallantry by fishermen', and they cover the period 1948–61. The files contain numerous reports, letters and newspaper cuttings describing various acts that resulted in awards, including British Empire Medals, commendations, and awards from the Royal Humane Society, the Royal National Lifeboat Institution and the Shipwrecked Fisherman's Society.

Other MAF files of interest include MAF 209/21, MAF 227/46, MAF 227/63 and MAF 284/154.

10.6.4 Prime Minister's Office
The records for post-1945 honours lists are in the series PREM 2 and these records are listed in CHAPTER 18 on New Year and Birthday Honours.

10.6.5 The Treasury
Records concerning recommendations for the George Cross for the post-1945 period can be found in the series T 350. However, many of the files are still closed. Included in the open files in T 350

is the recommendation for the George Cross to Violette Szabo in T 350/3.

10.6.6 Other Records

Long Service and Bravery Awards recommended by the British Railways Board from 1957 to 1987 can be found in AN 160/813.

Recommendations for gallantry awards submitted by the Ministry of Power can be found in the series POWE 8, with further recommendations in the series POWE 10 and POWE 14.

The Metropolitan Police Register of Awards is in MEPO 22 and some recommendations may be found in the series MEPO 2.

Records created by the National Dock Labour Board concerning awards for gallantry can be found in BK 2/733.

11   Awards by Operational Theatre (except WW1 and WW2)

11.1   INTRODUCTION

If the operational theatre or place in which an award for gallantry or meritorious service was earned is known, it is far more effective to look at records for a specific campaign than research the award generally. What follows are references relevant to the numerous operational theatres in which awards were won.

Where appropriate, the relevant campaign medal, which would have been qualified for at the same time as the award for gallantry or meritorious service, is shown in bold. Where no known campaign medal was awarded, the country in which an award for gallantry or meritorious service was won, is shown in plain type.

In the case of recommendations for awards, if the *London Gazette* (LG) date is known, it will be added to the description. If the document covers more than one *London Gazette* date, the first and last will be listed.

If you do not find references to awards granted for a particular battle or campaign, you may wish to consult WO 32 under Codes

O for overseas and then the country code, e.g. (AU) South Africa, or the records in WO 33 or WO 106. Keyword searching the Catalogue will produce plenty of results. Some recommendations for awards for service in the Middle East after the First World War can be found in the records of the Foreign Office.

For recommendations for RFC and RAF personnel, you may wish to look at AIR 1 and AIR 2. See CHAPTERS 12 and 16 on First World War Awards and Second World War Awards: RAF, respectively.

Many recommendations for awards to naval personnel can only be traced by using ADM 12. See CHAPTER 25 on Research Techniques for further information about how to do this.

This following list is not exhaustive, but at least it gives an idea of the types of records and in which records series they are most likely to be found. There will always, however, be exceptions to the rule!

11.2 OPERATIONAL THEATRES
Africa
Ashantee 1873–4

WO 32/7377	Victoria Cross (VC): Awards to Lt Lord Gifford 24th Regtand L/Sgt S. McGraw 42nd Regt for actions during Ashanti War; Recommendations in respect of other Officers and Men	1874

South Africa 1877–9

WO 32/7682	Recommendations for Awards and Promotion for Officers by General Cunyngham	1878
WO 32/7387	VC: Recommendations and Awards concerning Major E Leet, 13th Regt, Surgeon Major Reynolds, AMD, Capt and Brevet Lt Col R. Buller, 60th Rifles, Lt E. Browne 24th Regt and Pte Wassall, 80th Regt	1879
WO 32/7388	VC: Recommendations concerning C/Sgt A Booth, 80th Regt, and Ptes Flawn and Fitzpatrick, 94th Regt	1879
WO 32/7390	VC: Recommendations concerning Lt (now Capt and Brevet Major) G. Bromhead, Lt (now Capt etc.) J. Chard, Cpl W. Allen and Ptes Williams, Hook, Jones and Hitch of 24th Regt. Award to Cpl Schies of Natal Native Contingent for action at Rorke's Drift	1879
WO 32/7834	DCM: Recommendations for Pte Walkinshaw 58th Regt, late 90th Regt, for Action in Zulu War	1881–2

Egypt 1882–9

| WO 32/7410 | VC: Recommendation for Gunner A. Smith, Royal Artillery, at Abu Klea | 1885 |

East and West Africa 1887–1900

WO 32/3418	Recommendations for Awards of the Victoria Cross from General Office Commanding (GOC) South East Africa	1892
WO 32/7620	Operations against the Yonnis Tribe: Recommendations for Awards	1887–8
WO 32/7622	Niger-Sudan Campaign: Recommendations for Rewards for Services	1897
WO 32/7629	Sierra Leone: Recommendations for Awards	1898
WO 32/7630	Sierra Leone: Commendations	1898
WO 32/7635	Sierra Leone: Colonel Woodgate's Despatch: Recommendations for Awards	1899–1900

British South Africa Company 1890–7

WO 32/7419	VC: Award to Trooper Henderson 9th Lancers for Action during Matabele revolt. Recommendations by British South Africa Company in respect of Officers and Men	1896
WO 32/7840	Recommendations for Services rendered during rebellion in Matabeleland, Mashonaland and Rhodesia	1897
WO 32/7842	As above	
WO 32/7843	As above	

Central Africa 1891–8

WO 32/8487	Awards for Unyoro campaign Abyssinia	1895
WO 32/7375	VC: Recommendations for Drummer M. Magner and Pte J. Bergin 33rd Regt	1868
L/MIL/7/12878	British Mission to King Menelik. Decoration of two Officers with the Star of Ethiopia	1897

East and Central Africa Medal 1897–99

L/MIL/7/14438	Honours and Rewards. Medal for operations of the Indian Contingent in Uganda	1898
L/MIL/7/14446	Mutiny rebellion in Uganda: Services of Officers	1899
L/MIL/7/14459	1st Uganda Rifles: Good Service of, Reports on Operations, Rewards	1901–2

Sudan and Egypt 1896

L/MIL/7/12724	Defence of Suakin, Honours and Rewards for certain Officers	1896/97

Queen's South Africa Medal 1899–1902

The biggest problem when researching awards for gallantry
and meritorious service granted during the Boer War is which
records survive. There are many records dispersed across three
different records series as well as what can be found in
Parliamentary Papers.

ADM 116/641	Honours and Awards – South Africa	1899–1902
L/MIL/7/15687	Honours and Rewards	1900–02
WO 32/7114B	List of Officers present at the defence of Ladysmith	
WO 32/7437	VC: Award to Cpl F. McKay, Gord Hghrs	1900
WO 32/7444	VC: Award to Capt W. Gordon, Gordon Highlanders. Notice concerning Recommendations in respect of Cpl J. Shaul and Pte C. Ward	1900
WO 32/7451	VC: Recommendation concerning Pte A. Curtis and DCM for Pte T. Morton, East Surrey Regt	1900
WO 32/7463	VC: Lt E. Dugdale, 5th Lancers and Sgt W. Traynor, West Yorkshire Regt. Recommendations in respect of other Officers and Men for the DSO and DCM	1901
WO 32/7465	VC: Recommendation for Sgt H. Hampton, Liverpool Regt	1901
WO 32/7466	VC: Recommendation respect of Ptes H. Crandon 18 Hrs and Pte C. Kennedy, HLI, and other Recommendations and Awards	1901–2
WO 32/7467	VC: Recommendation for Pte E. Durrant, Rifle Brigade	1901
WO 32/7469	VC: Recommendations for Pte C. Ravenhill, Royal Scots Fusiliers; other Recommendations and Reports 1899–1900 related to the battle of Colenso	1901
WO 32/7470	VC: Recommendation for Capt H. Schofield	1901
WO 32/7473	VC: Recommendation for Driver F. Bradley, RFA for Action in Zululand. Recommendations and Awards in respect of Gunners Rabb, Boddy, Ball and Driver for the DCM	1901
WO 32/7475	VC: Recommendation concerning Sgt J. Rogers, South African Constabulary	1902
WO 32/7481	VC: Recommendation for Shoeing Smith A. Ind, RHA	1902
WO 32/7482	VC: Recommendation for Pte W. House, Royal Berkshire Regt	1902

WO 32/7892	Recommendations for gallantry at Colenso	1900
WO 32/7895	DCMs: Recommendations for Pte G. Day, Sgt A. Freeman, Pte S. Dodson and Pte A. Nunn, 6th Dragoon Guards	1899–1900
WO 32/7899	VC: Recommendations for Capt M. Micklejohn and Sgt Major W Robertson, 2 Gord Hghrs and 2 Lt L. Norwood, 5th Dragoon Guards	1899–1900
WO 32/7900	As above	
WO 32/7906	Recommendations for Awards and Mentions by General G. White for Services of various Officers and Men at Ladysmith	1900–1
WO 32/7952	VC: Recommendations for Cpl J. Shaul, HLI, Lt H. Douglas, RAMC ad C/Sgt D. Nelson and L/Cpl W. Hodgson, Gordon Highlanders	1900
WO 32/8076	Recommendations by General Buller for the Victoria Cross and other Decorations following the relief of Ladysmith	1900–1

WO 105 Roberts Papers

Despatches and Reports of Operations in South Africa 1899–1902 by Commander in Chief and Commanders in the Field

WO 105/5–12 contains Reports and Despatches concerning Operations including:

  5 Nicholson's Nek; Spion Kop; relief of Kimberley; Colesburg; and Arundel
  6 Modder River; Paardeberg; and Ladysmith.
  7 Sannah's Post, Mafeking and Wepener
  8 Rhodesian Field Force, Ladysmith and Johannesburg
  9 Honing's Spruit, Tweefontein and Laing's Nek
  10 Operations north of the Orange River and Pretoria
  11 Roodeval Station and Belfast
  12 Contains Roberts' Final Report and an Index of Despatches and Reports

WO 108 South African War Papers

WO 108/135 Nominal roll accompanying 1st Despatch
WO 108/136 Recommendations for Awards: 1st Despatch 8 March 1901
WO 108/137 Recommendations for Awards: 2nd Despatch 8 May 1901
WO 108/138 Recommendations for Awards: 3rd Despatch 8 July 1901
WO 108/139 Recommendations for Awards: 8th Despatch 8 December 1901
WO 100/140 Recommendations for Awards: 11th Despatch 8 March 1902
WO 108/141 Recommendations for Awards: 13th Despatch 1 June 1902
WO 108/142 Mentions in Despatches and Rewards Granted: 1901
WO 108/143 Acts of Gallantry and Awards made: Extracts from Lord

Kitchener's Despatches, 1901–1902
WO 108/145 Awards for Distinguished Service 1902
WO 108/179 Review of Awards and Omissions 1900–3
WO 108/237 South Africa Despatches: November 1899–June 1900

PARLIAMENTARY PAPERS
1902 LXIX.235 Spion Kop Despatches   Fiche No 108.605

Africa General Service Medal 1900–56

• Clasps: *SOMALILAND 1901, SOMALILAND 1902–4, JIDBALLI*
L/MIL/7/14513   Good Services of Officers and Men   1901
L/MIL/7/14547   Honours and Rewards for Natives (Indian soldiers)   1903–4
L/MIL/7/14582   Honours and Rewards   1904–8
L/MIL/7/14591   Rewards for Warrant Officers and NCOs   1904–6
WO 32/8440   Recommendations for Awards   1903–04

• Clasps: *AGS: CLASPS UNKNOWN*
L/MIL/7/15797   Promotion and Rewards for Men of the Madras Sappers and
                Miners
L/MIL/7/14634   Operations in Somaliland 1919, Recommendations 1919–21
                for Rewards

• Clasp: *SOMALILAND 1920*
AIR 2/204   Recommendations for RAF Z Unit   1920

• Clasp: *KENYA*
AIR 2/12423   Awards for Service in Kenya   1953–5
AIR 2/12424   Awards for Service in Kenya   1955–6
WO 373/120   Kenya: LG dates 14/08/1953–01/01/1955
WO 373/121   Kenya: LG dates 21/02/1955–19/07/1957

——UN Operations: Congo 1960–4
WO 373/124   LG dates 19/09/1961–16/10/1964

India, Afghanistan, Burma and South East Asia
Indian General Service Medal 1854–95

• Clasp: *BHOOTAN*
WO 32/7374   VC: Recommendations for Major W. Trevor
                and Lt J. Dundas   1867–8

• Clasp: *UMBEYLA*
L/MIL/7/10633 Sir N. Chamberlain's Despatch and names of   1863–4
Officers Recommended for Reward

• Clasp: *PERAK*
L/MIL/7/13458 Honours and Rewards: Proposed V C to Captain   1876
G.N. Channer

• Clasp: *PERSIA*
WO 32/7344 VC: Recommendations for Lt A. Moore and Lt J.   1860
Malcolmson

• Clasp: *JOWAKI 1877–8*
L/MIL/7/15379 Recommendations for Rewards   1878–9

• Clasp: *NAGA 1879–80*
L/MIL/7/13464 Report on Operations and Honours and Rewards   1881
to Officers

• Clasp: *BURMA 1885–1892*
L/MIL/7/9724 Military and Naval Officers recommended by the
Government of India   1887
L/MIL/7/9725 Reward of certain Officers of the Indian Marine   1887
L/MIL/7/9727 Rewards for Officers of the Royal Navy   1887
L/MIL/7/9728 Further Recommendations by the Government of India 1888
L/MIL/7/9729 Recommendations for Officers of the Army Veterinary 1888
Department
L/MIL/7/9730 Further Recommendations by the Government of India 1889
L/MIL/7/9732 Surgeon Hale and Captain Keary, DSO for   1891–92
Operations in Kachin 1889–90 and Wuntho 1891
L/MIL/7/9735 Recommendations by the Government of India   1893

• Clasp: *HAZARA 1888* and *SIKKIM 1888*
L/MIL/7/9621 Officers recommended for Rewards   1888–9
L/MIL/7/9954 Recommendations for 3 Nurses for the Royal   1891
Red Cross

• Clasp: *CHIN LUSHAI 1889–90*
L/MIL/7/1298 Recommendations for Awards   1890
L/MIL/7/15093 Honours and Rewards   1891–2

• Clasp: *SAMANA 1891*
L/MIL/7/15278 Despatch and Description of Operations   1891–2
L/MIL/7/15282 Honours and Rewards   1891–4

• Clasp: *HAZARA 1891*

| L/MIL/7/14705 | Honours and rewards | 1891 |

• Clasp: *HUNZA 1891*

L/MIL/7/13381   Officers recommended for the VC: Captain   1892–3
F. Aylmer RE, Lt G. Boisragon, 5th Gurkhas and
Lt J. Smith, Indian Staff Corps. Lt Badcock
recommended for the DSO

WO 32/7416   As above   1892

L/MIL/7/13383   Honours and Rewards other than the VC   1892–3

• Clasp: *N E FRONTIER 1891*

L/MIL/7/15111   V C to Lt C.J.W. Grant, Indian Staff Corps   1891–6

L/MIL/7/15112   Rewards for Native Troops   1891

• Clasp: *CHIN HILLS 1892–93* and *KACHIN HILLS 1892–93*

L/MIL/7/9736   Rewards to Officers for Service in Burma and   1893–4
Chin Hills

L/MIL/7/9737   VC to Surgeon Major O.P. Lloyd, Army Medical   1893–4
Staff

WO 32/7418   VC awarded to Surgeon Major O.P. Lloyd,   1893
Army Medical Staff

• Clasp: *WAZIRISTAN 1894–5*

L/MIL/7/15371   Officers recommended for Honours and Rewards   1895

L/MIL/7/11809   Operations against the Abors. Honours and   1894
Rewards for certain Officers

Indian Mutiny Medal 1857–8

WO 32/7314   VC: Recommendation for Lt J. Tytler   1858

WO 32/7315   VC: Recommendations for Sgt Majors P. Gill and   1858
M. Rosamond and Colour Sergeant W. Gardner

WO 32/7316   VC: Recommendations for Capt F. Aikman and   1858
Gunner W. Connelly

WO 32/7318   VC: Recommendations for Awards for Operations   1858
at Lucknow

WO 32/7321   VC: Recommendations for Awards for Officers   1858–9
and Men of the 8th Hussars

WO 32/7323   VC: Recommendations concerning Capt G. Renny   1859
and Lt P. Roddy

WO 32/7324   VC: Recommendations concerning Lt T. Hackett,   1859
C/Sgt S. McPherson, Ptes Fairhurst, Cotter, and
Gilmore and Drummer Flinn

WO 32/7328   VC: Recommendations concerning Ptes W. Cook   1859

	and D. Miller, 42nd Highlanders	
WO 32/7330	VC: Recommendations concerning Lts W. Cubitt and H. Jarrett and Pte J. McGovern	1859
WO 32/7331	VC: Recommendations concerning Lts J. Goldie and A. Bogle and Pte H. Addison	1859
WO 32/7333	VC: Recommendations and Awards in respect of various Officers and Men, including Major C. Gough and Capts H. Cloystoun and R. Shebbeare	1859
WO 32/7334	VC: Recommendations concerning Lts H. Lyster and H. Prendergast and Pte F. Whirlpool	1859
WO 32/7335	VC: Recommendation concerning Capt H. Jerome, Lt A. Cameron and six Men	1859
WO 32/7336	VC: Recommendations concerning Major S. Lawrence, Pte W. Dolwing, Cpl W. Oxenham with nine other Men	1859
WO 32/338	VC: Recommendations concerning Lt A. Heathcote, three Sergeants, four Privates and a Bugler	1859–60
WO 32/7340	VC: Recommendations concerning Capt W. Cafe, Lt F. Brown and Mr W. McDonnell	1859–60
WO 32/7341	VC: Recommendations for Pte J. Pearson	1860
WO 32/7342	VC: Recommendation concerning Lt G. Maker and Mr G. Chicken	1860
WO 32/7343	VC: Recommendations concerning Sgts H. Hartigan and R. Ewart and Pte P. McHale	1860
WO 32/7344	VC: Recommendations concerning Lt Col J. Forbes and Capt J. Wood	1860
WO 32/7347	VC: Recommendation concerning Lt E. Wood, 17th Lancers	1860
WO 32/7349	VC: Recommendations for Col J. Traves, Lt Col S. Browne, Lts C. Maclean, E. Thackeray and T. Cadell and Conductor J. Miller	1860

Second Afghan War Medal 1878–80

L/MIL/7/5675	Grant of Rewards for 1st phase of the war	1879–81
L/MIL/7/5676	Grant of Rewards for 2nd phase of the war	1881
L/MIL/7/5678	Further Grants for 1st and 2nd phases	1881
L/MIL/7/5679	Further List	1882
WO 32/7393	VC: Recommendation concerning Lt W. Cunyngham 92nd Highlanders	1879–81
WO 32/7400	VC: Award to Pte T. Ashford, Royal Fusiliers and Recommendations in respect of Lt W. Chase, Bombay Native Infantry, for Action at Kandahar	1880–2

India Medal 1895–1902

L/MIL/7/6889	Rewards to Officers employed at Chitral Fort and for Relief Operations	1895
L/MIL/7/6902	Rewards to Officers of the Chitral Relief Force	1895–7
L/MIL/7/15895	Tochi Operations, Honours and Rewards	1898
WO 32/6755	Recommendations and Awards for Operations on North West Frontier 1897–8	1899
WO 32/6756	As above	1899
WO 32/7421	VC to Lt Col R. Adams and Lt E. Costello, Indian Staff Corps, and L.A. Viscount Fircastle, 16th Lancers, for actions in Malakand and Recommendations in respect of other Men	1897
WO 32/7422	VC: Piper G. Findlater and Pte E. Lawson, Gordon Highlanders, and Pte E. Vickery, Dorset Regiment	1897–8
WO 32/7423	VC to Lt H. Pennell, Derbyshire Regiment. Recommendations for 3 DCMs	1897–8

• Clasp: *MALAKAND 1897*

L/MIL/7/15874	Honours and Rewards. Victoria Cross to certain Officers	1897–8
L/MIL/7/15900	Honours and Rewards for Native Princes	1898
L/MIL/7/15905	Honours and Rewards for Officers	1898–9
WO 32/7420	VC to Lt T. Watson RE and Lt J. Colvin.	1897–8
WO 32/7421	VC to Lt Col R. Adams and Lt E.	1897

Costello, Indian Staff Corps, Lt A. Viscount Fircastle,
16th Lancers. Recommendations in respect of other Men

• Clasp: *WAZIRISTAN 1901–2*

L/MIL/7/16825	Honours and Rewards to British Officers	1902–3

Tibet Medal 1903–04

L/MIL/7/16837	Honours and Rewards	1904–5

Indian General Service Medal 1908–35

• Clasp: *NORTH WEST FRONTIER 1908*

L/MIL/7/16850	Honours and Rewards	1908
WO 32/7506	DSO to Lt G. Waterworth, Warwickshire Regiment and 2 Lt W. Platt, Northumberland Fusiliers. DCM to NCOs and Men	1908

• Clasp: *ABOR 1911–12*

L/MIL/7/16873	Despatch	1912–13
L/MIL/7/16883	Honours and Rewards	1912

- Clasp: *AFGHAN NWF 1919*
L/MIL/7/946   Recommendations for Awards   1919

- Clasp: *WAZIRISTAN 1919–21*
L/MIL/7/16939   Recommendations for Rewards and Mentions   1920–2

- Clasp: *WAZIRISTAN 1921–24*
AIR 2/10162   Awards to RAF Officers in connection with   1921–2
                Waziristan Expedition
WO 32/5428   Recommendations for Awards from 8/5/1920–31/3/1921
WO 32/5429   Recommendations for Awards from 1/4/1921–31/12/1921
WO 106/58   Operations in Waziristan 1921–4: Awards granted

- Clasp: *NORTH WEST FRONTIER 1930–31*
L/MIL/7/16957   Honours and Rewards in connection with North   1931
                West Frontier Operations April–September 1930

- Clasp: *BURMA 1930–32*
L/MIL/7/16963   Honours and Rewards   1932

CHITRAL RELIEFS 1932
L/MIL/7/16964   Awards   1932

Indian General Service Medal 1936–9

AIR 2/2516   Operations in Waziristan 1937: Awards for   1937–9
                Gallantry and Meritorious Service
AIR 2/9404   Rewards for RAF personnel: Operations in Waziristan   1940
                December 1937–December 1939
L/MIL/7/16971   Waziristan Operations: Awards   1936–9
L/MIL/7/16972   Waziristan Operations: Awards   1936–37
L/MIL/7/16974   Waziristan Operations: Recommendations   1937–38
                for Awards
L/MIL/7/16975   As above   1937–38

General Service Medal 1918–62

- Clasp: *S.E ASIA 1945–46*
WO 373/92 LG date 04/04 /946

- Clasp: *MALAYA*
AIR 2/16814 Recommendations for Malaya: June 1950 onwards
   (Air Min Ref A 74854/51)
   The following recommendations for Malaya 1948–60 include some
   duplicate *London Gazette* dates and some that have been misplaced in
   the chronological sequence.
WO 373/128   LG dates 04/02/1949–24/03/1950 and 19/05/1950

WO 373/129 LG dates 11/04/1950–02/02/1951 and 27/04/1951
WO 373/130 LG dates 16/02/1951–12/02/1952
WO 373/131 LG dates 12/02/1952–01/05/1953
WO 373/132 LG dates 24/04/1953–26/10/1954
WO 373/133 LG dates 14/09/1954–08/05/1956
WO 373/134 LG dates 15/03/1956–20/05/1958
WO 373/135 LG dates 10/01/1958–30/12/1960
WO 373/136 LG dates 18/09/1951, 21/03/1952, 31/10/1952, 04/05/1954,
    29/10/1954, 20/05/1955, 11/10/1955, 08/05/1956, 10/09/1956, 11/06/1957,
    03/12/1957, 01/07/1958, 09/12/1958, 16/09/1959, 14/06/1960

Korea Medal

AIR 2/16815	Recommendations for Korea: December 1950 onwards (Air Min Ref A 80462/51)	
WO 32/14861	VC: Recommendation for Pte W. Speakman, KOSB	1951–8
WO 32/15193	VC: Recommendation for Lt P.K.E. Curtis, DCLI	1954
WO 373/114-120	LG dates 05/12/1950– 31/05/1956	

Vietnam Medal (*Australian and New Zealand Forces*)
WO 373/141   LG dates 26/02/1965–19/09/1969

General Service Medal 1962

• Clasp: *BORNEO*
WO 373/138–140 LG dates 09/07/1963–12/05/1967

• Clasp: *MALAY PENINSULAR*
WO 373/140 LG date 09/04/1965

China
Second China War Medal 1857–60

WO 32/7356	VC: Recommendations concerning Officers and Men for Operation at Taku Forts	1861
WO 32/7357	VC: Recommendation for Hospital Apprentice A. Fitzgibbon attached 67th Regt	1861

Third China War Medal 1900

L/MIL/7/16761	Honours and Rewards	1901–2
L/MIL/7/16762	Award of the Royal Red Cross to certain Ladies	1901–2
L/MIL/7/16791	Promotions and Rewards for Natives	1901–5
L/MIL/7/16808	Honours and Rewards	1902–3

Crimea and Baltic

The following WO 32 files all concern the Victoria Cross.

WO 32/7302	Statement of Services of Officers and Men of the Royal Navy and Marines recommended for Awards	1857
WO 32/7303	Lists of Officers and Men recommended for Awards	1857
WO 32/7304	Awards to Col C. Dickson, Capt G. Davis, Sgt D. Cambridge, and Ptes T. Grady and S. Evans	1857
WO 32/7305	Recommendations for Awards to Asst Sugn W. Sylvester, Lt C. Teesdale, Capts H. Jones and T. Esmonde and Sgt J. Malone	1857
WO 32/7306	Recommendations for Awards to Lt G. Symons, Ensign J. Craig, and QMS J. Farrell	1857–8
WO 32/7307	Claims from Lt H.E. Wood	1857–8
WO 32/7308	Awards to Capt H. Elphinstone, Sgn J. Mouat, Major M. Walker, C Sgts G. Gardiner, P. Leitch and H. McDonald, and Sgt H. Ramage	1858
WO 32/7326	VC: Recommendation for Sgt Major C. Wooden, 17th Lancers	1858

PARLIAMENTARY PAPERS

List of Officers, NCOs and Men selected to receive War Medals presented by the King of Sardinia to British Army in War in the East. Volume XXVII.215, Fiche Number 62.210

List of Officers and Men of the Royal Navy and Royal Marines selected to receive War Medals awarded by the King of Sardinia to British Naval Forces engaged in the Crimea. Volume XXXVII.557, Fiche Number 63.320

Supplemental List of Officers of the Army selected to receive War Medals presented by the King of Sardinia. Volume XXXVII.565, Fiche Number 63.320

The above lists all contain one or two lines about each recipient and what they did to receive the Al Valore Militari.

Middle East
General Service Medal 1918–66

• Clasp: IRAQ

AIR 2/2841	Recommendations for Decoration of Officers of the Mesopotamian Expeditionary Force	1918–20
FO 248/1228	Bushire-Shiraz Operations	1919
FO 248/1229	Bushire Situation	1919
L/MIL/7/16967	Recommendations for Awards in connection with Operations	1925

	in Mesopotamia, July–December 1920	
L/PS/15/42 file H26	British Empire Order: Honours for Natives etc. of Mesopotamia and British Officials in Mesopotamia (Part 1)	1919–21
L/PS/15/42 file H26	Indian Orders: Mesopotamia; Awards for Services rendered during India Office control of Civil Administration (Part 2)	1921
L/PS/15/42 file H42	Indian Orders: Awards in recognition of Services rendered in connection with Military Operations	1921
L/PS/15/43 file H134	Indian Order: Awards for Services rendered in Mesopotamia	1919

• Clasp: KURDISTAN

L/MIL/7/16947	Honours in connection with Operations in Kurdistan	1924–5
WO 32/5842	Despatches and Diary of Operations in Kurdistan: Recommendations for Awards	1923–4

• Clasp: PALESTINE

AIR 2/9404	Rewards to RAF personnel for Operations in Palestine 3 August–31 December 1939	1940
WO 32/4298	GOC Palestine to make immediate Awards of Medals	1936–9
WO 373/92	LG date 06/11/1936	
WO 373/146	LG date 11/05/1937	
WO 373/92	LG dates 11/03/1938–22/12/1939	

• Clasp: PALESTINE 1945–48

WO 373/146	LG date 23/07/1948

• Clasp: CYPRUS

WO 373/125–127 LG dates 23/12/1955–09/02/1965

• Clasp: ARABIAN PENINSULAR

WO 373/125   LG dates 22/02/1949–17/05/1960

General Service Medal 1962

• Clasp: SOUTH ARABIA

AIR 2/17390	Operations in South Arabia	1964

WO 373/137–138 LG dates 01/05/1964–09/07/1968

• Clasp: DHOFAR

WO 373/172 &187 LG dates unknown

New Zealand

WO 32/7355	VC: Claim and Recommendations concerning	1861

	C Sgt J. Lucas, 40th Regt	
WO 32/8258	Despatch announcing Termination of Operations. Recommendations for Awards	1861
WO 32/8256	Recommendations in respect of Action at Pukorokoro	1863
WO 32/7369	VC Awards to Capt H. Shaw 18th Regt and Recommendations for the DCM for Ptes Brandon, Clampitt, Kairnes and Graham	1865–6

12   First World War Awards

12.1   INTRODUCTION

In the history of orders, decoration and medals, the First World War is probably one of the most significant periods. Not only were a number of new awards created, but the honours system was also refined into something we can understand today.

The First World War is very important in relation to various aspects concerning awards for gallantry and meritorious service. During the period 1914–19 the Military Cross (MC), Distinguished Flying Cross (DFC), Air Force Cross (AFC), Distinguished Service Medal (DSM), Distinguished Flying Medal (DFM) and Air Force Medal (AFM) were all instituted. The naval award the Conspicuous Service Cross evolved into the Distinguished Service Cross (DSC) and the Meritorious Service Medal (MSM) could be awarded for non-operational gallantry or meritorious services in connection with the war. In 1917, the Most Excellent Order of the British Empire was created.

The most difficult problem associated with researching an award granted to personnel in the British Army for the First World War is one of sources. All awards to members of the Army were submitted on an Army Form W 3121. These forms survived the war, only to be destroyed by enemy action in September 1940, when, along with many of the service papers, they were destroyed in the first major German attack on London. However, without the forms for the Army, all is not lost, it just means that finding information becomes harder and the amount of information you find may be less.

A useful starting point concerning awards granted in the First World War is *Honours and Awards Army, Navy and Air Force 1914–1920* (Hayward, 1979), but please note that it does not list winners of the Military Medal.

12.2 THE *LONDON GAZETTE*

All awards to British and Empire forces should have been announced in the *London Gazette*. As the *London Gazette* is available at the National Archives in three different forms, it is discussed in CHAPTER 7.

12.3 THE ADMIRALTY

Many recommendations for awards and other information concerning awards to personnel under Admiralty authority exist in abundance. Whilst not all of the recommendations for awards have survived, there are a number of sources and techniques that will produce at least something.

12.3.1 Easy Sources (Officers)

All naval and marine officers who were decorated in the First World War had an Honours card. These cards are on open access in the Microfilm Reading Room and they are arranged in three key collections: Honours and Awards; MiDs; and Foreign Awards, all of which are in alphabetical order. At the bottom of an award card, it will give you the name, rank, award and gazette date. At the bottom of the card should be a sheet reference. This is an alphanumeric reference to the Honours sheets in ADM 171. On the Honours sheet will be information concerning the circumstances for which the award was granted. Examples of a card and sheet can be seen in PLATES 15 and 16 respectively.

ADM 171/78	1914–19	Sheets A–C
ADM 171/79	1914–19	Sheets D
ADM 171/80	1914–19	Sheets E–H
ADM 171/81	1914–19	Sheets I–L
ADM 171/82	1914–19	Sheets M–O
ADM 171/83	1914–19	Sheets P
ADM 171/84	1914–19	Sheets Q–S

ADM 171/85	1914–19	Sheets T–U
ADM 171/86	1914–19	Sheets V–W
ADM 171/87	1914–19	Sheets X 1–500
ADM 171/88	1914–19	Sheets X 501–958

On the back of the Honours card you may find the date the award was actually invested.

There are a number of pieces of ADM 171 concerning appointments to the Most Excellent Order of the British Empire.

ADM 171/135	1918	Names submitted for Appointment
ADM 171/136	1919	Civil Division
ADM 171/137	1919	Military Division
ADM 171/138	1918–19	Recommendations for post-war Honours

A list of awards granted to the Royal Naval Reserve from 1914 to 1918 can be found in ADM 171/77 *The Distinguished Service Order 1886–1923* by O' Moore Creagh and Humphris (Hayward, 1978), *The Roll of the DSC 1901–1938* by W.H. Fevyer (LSE, 1990) or *Fringes of the Fleet* by R. Witte (DNW, 1997), all three providing very useful information.

For information about all naval and marine recipients of the Victoria Cross, *The Naval VCs* by Stephen Snelling (Sutton, 2002) is recommended.

12.3.2 Easy Sources (Ratings)

Apart from Mentions in Despatches (MiD), researching other awards to naval ratings and other ranks of the Royal Marines is relatively simple.

The Distinguished Service Medal (DSM) was the most common award granted to service personnel under the authority of the Admiralty during the First World War. There are a number of different ways to approach this medal.

You can consult *The Distinguished Service Medal 1914–1920* by W.H. Fevyer (1982). This will provide you with many basic details, but most importantly the date the award was announced in the *London Gazette*.

You can look at the index of the DSM and the Conspicuous Gallantry Medal (CGM) in ADM 171/75. This volume is arranged alphabetically and gives you a medal number. Once you have the medal number, look at the roll in ADM 171/61 which will give you gazette date, name, rate or rank, number, the naming details that would have been put on the medal and how the medal was disposed of. The naming details on a DSM are very important, as they will give you further indicators that will help you with your research. Once you have all of the details from ADM 171/61 and the gazette date, you can then use ADM 12.

For recipients of the CGM, you can use the index to the roll in ADM 171/75, and then the roll in ADM 171/61. A further roll of the CGM can be found in ADM 1/25295.

The roll of the Immediate MSM to the Royal Navy can be found in ADM 171/61.

A large number of naval and marine personnel saw service ashore and received awards normally associated with the Army. For further information about Army awards, see 12.6 below.

A number of Admiralty files concerning honours and awards for the First World War can be found quite easily in the catalogue, including the following:

ADM 1/8461/154 Jutland Awards

ADM 1/8474/280 Jutland Awards

ADM 1/8518/77 Recommendations for specific Rewards re RAF in connection with King's Birthday Honours 1918

ADM 1/8526/149 Posthumous VC to Master of SS *Otaki*

ADM 1/8528/175 Birthday Honours 1919

ADM 1/8548/1 Order of the British Empire: Admiralty Recommendations for King's Birthday Honours List May 1918 and/or New Years Honours List 1919

ADM 116/1414 Awards for Special Services – Notations on Service Certificates 1915–17

ADM 116/1575 Birthday Honours 1918

ADM 116/1650 RNAS Honours and Awards for Service during the period ending 31 December 1917

ADM 116/1561 Awards to Torpedo Boat Destroyers and Torpedo Boat Flotillas to 31 December 1917

ADM 116/1562 As above

ADM 116/1620 North America and West Indies Station – 10 Cruiser Squadron. Honours and Awards for Services rendered during the period ending December 1917

ADM 116/1801   Recommendations for Periodic Awards 1917–19
ADM 116/1811   Zeebrugge and Ostend April/May 1918, Honours and
   Awards
ADM 137/1090   Awards to Submarine E 14
ADM 137/1149   Awards for Gallipoli Operations
ADM 137/2098   Dover Patrol Awards
ADM 137/2653   Anti-Submarine Division Reports: include Awards June 1917–
   October 1918
ADM 137/3925   Royal Marine Artillery Anti-Aircraft Brigade: Honours and
   Awards 1915–16
ADM 137/3928   Field Ambulance Units attached to 63 Division:
   Recommendations for Awards 1916–18
ADM 137/3943B   Anglo Russian Armoured Car Unit: Honours and Awards
   1917–18

12.3.3 Researching Further

In order to find a detailed recommendation for an award granted
to a member of the naval forces or Royal Marines, it is necessary
to use the Admiralty Index and Digest in ADM 12. This means
using an index of correspondence (ADM 12) to find an original
Admiralty reference to an award, and then looking for it in ADM
1, ADM 116 or ADM 137. For a full explanation of how to use
ADM 12, see CHAPTER 25 on Research Techniques.

12.4   THE AIR MINISTRY

The majority of records concerning honours and awards granted
to members of the Royal Flying Corps (RFC) and Royal Air Force
(RAF) are in the records series AIR 1. Records concerning the Royal
Naval Air Service (RNAS) may also be found in this series, they
may also be found amongst the Admiralty records. See above.

Until such time as the First World War index of RAF honours
and awards is transferred to the series AIR 81, researching an
award for the RFC or RAF will take time. Most of the files
concerning honours and awards are arranged by unit and it is very
important to know the unit the individual was serving on when he
earned the award.

To find the unit an individual served in, you may need to trace
their record of service first. See *Air Force Records: A Guide for
Family Historians* by William Spencer (TNA, 2008).

You can search the AIR 1 catalogue online using the terms 'honours', 'awards', 'decorations' or 'recommendations', and you will retrieve a lot of results.

Should you wish to resort to secondary sources first, you may wish to consult the following: *The Air VCs* by Peter Cooksley (Sutton, 1996); *For Valour: The Air VCs* by Chaz Bowyer (Kimber, 1978); *The Distinguished Flying Cross and How it was Won 1918–1995* by N. and C. Carter (Hayward, 1998); *The Distinguished Flying Medal: A Record of Courage* by Ian Tavender (Hayward, 1990); *The Meritorious Service Medal to The Aerial Forces* by Ian McInnes (Picton, 1984).

For the DSO 1886–1923 for RNAS awards of the DSC, see *The Roll of the DSC 1901–1938* by W.H. Fevyer (LSE, 1990) or *Fringes of the Fleet* by R. Witte (DNW, 1997).

Examples of the types of file you may find in AIR 1 include AIR 1/107/15/9/287 RAF Honours and Awards, August 1918–April 1919 and AIR 1/75/15/9/173 RNAS Dunkerque Command, Honours and Awards gained by Officers and Men, 1916–19. A good example of a file that could be used as a way to consult other AIR 1 files on honours and awards is AIR 1/878/204/5/584 Record of Honours Awarded: Unit Index Book, January 1917–June 1918.

12.5 THE INDIA OFFICE (BRITISH LIBRARY)

Many of the records concerning honours and awards held in the India Office Collection at the British Library are for operations within India's boundaries.

L/MIL/7/15937	Waziristan Operations against the Mahsuds: Honour and Rewards	1917
L/MIL/7/15938	Despatch for the above Operation	1917
L/MIL/7/16893	Marri Operations March–May 1918: Honours and Rewards	1918
L/MIL/7/16895	Minor Operations in India and Aden: Despatch and Honours and Rewards	1916–17
L/MIL/7/16897	Lardek Valley Operations October 1915: Awards	1918–19
L/MIL/7/16967	Mesopotamia Awards July–December 1918	1919
L/PS/15/41 file H122	List of Recommendations for the Grant of Honours to certain British Officers for Service in connection with the siege of Kut	1918

L/PS/15/41	Honours awarded for Service at Aden in connection	1918
file H197	with the war	
L/PS/15/53	Indian Honours: British Empire Order; Awards	1920–1
file H106	for Services rendered in Minor Operations in India	

By far the most useful published source concerning honours granted to the Indian Army is *Honours and Awards: Indian Army August 1914–August 1921*, (Hayward, 1974).

Another very useful book concerning the Indian Distinguished Service Medal is *The Indian Distinguished Service Medal* by Rana Chhina (2001), which is actually the roll for the medal.

12.6 THE WAR OFFICE
As already stated, many of the records concerning awards granted to Army personnel were destroyed in 1940. What follows, therefore, is a description of the surviving sources together with advice about using non-medal sources.

12.6.1 The Recommendation Process
The process by which an individual was recommended for an award, was administered by the Military Secretary's Branch of the War Office. Over the duration of the war, the system was improved. *Instructions Regarding Recommendations for Honours and Rewards* gives an insight into the system.

To recommend an individual for an award, an Army Form W3121 had to be completed and then sent up the chain of command. Depending on the award being recommended, approval for an award could be granted by a Lieutenant General commanding a Corps.

What is important to grasp about the system with regards to research is the timescale. By the time the award was announced in the *London Gazette*, as long as the person was not dead at the time of publication, they would have known about the award before the publication date. An example of local promulgation, a Fourth Army Order, can be seen in PLATE 12.

Local promulgation of awards would have been in General Routine Orders (GRO). Although no complete collections of GROs with all of the award lists are held at the National Archives, the records that have survived are now held in WO 123.

THEATRE	REFERENCE
France	WO 123/199–203
Italy	WO 123/279
Egypt	WO 123/280–282
East Africa	WO 123/288–289
Mesopotamia	WO 123/290
Salonika	WO 123/293

Another form of local promulgation of awards was the Illuminated Army Order. An example of which is seen in PLATE 12.

12.6.2 The Records

Information about the Victoria Cross can be found in the registers in the series WO 98. The registers in WO 98 have recently been digitized and placed on DocumentsOnline, and it is possible to search by name and then download the citation as it was published in the *London Gazette*.

There are a number of files concerning the Victoria Cross in the records series WO 32 under Codes 50D and 50M.

WO 32

3421	1934	Priority of the first five Awards (of the VC) during 1914–18 War: Lt M.J. Dease
4991	1915	Recommendation for Award of a bar to Victoria Cross of Captain A. Martin Leake
4993	1914–16	Recommendations for Awards by Sir J. French
4994	1915	Recommendations for Awards with regard to Operations at the Dardanelles
4995	1915–17	Recommendations for Awards to Men of 1st Lancashire Fusiliers for Operations at Gallipoli
21402	1915–16	VC: Award to Pte H. Christian, 2nd King's Own

Information concerning those who were awarded the Distinguished Service Order (DSO) can be found in the series WO 390. This series is the DSO register: it covers the period 1886–1945 and it is available on microfilm.

WO 390 *Distinguished Service Order*

| 1 | November 1886–June 1902 |

2	June 1902–January 1916
3	January 1916–December 1916
4	December 1916–June 1917
5	June 1917–October 1917
6	October 1917–September 1918
7	January 1918–September 1918
8	September 1918–January 1919
9	April 1919–August 1941
10	August 1941–July 1943
11	July 1943–December 1944
12	December 1944–September 1945
13	Honorary Appointments July 1915–October 1943

Records concerning the Military Cross can be found in the series WO 389 and the records in this series take two forms. The Gazette Books in WO 389/1–8 have one great strength. Within each volume are the lists of the awards as they were published in the *London Gazette*. For those awards that were not published as part of the New Year or Birthday Honours Lists, it is usual to find a citation. Added to the citations is the date and place, when and where the MC was won. This information can be used when consulting the Unit War Diaries in WO 95.

WO 389/9–24 is a name index and this provides name, rank, unit and gazette date. The index card will also tell you how the medal was disposed of.

WO 389 *Military Cross*

1	Gazette Book	9 November 1914–31 May 1916
2	Gazette Book	3 June 1916–25 November 1916
3	Gazette Book	11 December 1916–26 May 1917
4	Gazette Book	4 June 1917–25 August 1917
5	Gazette Book	17 September 1917–23 April 1918
6	Gazette Book	18 January 1918–24 August 1918
7	Gazette Book	26 July 1918–12 February 1919
8	Gazette Book	30 July 1919–1982
9	Name Index	Aar–Belt
10	Name Index	Bem–Bury
11	Name Index	Bus–Coston
12	Name Index	Cot–Dumper
13	Name Index	Dun–Garbutt

14	Name Index	Garc–Harford
15	Name Index	Harg–Huntriss
16	Name Index	Hurc–Lapthorne
17	Name Index	Lara–Marryat
18	Name Index	Mars–Morphy
19	Name Index	Morr–Pepys
20	Name Index	Per–Robson
21	Name Index	Roc–Smitton
22	Name Index	Smo–Tozer
23	Name Index	Tra–Wilks
24	Name Index	Will–Zorawar

Recipients of Bars to the Military Cross 1916–1920 and A List of Warrant Officers awarded the MC 1915–1919 by J.V. Webb (1988)

A register of the Distinguished Conduct Medal is in the series WO 391. There is also a card index of DCM recipients for the First World War. The card index is available on microfiche and it has also been digitized on DocumentsOnline.

Each DCM index card provides, name, rank, number, unit, gazette date and operational theatre in which the award was won.

WO 391 *Distinguished Conduct Medal*

1	Alphabetical Index	1854–1908
2	Awards announced	23 October 1914–3 July 1915
3	Awards announced	5 August 1915–11 March 1916
4	Awards announced	22 January 1916–26 September 1916
5	Awards announced	20 October 1916–25 August 1917
6	Awards announced	29 July 1917–7October 1918
7	Awards announced	21 October 1918–11 May 1920
7A	Awards announced	1 April 1920–15 December 1998

Awards of the Military Medal (MM) are recorded in the *London Gazette* and there is also a name index on microfiche. The name index provides name, rank, number, unit, gazette date and operational theatre. The index has been digitized and is available on DocumentsOnline, where it is possible to search for the MM by name.

Records of awards of the Meritorious Service Medal (MSM) are also available in the form of a card index. As with the DCM

and MM, the MSM index is available on microfiche and via
DocumentsOnline. An example of an MSM card can be seen in
FIGURE 11.

The Immediate MSM 1916–1928, Ian McInnes (1988)

On the DCM, MM and MSM index cards, the gazette date is
sometimes given as a numerical code. These are listed below.

GAZETTE CODE	GAZETTE DATE(S)
58	11 February 1919
59	11 February or 13 March 1919
60	18 or 24 or 30 January, or 22 February 1919
61	29 March 1919
62	14 May 1919
63	17 June 1919
64	3 July 1919
65	23 July 1919
66	20 August 1919
67	20 August 1919
68	20 October 1919
69	22 November 1919
70	18 December 1919
Peace Gazette	3 June 1919
POW Gazette	30 January 1920

Another card index available on microfiche in the Microfilm
Reading Room and on DocumentsOnline is that for Mention in
Despatches (MiD). The index is by no means complete, but where
a card exists, it does provide you with the gazette date for the MiD.

The register of the Royal Red Cross is available in the series WO
145 and it covers the period 1883–1994. There are three volumes,
each with an internal index. The register takes the form of
announcements extracted from the *London Gazette* and rarely
adds anything to the information that accompanied the announcement of the award.

WO 145 *Royal Red Cross*

1	Register of Awards	1883–1918
2	Register of Awards	1918–1943
3	Register of Awards	1943–1994

Recommendations for awards to officers of the Women's Auxiliary Army Corps during the period December 1918–December 1919 can be found in WO 162/65. Most of the awards were appointments to the Most Excellent Order of the British Empire.

A Mention in Despatches (MiD) was the lowest form of official recognition for deeds that would be announced in the *London Gazette*. Prior to the First World War, apart from the announcement in the *London Gazette*, there was no tangible proof that someone had a Mention in Despatches.

During the First World War, tangible proof of an MiD was created in the form of an oak leaf emblem to be worn on the ribbon of the Victory Medal. At the same time as the creation of the oak leaf emblem, it was decided to award a certificate, giving the service details of the recipient and the date the MiD was announced in the *London Gazette*. Information about the creation of the oak leaf emblem can be found in WO 32/5412.

A second level of MiD was the Class B mention which was only

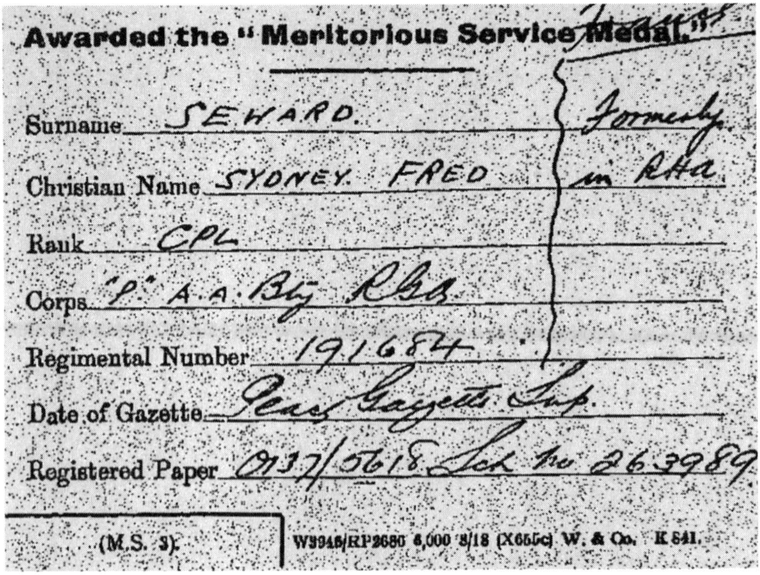
Awarded the "Meritorious Service Medal."
Surname SEWARD. Formerly
Christian Name SYDNEY FRED in RHA.
Rank CPL
Corps "P" A.A. Bty RGA
Regimental Number 191684
Date of Gazette Peace Gazette Sup.
Registered Paper
(M.S. 3)
W3948/RP2680 6,000 8/18 (X655c) W. & Co. K 841.

FIG 11. *The Meritorious Service Medal Index Card for Cpl S.F. Seward, Royal Garrison Artillery* [WO 372]

published in *The Times* newspaper. An individual who was given a Class B was not entitled to wear an oak leaf emblem. You can find the Class B announcements by searching *The Times* digital archive using the term 'brought to notice'.

Other recommendations for awards can be found in WO 32 and they include:

WO 32

| 5815 | 1915 | Despatch from General Wapshare on Operations on Mafia Island East Africa; Recommendations for Awards |
| 5817 | 1915 | Report by General Wapshare on Situation and Operations from 4 December 1914–12 April 1915 in East Africa and Uganda; Recommendations for Awards |

12.6.3 Using Unit War Diaries

As there are no published citations for nearly all of the Military Medals gazetted during the war, another source of information is needed. What follows can be used for all awards to the Army.

The easiest alternative source to access for information about awards are the unit war diaries in WO 95. As long as you have the unit of the recipient and the gazette date, all you need to do is find the appropriate war diary covering the gazette date. Using the gazette date as a starting point, work backwards chronologically. Hopefully you will find something within three months of the gazette date.

The amount of information in war diaries concerning awards varies. You may find nothing, you may find a list of awards, you may find a brief citation (especially for a VC action), you may find something that says 'the following awards have been announced for service on' and a date. By using that information, you can then look at the appropriate date in the diary.

12.7   THE WEST AFRICAN FRONTIER FORCE AND KING'S AFRICAN RIFLES DISTINGUISHED CONDUCT MEDAL

The most effective way to research a WAFF or KAR DCM is to consult John Arnolds' excellent book *The African DCM* (OMRS 1998). It lists all of the awards, giving unit, gazette date and the National Archives references to the recommendations as appropriate.

12.8 OTHER GOVERNMENT DEPARTMENTS

Although there are no consolidated collections of files concerning awards in the records of the non-military government departments, it does not mean that there are none. Many policy files concerning awards can be found by keyword searching the catalogue online. Recommendations for some awards of the Albert Medal to service personnel may be found in HO 45. Search the catalogue of HO 45 by name of the recipient.

There is currently an indexing project relating to the records of the Colonial Office and the cataloguing has thrown up at least one file of interest. CO 323/720 contains a file described as 'Military Medal: Applications for certain African and West Indian Forces, 1916'.

12.9 RECORDS HELD ELSEWHERE

The recommendations for awards to members of the 55th West Lancashire Division are held at Liverpool Central Library. The recommendations for the 29th Divisional Artillery are held by the Imperial War Museum.

12.10 CASE STUDIES

Hundreds and thousands of men and women were decorated for their service in the First World War and it is difficult to choose from them all. What follows, therefore, are three examples that are slightly different. The case studies represent different services, different operational theatres and they illustrate that you don't have to have all of the medals earned by an individual to discover an interesting story.

Frances Maud Rice

Frances Maud Rice was born in 1874, but very little is known about her prior to the First World War, apart from the fact that she was a nurse. On 28 August 1914, Frances offered her services to the War Office and she was soon enrolled in the Territorial Force Nursing Service.

As she was already qualified as a nurse, Frances was sent to France on 24 September 1914, joining 5 General Hospital on 26 September. By entering France prior to 22 November 1914, Sister Rice qualified for the 1914 Star, the British War Medal and Victory Medal.

Over the next two years, Sister Rice served at a number of hospitals and medical establishments before being invalided back to England in September 1916. After a period of convalescence she returned to 29 Casualty Clearing Station in France in November 1916.

For her devotion to duty as a nurse, Frances Maud Rice was awarded the Royal Red Cross (RRC) and it was announced in the *London Gazette* on 3 June 1917. The award can be found in the Register of the RRC in WO 145/1.

FIG 12. *Sister F.M. Rice leaving Buckingham Palace after being invested with her Royal Red Cross*

Sister Rice was presented with her RRC by King George V in February 1918. She was photographed leaving Buckingham Place after the investiture and the photograph was published in *The Nursing Times* on 16 February 1918 (see FIGURE 12). Her medals are shown in PLATE 13.

George Williams

George Williams is a significant individual in the history of the Victoria Cross because he was not a European, but a black Sudanese Christian soldier in the King's African Rifles (KAR).

George Williams' 5 clasp Africa General Service Medal was purchased at auction many years ago, and research soon revealed that he had won the KAR Distinguished Conduct Medal in the First World War. As 1925 Sergeant George Williams 1/3 KAR, the recommendation for Williams' KAR DCM can be found in CO 534/19. The medal was issued from the Royal Mint on 17 August 1915 (WO 102/24 refers).

George Williams was obviously a very brave soldier because it wasn't long before he was recommended for the Victoria Cross, and it was here that he becomes important in the history of that award. Although George Williams' bravery cannot be doubted, he or those recommending him fell foul of the VC statutes because, as a black African soldier, he wasn't eligible.

Having failed to be awarded the Victoria Cross because of a technicality, George Williams was awarded a bar to his KAR DCM. Unfortunately, having served almost continually in East Africa from 1900, George Williams was killed towards the end of the War.

George Williams' KAR DCM and 5 clasp AGS were reunited two years ago, the DCM having being sold at another auction. The reunited medals can be seen in PLATE 14.

The recommendations for George Williams' KAR DCM and bar and the letter concerning the VC are seen in FIGURES 13, 14 and 15.

Arthur William Sims Reeve

The single British War Medal as earned by Lt A.W.S. Reeve RNR is very common. See PLATE 8. Many naval personnel received a single British War Medal for their service in the First World War, so to see Reeve's medal for sale on its own did not cause any concern.

With all British War Medals awarded to naval officers, I always check the two awards card indexes in the Microfilm Reading Room at the National Archives. The cards are arranged alphabetically and the search for Reeve produced a result: he had been awarded an OBE in the *London Gazette* on 1 April 1919.

The Honours card for Reeve gave the sheet reference X 21 and said the award was 'Post War' as 'Executive Officer, HMS *Managem*', so it was necessary to look at ADM 171/87. This revealed that Reeve's OBE had been awarded for 'Special service in connection with intelligence organization in Palestine, Syria and Karamania'.

After scouring various sources at my disposal, the Imperial War Museum catalogue led me to a book called *Hard Lying* by Captain L.B. Weldon MC (Herbert Jenkins, 1925). Weldon had been the intelligence officer on HMS *Managem* and the book tells his and the ship's story about dropping and picking up our agents behind the Turkish Lines in Palestine and Syria.

In transmitting the enclosed correspondence recently received I am to state that there is no trace of the receipt of any recommendation for the award of the Victoria Cross to Colour-Sergeant George Williams, 3rd King's African Rifles, and in any case African Native Soldiers are ineligible for such distinction.

(1A).   Medal for Distinguished Conduct.

Name.	Regiment.	Action for which Commended.
GEORGE WILLIAMS.	3rd Bn: King's African Rifles.	For showing great courage and enterprise on the night of the 5th/6th September, 1914, at the action of Tsavo. This N.C.O. twice, at great personal risk, crept up to the German position and brought back information of the enemy's dispositions and strength.

-o-

Already recommended for a V.C. vide my No.242, dated 1st March, 1915. If V.C. has not been granted - recommended for an additional Bar.

1905	Color Sergeant.	GEORGE WILLIAMS, 3rd Bn: King's African Rifles.	He commanded "D" Company on the 18th January, 1915, at JASIN, after Lieut: Dean had been wounded and the Effendi killed. He succeeded in extricating the Co: and Machine Guns under a very heavy rifle and Machine Gun fire, after all their ammunition had been expended. This Non-Commissioned Officer has frequently come to notice for acts of gallantry and skill.

FIG 13. (top) *Colonial Office correspondence concerning the missing recommendation for C/Sgt George Williams' Victoria Cross* [CO 534/19]

FIG 14. (middle) *Recommendation for the King's African Rifles Distinguished Conduct Medal for C/Sgt George Williams, 3rd King's African Rifles* [CO 534/19]

FIG 15. (above) *The recommendation for the Victoria Cross for C/Sgt George Williams, subsequently downgraded to a bar to his King's African Rifles Distinguished Conduct Medal* [CO 534/19]

FIG 16. *The ship's company of HMS* Managem, *including front left Lt A.W.S. Reeve* RNR

Weldon's book contains a number of photographs with one of the crew, including Lt Reeve, see FIGURE 16.

Lt Reeve's Honours card and Honours sheet can be seen in PLATES 15 and 16.

Sydney Fred Seward

Very little is known about Sydney Fred Seward because his record of service is still retained by the Ministry of Defence. According to the 1901 Census, Seward was aged 5 when it was taken. By the outbreak of the First World War, Seward was almost old enough to see overseas service straight away, but as his date of entry into the Army is unknown, whether he lied about his age when he enlisted is still a mystery.

The Medal Index Card for Sydney Fred Seward states that he went to France on 28 August 1915 as 578825 Gunner Royal Field

Artillery. At a later point, Seward transferred to the Royal Garrison Artillery and it was with 'P' Anti Aircraft Battery, RGA, that he earned his Meritorious Service Medal. Seward's MSM index card can be seen in FIGURE 11.

Staying in the Army after the war, he was awarded his Long Service and Good Conduct medal in 1933. Seward's medals can be seen in PLATE 17.

Bertine Sutton

Air Marshal Bertine Sutton was born in 1886. By the end of 1914 he was serving as a soldier in the Inns of Court Officers' Training Corps (OTC).

Commissioned into the Westmoreland and Cumberland Yeomanry, by 1916 he had transferred to the Royal Flying Corps (RFC) as an observer, seeing service with 5 Squadron RFC. After retraining as a pilot, Bertine Sutton went on to see service with 9 and then 7 Sqdn RFC.

After being awarded the MC in January 1917, Sutton went on to receive the DSO in September 1917 and three MiDs, one in 1917 and two in 1918. In the New Year Honours List of 1919 Sutton was appointed an OBE, and on 15 July of the same year his Belgian Croix de Guerre was gazetted.

Awarded a permanent commission in the RAF on 1 August 1917, Sutton served in various staff appointments for the remainder of his career. These included OC No 1 Group India RAF for operations in Mohmand in 1933, for which he was awarded another MiD.

Whilst serving as Air Officer Commanding 22 Group, Sutton was appointed Companion of the Order of the Bath on 8 June 1939. Sutton's final appointment was as Air Member for Personnel. Knighted (KBE) on 11 June 1942, Sutton retired from the RAF on 7 June 1945.

The recommendations for the DSO and MC awarded to Bertine Sutton can be found in AIR 1/1032/204/5/1434 and AIR 1/1031/204/5/1433 respectively. Sir Bertine Sutton's medals can be seen in PLATE 31 and on the cover of this book.

13   Awards Given between the Wars

13.1   INTRODUCTION

Once the First World War was over, the armed forces returned to pre-war type duties. However, between 1919 and 1939, there were a number of military operations that resulted in the granting of awards for gallantry or meritorious service. Added to this is the continued granting of New Year and Birthday honours, and the recognition of civilian acts of gallantry, including those by the police.

If you do not find reference to what you are looking for in this chapter, you may wish to consult CHAPTER 11 on Awards by Operational Theatre.

13.2   THE RECORDS

There are so many files dispersed between the National Archives and the Oriental and India Office collections at the British Library that the only way to describe them effectively is to cover them by place of deposit, government department and chronologically.

As with all awards announced to British nationals and members of the colonies and dominions, the awards were announced in the *London Gazette* or the appropriate colonial or dominion gazette.

13.3   THE NATIONAL ARCHIVES

The records held at the National Archives cover all government departments, apart from the India Office and Burma, although there is a small amount of duplication, especially with regard to the British Army in India.

13.3.1 *The Admiralty*

The majority of files concerning honours and awards for the period 1919–38 can be found in ADM 1, ADM 116 and ADM 137. Most can be found by keyword searching the online catalogue or by using ADM 12. See CHAPTER 25 on Research Techniques for further information.

The following document references are the key files concerning honours and awards for the prescribed period.

ADM 137/1683 Baltic Honours 1919 (gazetted 8 March 1920)
ADM 116/2497 Wanhsien Incident 1927

13.3.2 The Air Ministry

Records containing recommendations for honours and awards to officers and men of the Royal Air Force can almost exclusively be found in AIR 2. Many of these recommendations concern non-operational flying such as long distance flights and flights of exploration.

The following document references are the key surviving files for honours and awards for the RAF for the inter-war period.

AIR 2/110	1919–20	Kenley to Cairo flight. Special Rewards List for flights to Egypt and for work on aerial routes to Africa
AIR 2/129	1919–20	Rewards for Atlantic Flight (Alcock and Brown)
AIR 2/142	1920	Policy regarding Awards in connection with England to Cape Town flights during January–February 1920
AIR 2/204	1920	Recommendations for Honours and Rewards for Z Expedition in Somaliland
AIR 2/119		Decorations to Captain Ross Smith and Crew for accomplishing first flight to Australia
AIR 2/109	1919	Presentation of the Air Force Cross for distinguished performances by Civilians
AIR 2/306	1927	Rewards for valuable flying. King's Birthday Honours List. June 1927
AIR 2/374	1930	Awards to French personnel who rendered Assistance in the R 101 Disaster
AIR 2/310	1937	Award of AFC to Charles Lindbergh in recognition of his New York to Paris Flight
AIR 2/318	1927	Award of AFC to Lt R.R. Bentley in recognition of his flight from England to Cape Town
AIR 2/331	1928	Awards of AFC to Mr Bert Hinkler in recognition of his flight from England to Australia
AIR 2/326	1928-1929	Appointments to the Most Excellent Order of the British Empire
AIR 2/333	1928	Recommendations for the Order of the Bath, King's Birthday Honours List 1928
AIR 2/448	1930–5	Recommendations for Honours and Awards in connection with Operations on the North West Frontier
AIR 2/1581	1919–30	Order of the Bath: Submissions
AIR 2/1582	1935–45	Order of the Bath: Submissions

AIR 2/2084	1937	Recommendation for the Award of the Royal Victorian Order: RAF Display 1937
AIR 2/2348	1936–7	New Years Honours list 1937
AIR 2/2489	1937–60	New Years Honours list: Awards for flying services in peace time
AIR 2/2516	1937–9	Operations in Waziristan 1937: Awards for Gallantry and Meritorious Service
AIR 2/3766	1938	King's Birthday Honours List: Awards for Valuable Services in peace time
AIR 2/4022	1939	Awards to RAF personnel in connection with long distance flights to Australia
AIR 2/3803	1938–9	Operations in Waziristan 1937: Awards of Decorations and Medals
AIR 2/8783	1930	R 101 Disaster: Awards
AIR 2/9315	1938–9	New Years Honours list, 1939: Rewards for Valuable Flying Services in peace time
AIR 2/9393	1938–40	Immediate Awards: Waziristan Operations 1938
AIR 2/10162	1920–1	Awards to RAF Officers in connection with Waziristan operations
AIR 2/10193	1923–4	Order of El Nahda: Awards to be gazetted
AIR 2/10194	1924	Awards of the OBE in recognition of flight around Australia by W/Cdr S. Goble and F/Lt I. McIntyre RAAF
AIR 2/10198	1924–5	Appointments to the Military Division of the Order of the British Empire: King's Birthday Honours List 1926
AIR 2/10207	1930–1	Rewards for Valuable Flying Services under peace-time conditions; New Year Honours 1931
AIR 2/10212	1939	RAF Recommendations for Appointments to KCB, KBE and CB: King's Birthday Honours List 1939

13.3.3 The War Office

There are remarkably few awards files for the inter-war period. Those that survive are either in WO 32 or WO 373, with the records in WO 373 being available on DocumentsOnline (see 15.2). Most that do survive are listed in CHAPTER 11, but some are listed below.

WO 32/3757 Report on Operations in Nubia mountains and
  Recommendations for Awards. 1926–7

Two significant award files for Ireland between 1921 and 1922 are WO 35/181 Rebel Outrages and Consequent Activities: Appreciation and Medal Awards 1921–2 and WO 141/54 Recommendations for Awards for Gallant Services rendered in Ireland 1921–2.

Many recommendations for awards concerning operations in India are in the series L/MIL/7 at the British Library.

13.3.4 Other Government Departments

Records of the Home Office in HO 45, the Board of Trade in BT 261 and the Ministry of Transport in MT 9 all contain recommendations for honours and awards. It is possible to find most of them by keyword searching on the online catalogue.

The series BT 261 is listed in CHAPTER 21 on Gallantry (Life Saving) Awards.

13.4   INDIA OFFICE RECORDS (BRITISH LIBRARY)

Amongst the records at the British Library are a number of files concerning honours and awards granted for operations between 11 November 1918 and 3 September 1939. The majority of files concerning military awards from between the wars are listed in CHAPTER 11 on Awards by Operational Theatre.

Most of the awards files in the India Office collection are in the series L/PS/13, L/PS/15 and L/MIL/7. They cover such items as appointment to the Indian Orders: the Star of India and Indian Empire. There are numerous files on the Kaisar I Hind, the Imperial Service Order and Imperial Service Medal.

13.5   CASE STUDY
Clarence Howells

Clarence Howells joined the Royal Air Force as a boy apprentice on 9 April 1919. Very little is known of his service until he received the Indian General Service Medal 1908–35 with the clasp NORTH WEST FRONTIER 1930–31. At the time he earned the medal, Clarence was Sergeant.

On the medal ribbon of his first medal is an oak leaf emblem denoting a Mention in Despatches (MiD). In the file AIR 2/448, Recommendations for Honours and Awards in connection with Operations on the North West Frontier 1930–5, there is a recommendation for the award of the British Empire Medal to Sergeant Howells. However, this was obviously not granted and the award was downgraded to the MiD that Sergeant Howells was eventually to receive.

Earning his Long Service and Good Conduct Medal in 1937, Clarence Howells was commissioned into the RAF Technical Branch in 1940. Awarded another MiD in 1945, Wing Commander Clarence Howells retired from the RAF in 1945, but he was re-employed from 1947 to 1954, during which time he also received the 1952 Coronation Medal. Clarence Howells retired for a second time on 17 May 1954 and he died on 17 February 1981.

The recommendation for Clarence Howells' downgraded BEM can be seen in FIGURE 17 (p. 163) and his medals can be seen in PLATE 18.

14   Second World War Awards: Royal Navy and Royal Marines

14.1   INTRODUCTION

Records concerning honours and awards granted to naval and marine personnel during the Second World War also cover, in some cases, personnel of the Merchant Navy and civilians employed under Admiralty authority. Not all of the Admiralty recommendations for honours and awards survive, but, unlike the records of the Army in WO 373, there are more chances of finding a Mention in Despatches (MiD).

14.2   FIRST STEPS

As when researching any award for gallantry or meritorious service, the most important item you really need to know is when the award was gazetted. The gazette date will dictate where to start looking in ADM 12, ADM 1 and ADM 116.

There are a number of volumes in ADM 171 that will help you to obtain the gazette date of a number of awards.

| ADM 171/164 | 1942–6 | Lists awards of the OBE, MBE, DSC, GM, DSM, MM and BEM |
| ADM 171/165 | 1946–72 | As above |

There is also:

| ADM 1/25295 | 1855–1946 | Conspicuous Gallantry Medal, roll of Awards |
| BT 164/23 | 1939–46 | RNR Officers Awards |

The published roll of the DSM, *The Distinguished Service Medal 1939–1946* by W.H. Fevyer (Hayward, 1981), is also of use.

Another very good series of books about awards to naval and marine personnel that provides the ship, squadron or unit, and the gazette date, are the *Seedies Rolls of Awards to...* series by W.W.F. Chatterton-Dickson (various dates). These books are sadly let down by the fact that they do not provide the original Admiralty File References which are present on the source material used to compile them.

14.3   ORIGINAL CREATION OF THE RECORDS

The majority of recommendations for awards discussed in this chapter are in the series ADM 1 (Series 1, Code 85, Series 2, Code 85 and the Numerical List), with a number in ADM 116 (Admiralty Case Papers) and an even smaller number in ADM 199. ADM 1 Series 1 is predominantly for awards up to 1945 and Series 2 for awards from 1946 onwards. The ADM 1 Numerical list contains many honours and awards files missing from the two ADM sections, together with many files for post-Second World War honours.

During the Second World War, a number of Admiralty departments submitted files relating to awards, and their departmental codes can be found in the original Admiralty file references, including the Commission and Warrant (CW) Branch. By 1941, the majority of awards files had the abbreviation H&A (Honours and Awards) in their original Admiralty file references. The most effective way to pursue an award recommendation is to find the original Admiralty file reference in ADM 12 and then apply that reference to ADM 1, ADM 116 or ADM 199.

At the National Archives, the old Admiralty references are called 'former references' and they usually appear on the right-hand side of the page in the paper catalogue. It is possible to use the former reference to search the catalogue online. This can be done by putting it in the box 'type reference here' in the top left-hand corner of the catalogue page, and then clicking on the 'go to reference' button.

There is a problem when using the former reference when trying to trace an Admiralty file amongst the records in ADM 116 and ADM 199. The papers in ADM 116 are Admiralty Case Papers, and the former reference is nearly always a Case number. In examples such as these it is very important to use ADM 12, as it will tell you the Case number that an awards file has been put in.

The three files in ADM 199 are given their Second World War 'War History and Cases' reference as their former reference. As there are only two pieces of ADM 199 that contain significant H&A files, they are listed below.

For a full explanation of how to use ADM 12, see CHAPTER 25 on Research Techniques. An alternative method to using ADM 12 is to keyword search the ADM 1 catalogue online, using terms such at the name of the ship, operation, convoy number, place or type of award. This method will produce results, but I would still use ADM 12 as well.

Some recommendations for awards for Combined Operations may be found in the series DEFE 2 and some recommendation for awards to pilots of the Fleet Air Arm, employed by the RAF, may be in the series AIR 2.

14.4   EXAMPLES IN ADM 1, ADM 116 AND ADM 199

The number of files in ADM 1 and ADM 116 are too great to list here. What follows are a selection of files listed in ADM 1 and ADM 116, together with the three files concerning Operation Husky in ADM 199.

ADM 1		DESCRIPTION	FORMER REFERENCE
10481	1940	Operations Cycle and Aerial, evacuation of troops from Le Havre: Awards to RN and MN Officers and Men	Admiralty 479/1940
10488	1940	Battle of the River Plate: Recommendations for Awards	Admiralty 487/1940

ADM 1

10490	1940	First battle of Narvik 10 April: Awards to Naval personnel: Award of first Royal Naval VC of World War II to Captain Warburton-Lee	Admiralty 489/1940
10492	1940	Loss of HMS *Foylebank* 4 July 1940: Awards to Naval Ratings and award of VC to L/Sea Jack F. Mantle	Admiralty 496/1940
10496	1940	Sinking of HMS *Jervis Bay*: Posthumous Award of VC to Cdr (acting Capt) E.S.F. Fegen	Admiralty 501/1940
11260	1941	Sinking of German battleship *Bismark*: issue of Honours and Awards to participants	Admiralty 462/1941
11369	1941	Awards to personnel of HMS *Torbay* following successful war patrols, June and July	CW 29459/1941
11377	1941/42	Battle of Cape Matapan: Recommendations and Awards	CW 19668/1941
11394	1941	Awards to personnel of 6th MGB Flotilla for Good Services in Actions against enemy E Boats	CW 24101/1941
11439	1941	Awards to Naval personnel and Civilians for Gallant Services during air attack on Portsmouth March 10–11	CW 15106/1941
11886	1942	Operation Pedestal, convoy to Malta: Awards to Army and Navy personnel	Admiralty 415/1942
11888	1942	Operation Chariot: HM Ships *Cambletown*, *Athestone*, *Tynedale* and other small craft in attack on St Nazaire: Recommendations for Awards including VC. (There is a nominal roll of all participants in this file.)	Admiralty 418/1942
12212	1942	Lt W.N. Bennet RNVR awarded George Cross for mine disposal	H&A 92/1942

12229	1942	S/Lt (A) R.C. Mckay	Airman H&A 281/1942
		RNVR and A/Ldg D.H. Stockman	
		FAA, both killed in Action at Suda Bay,	
		awarded posthumous Mentions	
		in Despatches	
14511	1943	Awards to personnel for Mine	H&A 970/1943
		Clearance Operations	
14522	1943	Destruction of enemy submarine	H&A 1002/1943
		by HMS *Sennen* in defence of	
		convoy SC 130: Awards	

ADM 116

PIECE	DATE	DESCRIPTION	CASE NUMBER
4649	1941	Operation Dynamo (Evacuation	6801 Vol 1
		from Dunkirk): Reports and	
		Recommendations for	
		Includes H&A 245/1941 Awards	
4504	1941	As above	6801 Vol 2
4546	1939–42	Awards to Merchant Navy and	5706
		Fishing Fleets: Reports by Treasury	
		Committee	
		Includes H&A 296, and Admiralty	
		Committee on Honours 297, 298, 300	
		& 301/1941 and Awards	
4953	1944	Operation Neptune: Recommendations	6271 Vol 1
		for Awards	
4954	1944	As above	6271 Vol 2

Both the above files incorporate H&A 815 and 1014/1944.

5232	1945–6	European war 'Wind Up' Operational	6747 Vol 1*
		Awards	
5233	1945–6	As above	6747 Vol 2**

The above files contain H&A 732*, 900*, 901*, 905*, 931**, 935*, 936*, 951*, 952*, 966* and 975*/1945.

ADM 199

Operation Husky (the invasion of Sicily): Recommendations for Awards are in ADM 199/855 and 856 (former refs H&A 912/43, H&A 1082/43 and H&A 1106/43).

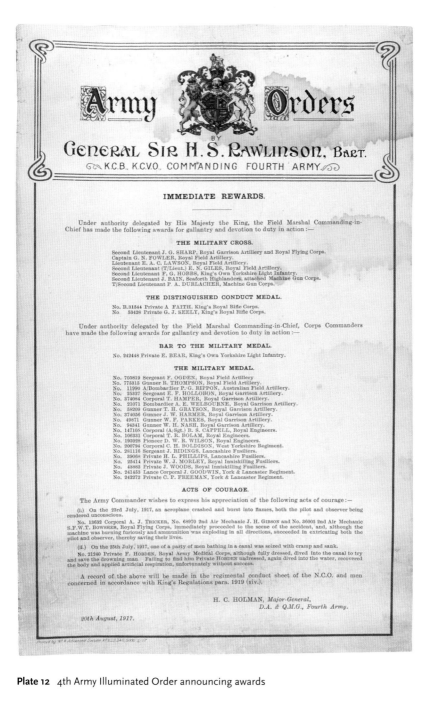

Plate 12 4th Army Illuminated Order announcing awards

Plate 13 (*left to right*) The Royal Red Cross, 1914 Star, British War Medal and Victory Medal earned by Sister F.M. Rice

Plate 14 (*facing page, left to right*) The King's African Rifles Distinguished Conduct Medal and bar and 5 clasp Africa General Service Medal earned by Colour Sergeant George Williams, 3rd King's African Rifles

NAME Reeve Arthur W. S.   RNR BRANCH

RANK Lieut.

AWARD	DATE OF GAZETTE	SERVICE WITH DATE.
OBE (Mil)	1. 4. 19.	Post War. Executive officer HMS. "Managrin."
		9. 195. Service book Sheets. X. 21

NOTE RECORDS.   SERVICE IN PAPERS.   L1.
                                                 cw/M. 0610   1919.

NAME	RANK AND SENIORITY	SHIP	RECOMMENDED BY	NATURE OF SERVICES	GAZETTE DESPATCH OR REPORT G D or R	AWARD IF ANY
Arthur W. S. Reeve 9-195.	Lieut. RNR 27-7-18.	HMS Managrin	Brit. C in C Mediterranean	Special Service in connection with intelligence organisation in Palestine, Syria and Karamania	Gazette 1. 4. 19.	O. BE (Mil).
Lieut. Roger F. Shotton 6 Nov	Lt. R NR. 10 Nov. 17.	HMS 'Kwaney''	"	Special Service in connection with intelligence organisation in Palestine, Syria, and Karamania	Gazette 1. 4. 19.	

Plate 15 (*above, top*) The Royal Navy honours card for Lt A.W.S. Reeve RNR giving the sheet reference X21

Plate 16 (*above*) Royal Navy honours sheet X21 for Lt A.W.S. Reeve RNR ADM 171/87

Plate 17 (*left to right*) The medals of Sgt S.F. Seward RA. 1914/15 Star, British War Medal, Victory Medal, Army LSGC Medal and Meritorious Service Medal

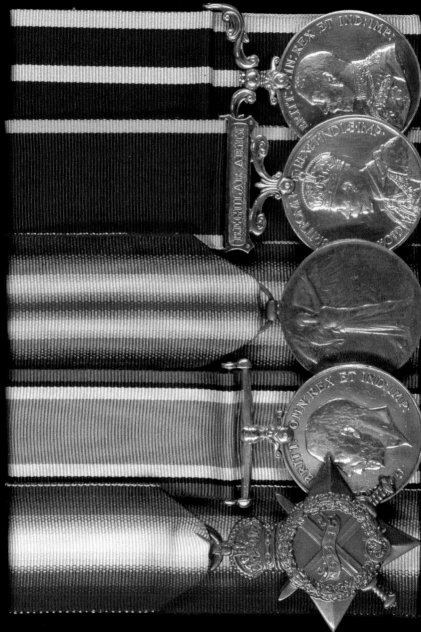

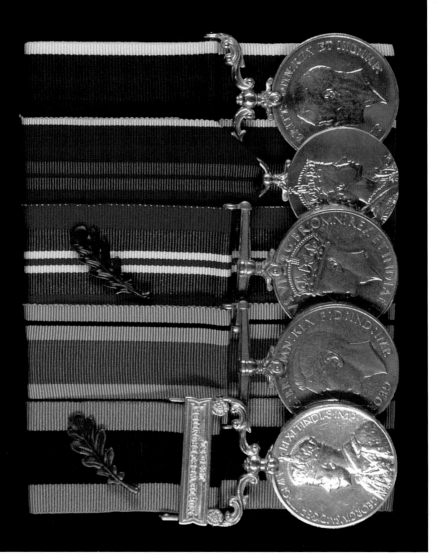

Plate 18 (*left to right*) The medals earned by Clarence Howells. IGS 1908–35 with clasp for *NORTH WEST FRONTIER 1930–31* and an MiD oakleaf, Defence Medal 1939–45, War Medal 1939–45, 1953 Coronation Medal and RAF LSGC Medal

Plate 19 (*left to right*) The medals earned by Percy Brown. OBE, British War Medal, Victory Medal, IGS 1908–35 with clasp *NORTH WEST FRONTIER 1935*, Defence Medal 1939–45, War Medal 1939–45 with MiD oakleaf and RAF LSGC Medal

Plate 20 (*above, left to right*)
Territorial Force Efficiency
Medal and Japanese Order
of the Rising Sun awarded
to Pipe Major Alexander
Stewart, Scottish Horse

14.5   FILES IN NON-ADMIRALTY RECORDS

Some files concerning awards to members of Combined Operations can be found in the series DEFE 2. In many cases the information is duplicated in either ADM 1 or WO 373.

A number of files concerning recommendations for awards to members of the Royal Navy and Royal Marines can be found in the series WO 373. Most of the awards were for services ashore or for escaping from POW camps. The majority of these recommendations are in WO 373/88 and cover gazette dates from April 1941 to July 1946 and the awards include the CBE, DSO, OBE, MBE, MC, DCM, MM, BEM and some MiDs. The other file of a similar nature is WO 373/101.

During the Second World War, a committee existed to assess all recommendations for the George Cross, George Medal and the British Empire Medal from all three services. The papers of the Central Selection Committee for the George Cross, George Medal and British Empire Medal are in the records series AIR 2. The following list of AIR 2 files contains the committee's papers for the period 1940–6. They are listed in original Air Ministry file number order.

AIR 2

	DATE(S) OF CONTENTS	FORMER REFERENCE
8883	1940	A74130/40
9429	1940	A84049/40
9504	1941–3	A161263/41
9537	1939–40	A194732/41
6262	1941–2	A265611/41
8908	1941–2	A321475/41
9575	1941–2	A334893/41
9001	1943–4	A618286/43
9013	1944	A670891/44
9029	1944–5	A719359/44
9040	1944	A738920/44
9094	1945	A790930/45
9288	1945–6	A821315/45
9289	1945–6	A834269/45
9700	1946–7	A890183/46

14.6   NAME INDEX

A name index of all the recommendations in ADM 1, ADM 116 and ADM 199 is currently being created. For further information contact paulbaillie@tiscali.co.uk .

15   Second World War Awards: Army

15.1   INTRODUCTION

Almost all of the surviving recommendations for awards for gallantry or meritorious service granted to Army personnel of the British and Indian Armies, Australian, Canadian, New Zealand and South African forces for the Second World War are preserved in the records series WO 373, at the National Archives. A number of other records series contain recommendations for Army personnel and these will be discussed after WO 373.

15.2   WO 373

The Army Forms W 3121 and other forms of recommendation preserved in WO 373 detail the deeds for which an individual was granted an award. Many of the recommendations provide detailed accounts of an individual's activities, many giving place names and dates that can be used with other sources.

Included in WO 373 are the recommendations for the British Army, Australian, Canadian and South Africa Army personnel and the Indian Army. The series also contains recommendations for a number of RN, RM and RAF personnel where the authority for granting certain awards was vested in the War Office. The RN, RM and RAF pieces of WO 373 are listed in the appropriate service chapter.

WO 373 is arranged under a wide variety of headings, the majority of which are the operational theatres in which the award was won. The recommendations for awards for gallantry in a

FIG 17. (facing) *Recommendation for the British Empire Medal for Sgt Clarence Howells, subsequently downgraded to a Mention in Despatches* [AIR 2/448]

CONFIDENTIAL.

RECOMMENDATIONS FOR HONOURS AND AWARDS.

Christian Names. Clarence.   **Surname.** HOWELLS.

Rank. Sergeant.   **Official Number.** 330121.

Area.   **Unit.** No. 60 (Bomber) Squadron.

I wish to recommend No. 330121 Sergeant Howells for award of the "Medal of the Order of the British Empire" for his very meritorious services during recent operations.

As Fitter Sergeant in "A" Flight of this Squadron he has maintained a very high standard of work, energy, keeness and efficiency in his Flight. Owing to the presence of the special photographic machine in this Flight, it was necessary to maintain 100 per cent serviceability of engines day by day. Although personnel were unfamiliar with the Jupiter engine at the commencement of operations, Sergeant Howells by his ability, energy and example enabled this remarkably high percentage of serviceability to be almost invariably maintained in the Flight.

He is a reserve Sergeant Pilot, and a very good and experienced one, and was thus invaluable in carrying out test flights whenever required in the absence of other flying personnel on operations.

He never has any difficulty in obtaining the best results from the men working under him.

State what recognition is recommended:- Medal of the Order of the British Empire.

State appointment held or how employed.   Sergeant - Fitter A.E.

Signature of Commanding Officer,

Rank. Squadron Leader.

Unit. No. 60 (Bomber) Squadron, Royal Air Force....Kohat.

Date. 26.10.30.

Covering remarks of Air Officer Commanding, or senior Officer.

Recommended.

Air Marshal,
Air Officer Commanding,
Royal Air Force, India.

Date:- 1.11.1930.

given operational theatre are separated from those for meritorious service. An example of a WO 373 can be seen in FIGURE 18. This series has been digitized and placed on DocumentsOnline. It is indexed by name, rank, number, regiment/corps, award and operational theatre. It is possible to search by any of the index terms.

Each piece of WO 373 is usually arranged in gazette date order. At the beginning of each section, you should find a marker that will give you the operational theatre and gazette date and there should be a copy of the relevant gazette page(s). If any recommendations are missing, it will be noted on the copied gazette page(s).

The awards under each gazette date are then arranged in order of precedence by award. The arrangement of each award section is then either in alphabetical order, in order of seniority by rank or in regimental order of precedence.

Some of the recommendations for awards for North West Europe 1944–5 are now wildly displaced from their original positions. An indexing project of WO 373/48–56 is currently in progress and the information is being placed in the Catalogue. It is possible to search this index by name and in return it will tell you the specific place to look in WO 373. Now that WO 373 is digitized, it is far easier to locate a recommendation in WO 373.

What follows is a listing of all the appropriate files for each operational theatre, giving both the awards for gallantry and those for meritorious service.

British Expeditionary Force (Gallantry)
WO 373   15, 16, 92 and 146

British Expeditionary Force (Meritorious Service)
WO 373   75

Burma (Gallantry)
WO 373   30–43, 47, 91, 92 and 146

Burma (Meritorious Service)
WO 373   79–81

Combined Operations (Gallantry and Meritorious Service)
WO 373   46 and 87

Escape and Evasion (including Awards to the RAF)
WO 373   60–65

Far East (Dutch East Indies) (Gallantry)
WO 373   92

Hong Kong (Gallantry)
WO 373   47 and 92

Hong Kong (Meritorious Service)
WO 373   87

India (Gallantry)
WO 373   43

Italy (Gallantry)
WO 373   4–14, 43, 47, 90 and 146

Italy (Meritorious Service)
WO 373   71–73, 75 and 146

Java 1942 (Gallantry* and Meritorious Service**)
WO 373   47* and 87**

The London Omnibus List (Gallant and Distinguished Services
in the Field)
   The London Omnibus List contains recommendations for awards
   which, when published in the *London Gazette*, were always published
   under the heading 'Gallant and Distinguished Services in the Field'. This
   heading was used to hide the numerous special operations that took
   place during the war and was also a way of hiding awards for escapes
   and other reasons that the military did not want to disclose.
   The following pieces are arranged in chronological order, but please note
   that WO 373/99 is still retained by the Ministry of Defence.

WO 373   93 (earliest Gazette date 27/05/1941) to 105 (latest Gazette date
               06/10/1950)

Malaya and Singapore (Gallantry)
WO 373   47 and 65

Malaya/Singapore (Meritorious Service)
WO 373   47 and 87

Middle East (East Africa and Madagascar, Gallantry)
WO 373   28 and 29, 88 and 146

Middle East (East Africa and Madagascar, Meritorious Service)
WO 373   79 and 146

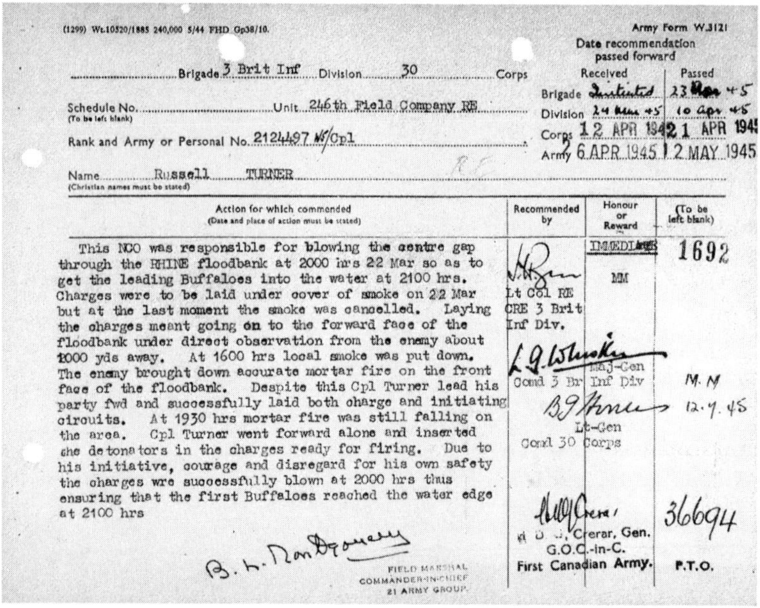
(1299) Wt.10520/1885 240,000 5/44 FHD Gp38/10.

Army Form W.3121

Date recommendation passed forward

	Received	Passed
Brigade	[illegible]	23 [illegible] 45
Division	24 [illegible] 45	10 Apr 45
Corps	12 APR 1945	21 APR 1945
Army	26 APR 1945	12 MAY 1945

Brigade 3 Brit Inf Division 30 Corps

Schedule No. (To be left blank) Unit 246th Field Company RE

Rank and Army or Personal No. 2124497 L/Cpl

Name (Christian names must be stated) Russell TURNER

Action for which commended (Date and place of action must be stated)	Recommended by	Honour or Reward	(To be left blank)
This NCO was responsible for blowing the centre gap through the RHINE floodbank at 2000 hrs 22 Mar so as to get the leading Buffaloes into the water at 2100 hrs. Charges were to be laid under cover of smoke on 22 Mar but at the last moment the smoke was cancelled. Laying the charges meant going on to the forward face of the floodbank under direct observation from the enemy about 1000 yds away. At 1600 hrs local smoke was put down. The enemy brought down accurate mortar fire on the front face of the floodbank. Despite this Cpl Turner lead his party fwd and successfully laid both charge and initiating circuits. At 1930 hrs mortar fire was still falling on the area. Cpl Turner went forward alone and inserted the detonators in the charges ready for firing. Due to his initiative, courage and disregard for his own safety the charges were successfully blown at 2000 hrs thus ensuring that the first Buffaloes reached the water edge at 2100 hrs	Lt Col RE CRE 3 Brit Inf Div. Maj-Gen Comd 3 Br Inf Div Lt-Gen Comd 30 Corps H. D. G. Crerar, Gen. G.O.C.-in-C. First Canadian Army.	IMMEDIATE MM	1692 M.M 12.7.45 36694 P.T.O.

B. L. Montgomery FIELD MARSHAL COMMANDER-IN-CHIEF 21 ARMY GROUP

Fig 18. *A typical example of an Army Form W3121, Recommendation for Awards, found in* WO 373

Middle East (Egypt and Libya, Gallantry)
WO 373 17–26, 88, 92 and 146

Middle East (Egypt and Libya, Meritorious Service)
WO 373 75–77 and 146

Middle East (Greece and Crete, Gallantry)
WO 373 27, 88 and 146

Middle East (Greece and Crete, Meritorious Service)
WO 373 77

Middle East (Malta, Gallantry)
WO 373 29 and 88

Middle East (Malta, Meritorious Service)
WO 373 78

Middle East (Iran, Iraq and Syria) (Gallantry)
WO 373 27, 88 and 146

Middle East (Iran, Iraq and Syria) (Meritorious Service)
WO 373   78 and 146

Middle East (Special Operations and Escapes)
WO 373   46, 47, 78 and 146

Mediterranean (Gallantry* and Meritorious Service**)
WO 373   46*, 75**, 90*, and 146* and **

Non-Combat Gallantry
    The recommendations under the heading 'Non-Combat Gallantry'
    cover such things as bomb and mine clearance and disposal, life saving
    and rescues during air raids, etc. The earliest gazette date in this
    collection is pre-Second World War 23/06/1936 and the most recent
    13/11/1990. Only the Second World War pieces are listed here.
WO 373   66, 67, 68, 69, 70 and 142

North Africa (Gallantry)
WO 373   1–2 and 90

North Africa (Meritorious Service)
WO 373   71 and 146

North West Europe 1944–5 (Gallantry)
WO 373   48–56, 90–92

North West Europe 1944–5 (Meritorious Service)
WO 373   83–86 and 146

Norway (Gallantry* and Meritorious Service**)
WO 373   15*, 75** 88* and 146**

Repatriated Prisoners of War
WO 373   57 LG Dates 08/11/9145 pages 5432–3   pages 5789–91
                   and 29/11/1945
               59 LG Dates 12/12/1945 pages 6163–4 and   pages 749–50
                   14/02/1946

Services While a Prisoner of War
WO 373   47, 65, 87, and 125

Sicily
WO 373   3, 71 and 146

South West Pacific (Gallantry)
WO 373   44, 45, 65 and 146

South West Pacific (Meritorious Service)
WO 373 87 and 146

For Distinguished Conduct in the Field: Register of the DCM 1920–1992 by P.
  McDermott (Hayward, 1994). This book is in alphabetical order, but does
  not contain references to WO 373.
The Military Cross Awarded to Officers and Warrant Officers, 1937–1993 by
  R.M. Kamaryc (Harlow, 1993)
For Bravery in The Field by C.K. Bate and M.G. Smith (Bayonet, 1991)

15.3   OTHER RECORDS

A small number of recommendations for Second World War
awards can be found in WO 32, amongst which are the recommendations for the VC and bar to the VC for Captain Charles Upham
in WO 32/11643 and 11644. Recommendations for awards for
service in Waziristan covering the period 1 January–24 May 1940
can also be found in WO 32/9948

Some information about Mentions in Despatches to Indian Army
personnel can be found in L/MIL/7/967–984 at the British Library.

For recommendations for the Glider Pilot Regiment and the
Army Air Corps you may also wish to consult CHAPTER 16 on
Second World War awards to the RAF.

Recommendations for Army personnel who served under
Admiralty authority, such as Defensively Equipped Merchant Ships
(DEMS) gunners of the Royal Artillery, may be found in ADM 1.
See CHAPTER 14 on Second World War awards to the Royal Navy.

If the person was employed by and honoured whilst serving
with the Special Operations Executive (SOE), you may wish to
look at HS 12/1 and the other honours files in HS 8.

16   Second World War Awards: RAF

16.1 INTRODUCTION

The vast majority of records concerning RAF awards for the Second World War are in the records series AIR 2. In the context of awards, the term RAF also encompasses the air forces of Australia, Canada, New Zealand, South Africa and Southern Rhodesia, and all those who saw service under RAF authority.

One of the most numerous gallantry awards granted in the Second World War was the Distinguished Flying Cross. Between 1939 and 1945, some 20,354 DFCs, 1,550 first bars and 42 second bars were awarded, which illustrates not only the bravery of flying personnel but also the changing nature of warfare.

Whilst a number of recommendations for the Fleet Air Arm, Army Air Corps and Glider Pilot Regiment can be found in AIR 2, the majority are RAF.

16.2 INDEX

In order to access the records in AIR 2 effectively, you really need to have the original AIR Ministry file reference that can then be converted into a National Archives reference.

An index of honours and awards currently held by the Ministry of Defence only relates to successful awards, and in the cases of Mentions in Despatches some are not recorded. However, many of the files to which their index refers no longer survive or they have been absorbed into another file.

Within the awards files in AIR 2 are many hundreds of individual recommendations that were not successful, yet they record the deeds of individuals and their unit at the time of submission. A complete name index of all the awards files in AIR 2 has been created and is in private hands. For further information contact:

Mr P Baillie
14 Wheatfields
St Ives, Huntingdon
CAMBS, PE17 6YD
paulbaillie@tiscali.co.uk

16.3 ARRANGEMENT OF AIR 2

The vast majority of awards granted to RAF flying personnel fall into two distinct categories: Immediate and Non-Immediate. 'Immediate' means an award for an act or acts that warranted recognition within a short period of time from when the deed(s) occurred.

The term 'Non-Immediate' is used to describe an award that was for bravery over a longer period of time, usually a tour of operations, and the award came soon after the end of a tour.

A number of other award categories can be found in AIR 2. 'Ground Gallantry' relates to recommendations for awards where the deed was not performed in the air. Interestingly, I have found a recommendation in a Ground Gallantry file for an honorary MBE to an American for rescuing an RAF airman at sea, after their ship had been torpedoed – despite the fact it was not on the ground!

Many of the files containing recommendations for New Year and Birthday Honours are further described 'Higher' and 'Lower' awards. 'Higher' awards contain recommendations for the CBE and above. 'Lower' awards contain recommendations for the OBE and below.

To complicate matters further, many of the AIR 2 files are also arranged by the different RAF Commands, such as Bomber, Fighter, Coastal, Army Co-operation, West Africa, North Africa and Middle East. The file descriptions can also mention a wide variety of other unit designations, the colonies and dominions, foreign countries and places.

16.4 CONTENT OF AIR 2

AIR 2 does not just contain recommendations for operational flying. There are recommendations for non-operational flying in such roles as instructing and test flying, award recommendations for bomb and mine disposal, awards for services as POWs, civilian gallantry and awards to and from foreign countries.

Recommendations for the Victoria Cross can be found in AIR 2 in the following files:

AIR 2/5686	VC: Recommendations September 1939–July 1942	1940–2
AIR 2/4890	VC: Recommendations	1942–60
AIR 2/5010	VC: Recommendations	1943–4

AIR 2/5867   VC: Recommendations December 1944   1944–6
                –October 1946

16.5   USING AIR 2

The most effective way to use AIR 2 is to have the Air Ministry File reference for the file containing the recommendation you seek. See 16.2 for further advice.

If you don't have the Air Ministry File reference, find as much additional information as you can. You will need to know when the award was announced in the *London Gazette*, the type of award and the squadron, unit or station where the individual was serving at the time of the award. If you know the squadron, try and find out which command it came under, as many of the recommendations are also arranged by Command.

There are a number of useful books that will help you in your quest for the additional information with which to use AIR 2.

Honour the Air Forces: Honours and Awards to the RAF and Dominion Air Forces During WWII by Michael Maton (Token, 2005) is quite a useful place to start as it gives you the squadron and *London Gazette* dates. However, the book does miss some awards announced in 1946, when many of the awards for the last year of the war were gazetted!

The Distinguished Flying Cross and How it Was Won 1918–1945 by N. and C. Carter (Savannah, 1998) provides the unit and gazette information, together with the citations for the immediate awards.

In Action With the Enemy: The Holders of the Conspicuous Gallantry Medal (Flying) by A.W. Cooper (Kimber, 1986)

The DFM Registers for the Second World War by Ian Tavender (Savannah, 1999) is very useful, as it provides not only the unit and gazette data for the awards, but also the AIR 2 references.

In Adversity – Exploits of Gallantry and Awards to the RAF Regiment and its Associated Forces 1921–1995 by S. and N.L.G. Tucker (1997)

You can do a keyword search on the AIR 2 catalogue online and it will produce plenty of results. Be prepared for a long search, however, if you don't have the Air Ministry File reference.

16.6   CASE STUDY
Percy Brown

Percy Brown enlisted into the Royal Naval Air Service as F 41914,

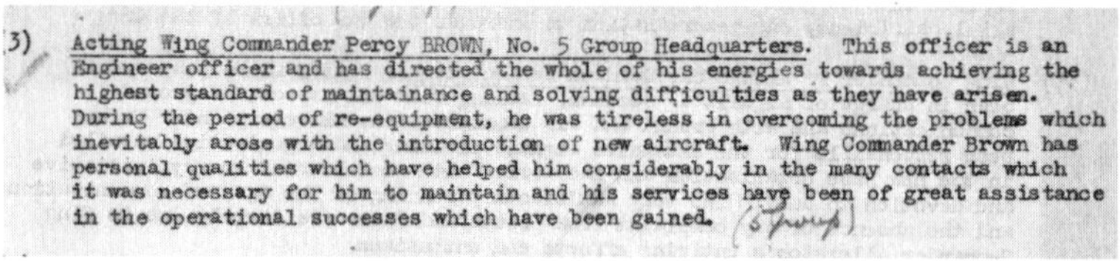

3) Acting Wing Commander Percy BROWN, No. 5 Group Headquarters. This officer is an Engineer officer and has directed the whole of his energies towards achieving the highest standard of maintainance and solving difficulties as they have arisen. During the period of re-equipment, he was tireless in overcoming the problems which inevitably arose with the introduction of new aircraft. Wing Commander Brown has personal qualities which have helped him considerably in the many contacts which it was necessary for him to maintain and his services have been of great assistance in the operational successes which have been gained.

FIG 19. *Recommendation for Percy Brown's Officer of the Most Excellent Order of the British Empire* [AIR 2/9004]

Boy Mechanic on 5 November 1917. Percy, like most other RNAS personnel, transferred to the RAF upon creation on 1 April 1918. As with most ex-RNAS men, Percy's number changed, in his case to 241914. Although there is a record for Percy in ADM 188 up to 31 March 1918, as he saw service beyond 1925, the rest of his record of service is still held by the RAF.

From the rest of his medal group, it transpires that Percy Brown saw service in India in 1935, as he has an Indian General Service Medal 1908–35 with the clasp NWF 1935. This medal is named to Percy as a Flight Sergeant.

The next medal Flight Sergeant P. Brown received was his RAF Long Service and Good Conduct Medal and this was announced in Air Ministry Order N 210/1936.

Commissioned as an Engineering Officer in 1940, Percy Brown went on to receive the Defence Medal and War Medal 1939–45, on which can be seen an oak leaf emblem denoting that Percy Brown had a Mention in Despatches (MiD). Percy Brown was actually awarded five MiDs.

For his high quality of service as an Engineering Officer, Percy Brown was appointed an Officer of the Most Excellent Order of the British Empire (OBE) on 8 June 1944. The recommendation for Percy Brown's OBE from AIR 2/9004 can be seen in FIGURE 19.

Percy Brown retired from the RAF as a Wing Commander on 12 May 1946. His medal group can be seen in PLATE 19.

17   Second World War Awards: Civilians

17.1 INTRODUCTION

During the Second World War, many thousands of men and women were recognized for their bravery or service above and beyond that normally expected. From the George Cross to Commendations for Brave Conduct, to appointments to the Orders of Chivalry, the types of awards and the associated records are just as diverse as those for service personnel. This chapter deals with awards granted primarily to British nationals. For information about British awards granted to foreign nationals, see CHAPTER 19.

In order to use the following records effectively, it can help if you know something about the recipient, their occupation and where they lived and worked, and when the award was gazetted.

Although it might be assumed that only one government committee dealt with honours and awards, that was not the case. The Home Office was the key department responsible for most matters concerning awards to civilians, but the Prime Minister's Office, the three armed services and, most significantly, the Treasury all had an input.

All awards to British, colonial and dominion civilians were announced in the *London Gazette* or the appropriate colonial, dominion or Indian Gazette. See CHAPTERS 7 and 8 for further information.

17.2 THE RECORDS

Although there are a number of logical places to look for information regarding awards to civilians, such is the nature of the subject that once you have looked in the most likely places, the unlikely places may eventually prove almost as rewarding.

17.2.1 The Admiralty

Recommendations for awards to civilians employed by the Admiralty can be found in the series ADM 1. Many files contain recommendations for bravery during attacks on naval dockyards and other Admiralty establishments. There are also many files concerning awards to Merchant Seamen.

The best way to locate recommendations in ADM 1 and ADM 116 is to use ADM 12. See CHAPTER 25 on Research Techniques for further information.

ADM 1 file examples concerning civilians include:

11242	1940–1	Awards for Gallantry in Civil Defence in bombing of Chatham Dockyard on 3 December 1940
11395	1942	Award of MBE to Mr C.D. Gilchrist, Third Officer of SS *City of Shanghai*
11514	1941–2	Award of MBE to Chief Officer of SS *Empire Wave* for bringing part of Crew to safety 14 days after ship was sunk
12217	1942	Mr A.C.J. Carpenter awarded a Commendation for Services in Civil Defence
14307	1943	SS *Idar*: Awards to Indian personnel
14587	1943	Award to Mr Desmond Tighe, Reuter's accredited war correspondent in Operation Husky

17.2.2 *The Air Ministry*

Although the majority of the honours and awards files in AIR 2 concern RAF personnel, there are a number of files which relate to civilians under Air Ministry authority. You can search AIR 2 by the terms 'civil*' and 'award*' or 'hon*'.

What follows are examples of award files in AIR 2 for civilians.

AIR 2/4751	1941	Medals awarded to Civilians for acts of merit and bravery during enemy action at fuel depots
AIR 2/5760	1945–6	Honorary C.B.E. to Professor Rene L. Varim
AIR 2/9258	1941	Civilian Gallantry Awards Committee: Recommendations
AIR 2/9264	1942	Civilian Gallantry Awards Committee: Recommendations
AIR 2/5904	1945–7	Proposed award of George Medal to Mlle. Andrée de Gough
AIR 2/6347	1940–1	Civilian Gallantry Awards: Publicity
AIR 2/6359	1939–53	British Empire Medal (Civil): Recommendations
AIR 2/6360	1939–48	British Empire Medal (Civil): Recommendations
AIR 2/6361	1933–45	MBE Civil Division
AIR 2/6362	1945–6	MBE Civil Division
AIR 2/6363	1941–6	Honours in respect of members of the Royal

		Observer Corps: Recommendations
AIR 2/6365	1941–3	Honours for Red Cross and St John's Ambulance Organizations
AIR 2/6585	1944–53	Awards for War Correspondents and Cameramen: Eligibility
AIR 2/6962	1945–6	Award of Commendation to Civilians who assisted an RAF aircraft crashed on the Isle of Mull
AIR 2/8911	1942	Civilian Gallantry Awards Committee: Recommendations
AIR 2/8912	1942	As above
AIR 2/8913	1942	As above
AIR 2/8914	1942	As above
AIR 2/8916	1942	As above
AIR 2/8917	1942	As above
AIR 2/8918	1942	As above
AIR 2/8922	1942	As above
AIR 2/8923	1942	As above
AIR 2/8991	1943–5	Honours and Awards: Civilian Technical Corps
AIR 2/9248	1940–1	Question of Awards to three Civilians for Services rendered on the occasion of aircraft accident at Kidlington. 29 September 1940
AIR 2/9258	1941	Civilian Gallantry Awards Committee: Recommendations
AIR 2/9264	1942	Civilian Gallantry Awards Committee: Recommendations
AIR 2/10025	1945–6	Civil Operational Awards for War Correspondents
AIR 2/10680	1945–7	Civilian Gallantry Awards: Faulds Explosion

17.2.3 The Board of Trade

Details concerning awards granted by the Board of Trade can be found in the series BT 261. By the time of the Second World War, the major award being granted by the Board of Trade was the Sea Gallantry Medal.

The pieces of BT 261 covering the Second World War period are listed below.

BT 261

7	1932–81	Register of Awards given by HM Government
8	1909–73	Register of Awards given to British Seamen by Foreign Governments
10	1935–41	Cases of Gallantry at Sea considered for Awards:

		Accounts of Actions and subsequent Awards
11	1941–3	As above
12	1942–4	As above
13	1944–6	As above
14	1941–9	Alphabetical Register of Awards given to Seamen
15	1944–6	Accounts of Cases submitted for consideration by Honours and Awards Committee
16	1944–5	As above

17.2.4 The Foreign Office

Information concerning foreign awards to British civilians and British awards to foreign civilians is discussed in CHAPTER 19.

17.2.5 The Home Office

A register of all gallantry awards to the Fire Service for the Second World War can be found in HO 187/1838. The register actually covers the period 1940–70. The register has a name index giving page numbers within the register. Each entry provides the name of the recipient in full, their rank, brigade, the award, the *London Gazette* date and the citation in full (where available).

The Fire Service Gallantry Award Register contains awards for gallantry after the Second World War and it covers the whole of the United Kingdom.

A large number of recommendations for awards for the police can be found in HO 45. The majority of recommendations are for the King's Police Medal, but other recommendations for the Albert Medal and British Empire Medal can be found in HO 45.

For those officers who received the King's Police Medal for gallantry, it is recommended that you consult *Police Gallantry* by J. Peter Farmery. This book not only contains personal information and photographs of the recipients, it may also contain the HO 45 document reference for the award.

A large number of Civil Defence Organization files concerning awards can be found in HO 207. Even though most of the files concern deeds performed in the Second World War, a significant number of the files remain closed for 75 years. Many of the honours files in HO 207 include awards announced in the New

Year and Birthday Honours Lists.

The awards files in HO 207 are dispersed throughout the series, so the best way to locate a file is to keyword search HO 207 on the online catalogue using the term 'awards'. Many of the awards are by Civil Defence Region, so if you know where in the country the award was won, you may wish to do a combined search using 'AND' with 'awards' and the region number.

A full list of the Civil Defence regions is given below.

REGION NUMBER	AREA COVER	HEADQUARTERS
1	Northern	Newcastle
2	North Eastern	Leeds
3	North Midland	Nottingham
4	Eastern	Cambridge
5	London	London
6	Southern	Reading
7	South Western	Bristol
8	Wales	Cardiff
9	Midland	Birmingham
10	Scotland	Edinburgh
11	South Eastern	Tunbridge Wells

The records of the Inter-departmental Committee on Civil Defence Gallantry Awards are in the records series HO 250. The records consist of minutes and recommendations for awards and are arranged from batch number I in HO 250/1 to batch number CX in HO 250/110/1. From HO 250/57–106, the file descriptions include the case file numbers. There is no name index to HO 250, but the author is aware of an index in private hands. The records in HO 250 are almost certainly duplicated by the records in T 336 (see 17.2.9).

17.2.6 The Ministry of Transport

Many files containing recommendations for awards to Merchant Navy personnel can be found in the Ministry of Transport Marine Crews (MC) series of records in MT 9. This series is arranged by numerical subject codes, with awards being code 6. Many of the file descriptions contain ships' names, convoy numbers and the names of some people.

17.2.7 The Prime Minister's Office

The majority of the records of the Prime Minister's Office concerning awards are in the series PREM 2 and, as most of the lists concern New Year and Birthday Honours Lists, the records are discussed in CHAPTER 18.

17.2.8 Railway Records

During the Second World War, railways companies created their own records concerning acts of gallantry by railwaymen. RAIL 360/1208 covers acts of gallantry of railwaymen between 1941 and 1944. RAIL 425/2 contains recommendations for New Year and Birthday Honours during the war. Further recommendations are in RAIL 1172.

RAIL 1172

2318	Sept 1940–Oct 1945	Awards for Gallantry: General Correspondence
2319	Sept 1940–Jul 1941	As above
2320	Jul 1941–Sept 1941	As above
2321	Oct 1941–Jan 1944	As above
2322	Jan 1944–Oct 1946	As above
2323	Jan 1941–Nov 1944	Awards for Gallantry: Individual Recommendations

17.2.9 The Treasury

Records created by the Treasury concerning honours and awards can be overlooked, yet they are often very informative. The Ceremonial Branch of the Treasury was primarily responsible for the financial aspects relating to the scales (numbers) of awards that could be granted over specified periods for particular incidents. This meant that in order to ensure that not too much money was spent on honours and awards, certain financial criteria had to be complied with.

Although the majority of Treasury files concern nothing more than the financial aspects of the honours system, information relating to the deeds for which awards were granted and the recipients of such awards may be more prevalent in some Treasury records than others. Two Treasury records series in particular relate to awards granted in the Second World War: one for the

Merchant Navy and one for the Civil Defence.

T 335 is the series of records of the Treasury Ceremonial Branch concerned with awards to the Merchant Navy. The series contains files in which can be found descriptions of the actions for which awards were granted and they include fishermen, army gunners from Defensively Armed Merchant Ships (DEMS) and some foreign nationals. The series includes a number of general files, but the majority are arranged in gazette date order.

T 335

PIECE	DATE RANGE	GAZETTE DATE OR CONTENT	FORMER REFERENCE
1	20/11/1940–3/8/1944	General file	MN (G)
2	19/2/1941–29/11/1945	Statistics and Correspondence	
3	13/10/1939–27/6/1947	Gazettes	
4	18/10/1940–29/11/1940	13/12/1940	MN 23
5	19/11/1940–11/2/1941	7/1/1941	MN 24
6	16/12/1940–24/12/1940	1/1/1941	MN 25
7	11/12/1940–17/1/1941	4/2/1941	MN 26
8	22/11/1940–6/2/1941	25/2/1941	MN 27
9	8/1/1941–21/2/1941	18/3/1941	MN 28
10	22/10/1940–19/3/1941	1/4/1941	MN 29
11	24/3/1941–29/7/1941	13/5/1941	MN 30
12	28/2/1941–29/5/1941	10/6/1941	MN 31
13	22/5/1941–24/6/1941	9/7/1941	MN 32
14	30/5/1941–25/7/1941	29/7/1941	MN 33
15	10/6/1941–29/9/1941	19/8/1941	MN 34
16	29/7/1941–14/8/1941	26/8/1941	MN 35
17	11/7/1941–26/8/1941	9/9/1941	MN 36
18	5/8/1941–19/9/1941	22/9/1941	MN 37
19	13/8/1941–12/101/1941	7/10/1941	MN 38
20	15/5/1941–30/10/1941	21/10/1941	MN 39
21	19/9/1941–28/11/1941	4/11/1941	MN 40
22	30/7/1941–1/11/1941	18/11/1941	MN 41
23	5/9/1941–21/1/1946	2/12/1941	MN 42
24	22/10/1941–16/12/1941	16/12/1941	MN 43
25	19/11/1941–2/1/1942	6/1/1942	MN 44
26	2/12/1941–16/1/1942	20/1/1942	MN 45
27	8/5/1941–16/1/1942	20/1/1942	MN 45A
28	20/7/1941–31/1/1942	3/2/1942	MN 46

29	20/7/1941–26/2/1942	17/2/1942	MN 47
30	22/1/1942–13/2/1942	3/3/1942	MN 48
31	29/10/1941–3/3/1942	17/3/1942	MN 49
32	29/10/1941–18/3/1942	31/3/1942	MN 50
33	17/1/1942–14/4/1942	14/4/1942	MN 51
34	26/1/1942–28/4/1942	28/4/1942	MN 52
35	9/4/1942–12/5/1942	12/5/1942	MN 53
36	2/4/1942–22/5/1942	26/5/1942	MN 54
37	3/2/1942–5/6/1942	9/6/1942	MN 55
38	38/5/1942–31/8/1942	23/6/1942	MN 56
39	20/5/1942–1/7/1942	7/7/1942	MN 57
40	22/6/1942–2/10/1942	21/7/1942	MN 58
41	25/4/1942–24/8/1942	4/8/1942	MN 59
42	4/6/1942–10/8/1942	18/8/1942	MN 60
43	22/6/1942–20/11/1942	1/9/1942	MN 61
44	16/8/1942–24/9/1942	8/9/1942	MN 61A

Malta Convoy

45	16/4/1942–22/9/1942	15/9/1942	MN 62
46	1/8/1942–25/9/1942	29/9/1942	MN 63
47	29/7/1942–28/9/1942	6/10/1942	MN 63A

Soviet Convoys

48	31/8/1942–13/10/1942	13/10/1942	MN 64
49	7/9/1942–27/10/1942	27/10/1942	MN 65
50	12/9/1942–10/11/1942	10/11/1942	MN 66
51	12/9/1942–24/11/1942	24/11/1942	MN 67
52	2/11/1942–16/12/1942	8/12/1942	MN 68
53	20/10/1942–18/12/1942	22/12/1942	MN 69
54	6/11/1942–22/3/1942	5/1/1943	MN 70
55	2/11/1942–19/1/1943	19/1/1943	MN 71
56	2/1/1943–2/2/1943	2/2/1943	MN 72
57	24/11/1942–11/9/1943	16/2/1943	MN 73
58	6/11/1942–26/6/1943	2/3/1943	MN 74
59	19/1/1943–16/3/1943	16/3/1943	MN 75
60	2/3/1943–30/3/1943	30/3/1943	MN 76
61	16/3/1943–13/4/1943	13/4/1943	MN 77
62	30/3/1943–7/5/1943	27/4/1943	MN 78
63	30/3/1943–1/9/1943	11/5/1943	MN 79
64	25/5/1943–15/6/1943	22/5/1943	MN 80
65	13/5/1943–8/6/1943	8/6/1943	MN 81
66	18/5/1943–6/7/1943	6/7/1943	MN 82
67	28/5/1943–11/12/1944	6/7/1943	MN 83
68	13/8/1943–27/10/1943	20/7/1943	MN 84

69	7/6/1943–17/11/1944	3/8/1943	MN 85
70	8/5/1943–17/8/1943	17/8/1943	MN 86
71	2/7/1943–31/8/1943	31/8/1943	MN 87
72	7/7/1943–14/7/1943	14/9/1943	MN 88
73	6/8/1943–28/9/1943	28/9/1943	MN 89
74	16/6/1943–12/10/1943	12/10/1943	MN 90
75	11/10/1943–9/11/1943	9/11/1943	MN 91
76	9/9/1943–3/2/1945	23/11/1943	MN 92
77	28/9/1943–16/1/1946	7/12/1943	MN 93
78	25/11/1943–21/12/1943	21/12/1943	MN 94
79	10/12/1943–18/7/1943	11/1/1944	MN 95
80	13/12/1943–18/7/1944	25/1/1944	MN 96
81	4/1/1944–23/2/1944	8/2/1944	MN 97
82	27/1/1944–22/2/1944	22/2/1944	MN 98
83	9/2/1944–7/3/1944	7/3/1944	MN 99
84	25/2/1944–21/3/1944	21/3/1944	MN 100
85	7/3/1944–4/4/1944	4/4/1944	MN 101
86	7/3/1944–18/4/1944	18/4/1944	MN 102
87	2/4/1944–2/5/1944	2/5/1944	MN 103
88	3/4/1944–16/5/1944	16/5/1944	MN 104
89	28/4/1944–30/5/1944	30/5/1944	MN 105
90	7/10/1942–13/6/1944	13/6/1944	MN 106
91	19/5/1944–27/6/1944	27/6/1944	MN 107
92	14/6/1944–11/7/1944	11/7/1944	MN 108
93	8/5/1944–25/7/1944	25/7/1944	MN 109
94	12/7/1944–/27/3/1945	15/8/1944	MN 110
95	4/8/1944–29/8/1944	29/8/1944	MN 111
96	11/8/1944–12/9/1944	12/9/1944	MN 112
97	31/8/1944–26/9/1944	26/9/1944	MN 113
98	11/8/1944–10/10/1944	10/10/1944	MN 114
99	26.9.1944–24/10/1944	24/10/1944	MN 115
100	19/10/1944–7/11/1944	7/11/1944	MN 116
101	19/10/1944–21/11/1944	21/11/1944	MN 117
102	27/10/1944–5/12/1944	5/12/1944	MN 118
103	21/11/1944–12/1/1945	19/12/1944	MN 119
104	7/12/1944–24/1/1945	9/1/1945	MN 120
105	5/4/1944–24/2/1945	23/1/1945	MN 121
106	20/1/1945–6/2/1945	6/2/1945	MN 122
107	6/2/1945–6/3/1945	6/3/1945	MN 123
108	7/2/1945–20/3/1945	20/3/1945	MN 124
109	26/3/1945–24/4/1945	24/4/1945	MN 125
110	4/4/1945–8/5/1945	8/5/1945	MN 126

111	23/4/1945–12/7/1945	26/6/1945	MN 127
112	22/5/1945–17/7/1945	17/7/1945	MN 128
113	29/6/1945–14/8/1945	14/8/1945	MN 129
114	5/7/1945–4/9/1945	4/9/1945	MN 130
115	9/8/1945–18/9/1945	18/9/1945	MN 131
116	13/8/1945–16/10/1945	16/10/1945	MN 132
117	12/9/1945–30/10/1945	30/10/1945	MN 133
118	1/11/1945–30/11/1945	30/11/1945	MN 134
119	23/10/1945–14/6/1946	11/12/1945	MN 135
120	5/12/1945–15/2/1946	221/1/1946	MN 136
121	13/12/1945–5/2/1946	5/2/1946	MN 137
122	19/2/1946–26/3/1946	26/3/1946	MN 138
123	9/3/1946–23/4/1946	23/4/1946	MN 139
124	10/4/1946–25/5/1946	23/5/1946	MN 140
125	21/5/1946–4/6/1946	4/6/1946	MN 141
126	16/3/1946–30/7/1946	25/6/1946	MN 142
127	11/6/1946–30/7/1946	30/7/1946	MN 143
128	11/7/1946–1/10/1946	1/10/1946	MN 144
129	18/10/1946–29/10/1946	29/10/1946	MN 145
130	25/10/1946–3/12/1946	3/12/1946	MN 146
131	7/9/1946–4/2/1947	4/2/1947	MN 147
132	20/6/1947–1/7/1947	1/7/1947	MN 148

T 336 is the series of records of the Treasury Ceremonial Branch concerned with awards to the Civil Defence organization, Police, National Fire Service, Red Cross, Young Men's Christian Association and a number of foreign nationals who assisted the Allied war effort in occupied countries and after the liberation of Europe.

T 336

PIECE	DATE RANGE	GAZETTE DATE OR CONTENT	FORMER REFERENCE
1	28/9/1938–28/4/1941	Wartime Awards to Civilian Defence	GCD (General)
2	3/5/1940–30/10/1940	30/9/1940	GCD 1
3	12/9/1940–4/10/1940	4/10/1940	GCD 2
4	11/10/1940–12/12/1940	22/10/1940	GCD 3
5	8/9/1940–29/1/1941	15/11/1940	GCD 4
6	30/9/1940–16/8/1941	3/12/1940	GCD 6
7	10/1/1940–19/8/1941	13/12/1940	GCD 7
8	9/10/1941–24/4/1941	17/12/1940	GCD 8

9	4/10/1940–9/1/1941	3/1/1941	GCD 9
10	27/9/1940–17/1/1941	17/1/1941	GCD 10
11	12/11/1940–16/1/1942	24/1/1941	GCD 11
12	16/10/1940–28/1/1941	28/1/1941	GCD 12
13	20/9/1940–15/1/1949	31/1/1941	GCD 13
14	18/10/1940–14/2/1941	7/2/1941	GCD 14
15	11/1/1941–25/5/1941	14/2/1941	GCD 15
16	6/1/1941–21/2/1941	21/2/1941	GCD 16
17	31/1/1941–28/2/1941	28/2/1941	GCD 17
18	8/2/1941–7/31941	7/3/1941	GCD 18
19	21/2/1941–21/4/1941	14/3/1941	GCD 19
20	11/2/1941–21/3/1941	21/3/1941	GCD 20
21	17/3/1941–28/8/1945	28/3/1941	GCD 21
22	13/3/1941–4/4/1941	4/4//1941	GCD 22
23	28/3/1941–4/4/1941	4/4/1941	GCD 22A
24	28/3/1941–25/7/1941	11/4/1941	GCD 23
25	18/3/1941–12/12/1941	18/4/1941	GCD 24
26	10/4/1941–1/5/1941	21/4/1941	GCD 25
27	21/4/1941–2/5/1941	2/5/1941	GCD 26
28	18/3/1941–9/5/1941	9/5/1941	GCD 27
29	3/5/1941–24/7/1941	16/5/1941	GCD 28
30	9/5/1941–24/2/1944	23/5/1941	GCD 29
31	11/2/1941–24/2/1944	30/5/1941	GCD 30
32	8/4/1941–21/10/1943	6/6/1941	GCD 31
33	13/9/1940–19/6/1941	13/6/1941	GCD 32
34	7/5/1941–8/8/1945	20/6/1941	GCD 33
35	7/2/1941–17/7/1941	27/6/1941	GCD 34
36	14/3/1941–10/10/1946	7/7/1941	GCD 35
37	11/2/1941–19/11/1945	11/7/1941	GCD 36
38	21/4/1941–29/7/1941	18/7/1941	GCD 37
39	29/4/1941–17/12/1945	25/7/1941	GCD 38
40	3/6/1941–14/2/1944	1/8/1941	GCD 39
41	11/7/1941–11/1/1943	8/8/1941	GCD 40
42	15/5/1941–15/8/1941	15/8/1941	GCD 41
43	9/8/1941–22/2/1950	22/8/1941	GCD 42
44	18/6/1941–12/12/1941	29/8/1941	GCD 43
45	24/4/1941–7/1/1943	5/9/1941	GCD 44
46	16/6/1941–29/10/1941	12/9/1941	GCD 45
47	30/6/1941–1/12/1941	19/9/1941	GCD 46
48	5/8/1941–12/7/1947	26/9/1941	GCD 47
49	28/5/1941–31/8/1943	3/10/1941	GCD 48
50	23/5/1941–2/8/1945	10/10/1941	GCD 49
51	16/6/1941–29/10/1941	17/10/1941	GCD 50

52	28/6/1941–29/10/1941	24/10/1941	GCD 51
53	16/10/1941–16/12/1941	31/10/1941	GCD 52
54	13/8/1941–15/11/1941	7/11/1941	GCD 53
55	16/8/1941–2/2/1944	14/11/1941	GCD 54
56	28/10/1941–21/11/1941	21/11/1941	GCD 55
57	19/8/1941–16/12/1941	28/11/1941	GCD 56
58	1/1/1941–2/1/1942	5/12/1941	GCD 57
59	20/8/1941–20/12/1941	12/12/1941	GCD 58
60	2/9/1941–18/4/1942	19/12/1941	GCD 59
61	23/6/1941–15/1/1942	2/1/1942	GCD 60
62	28/11/1941–21/1/1942	9/1/1942	GCD 61
63	5/11/1941–22/1/1942	16/1/1942	GCD 62
64	19/1/1942–13/2/1942	30/1/1942	GCD 63
65	3/10/1941–13/2/1942	13/2/1942	GCD 64
66	3/12/1941–27/2/1942	27/2/1942	GCD 65
67	16/9/1940–13/3/1942	13/3/1942	GCD 66
68	29/4/1941–2/4/1942	27/3/1942	GCD 67
69	3/12/1941–16/4/1942	16/4/1942	GCD 68
70	23/2/1942–24/4/1942	24/4/1942	GCD 69
71	24/4/1942–8/5/1942	8/5/1942	GCD 70
72	11/9/1940–22/11/1945	22/5/1942	GCD 71
73	6/5/1942–9/6/1942	5/6/1942	GCD 72
74	22/5/1942–19/6/1942	19/6/1942	GCD 73
75	12/5/1942–3/7/1942	3/7/1942	GCD 74
76	19/6/1942–17/8/1942	17/7/1942	GCD 75
77	15/5/1942–31/7/1942	31/7/1942	GCD 76
78	16/7/1942–14/8/1942	14/8/1942	GCD 77
79	19/7/1942–28/7/1942	28/8/1942	GCD 78
80	23/6/1942–11/9/1942	11/9/1942	GCD 79
81	9/5/1942–6/10/1942	25/9/1942	GCD 80
82	8/7/1942–15/10/1942	9/10/1942	GCD 81
83	3/5/1942–30/10/1942	23/10/1942	GCD 82
84	8/10/1942–31/8/1942	6/11/1942	GCD 83
85	10/11/1942–28/11/1942	28/11/1942	GCD 84
86	12/7/1942–4/12/1942	4/12/1942	GCD 85
87	18/10/1942–18/12/1942	18/12/1942	GCD 86
88	4/12/1942–11/1/1943	4/1/1943	GCD 87
89	16/2/1942–15/1/1943	15/1/1943	GCD 88
90	5/1/1943–29/1/1943	29/1/1943	GCD 89
91	5/12/1941–15/2/1943	12/2/1943	GCD 90
92	24/10/1940–9/11/1945	26/2/1943	GCD 91
93	3/3/1943–12/3/1943	12/3/1943	GCD 92

94	24/2/1943–26/3/1943	26/3/1943	GCD 93
95	28/2/1943–6/4/1943	6/4/1943	GCD 94
96	3/10/1940–11/5/1943	7/5/1943	GCD 95
97	27/2/1943–21/5/1943	21/5/1943	GCD 96
98	31/3/1943–15/6/1943	11/6/1943	GCD 97
99	15/6/1943–2/7/1943	2/7/1943	GCD 98
100	26/6/1943–2/7/1943	2/7/1943	GCD 99
101	5/5/1943–14/9/1944	16/7/1943	GCD 100
102	21/7/1943–30/7/1943	30/7/1943	GCD 101
103	5/8/1943–13/8/1943	13/8/1943	GCD 102
104	5/8/1843–30/8/1943	27/8/1943	GCD 103
105	3/8/1943–18/9/1943	10/9/1943	GCD 104
106	19/7/1943–24/9/1943	24/9/1943	GCD 105
107	8/1/1941–18/10/1943	8/10/1943	GCD 106
108	19/8/1943–15/11/1943	5/11/1943	GCD 107
109	10/11/1943–29/11/1943	19/11/1943	GCD 108
110	24/11/1943–3/12/1943	3/12/1943	GCD 109
111	16/12/1943–21/12/1943	21/12/1943	GCD 110
112	6/10/1943–24/1/1944	21/1/1944	GCD 111
113	25/1/1944–5/2/1944	4/2/1944	GCD 112
114	21/1/1944–15/3/1944	22/2/1944	GCD 113
115	14/6/1943–10/3/1944	7/3/1944	GCD 114
116	3/11/1943–24/3/1943	21/3/1944	GCD 115
117	2/2/1944–6/4/1944	4/4/1944	GCD 116
118	8/3/1944–18/4/1945	18/4/1944	GCD 117
119	20/4/1944–2/5/1944	2/5/1944	GCD 118
120	8/5/1944–16/5/1944	16/5/1944	GCD 119
121	15/3/1944–9/6/1944	30/5/1944	GCD 120
122	1/3/1944–21/6/1945	13/6/1944	GCD 121
123	30/1/1944–27/6/1966	27/6/1944	GCD 122
124	27/6/1944–11/7/1944	11/7/1944	GCD 123
125	28/3/1944–25/7/1944	25/7/1944	GCD 124
126	27/7/1944–15/8/1944	15/8/1944	GCD 125
127	9/8/1944–29/8/1944	29/8/1944	GCD 126
128	30/8/1944–12/9/1944	12/9/1944	GCD 127
129	22/6/1944–26/9/1944	26/9/1944	GCD 128
130	27/9/1944–24/5/1945	10/10/1944	GCD 129
131	1/9/1944–7/11/1944	24/10/1944	GCD 130
132	25/10/1944–21/11/1944	7/11/1944	GCD 131
		21/11/1944	GCD 131A
133	30/11/1944–7/3/1945	5/12/1944	GCD 132
134	11/8/1944–3/1/1945	19/12/1944	GCD 133

135	6/10/1944–9/1/1945	9/1/1945	GCD 134
136	11/1/1945–23/1/1945	23/1/1945	GCD 134A
137	28/12/1944–6/2/1945	6/2/1945	GCD 135
138	16/12/1944–6/3/1945	20/2/1945	GCD 136
		6/3/1945	GCD 136A
139	7/2/1945–20/3/1945	20/3/1945	GCD 137
140	26/31945–17/4/1945	10/4/1945	GCD 138
141	12/4/1945–24/4/1945	24/4/1945	GCD 139
142	26/4/1945–8/5/1945	8/5/1945	GCD 139A
143	30/3/1945–28/6/1945	12/6/1945	GCD 140
144	10/5/1945–28/6/1945	26/6/1945	GCD 141
145	18/5/1945–20/2/1946	17/7/1945	GCD 142
146	1/8/1945–14/8/1945	14/8/1945	GCD 142A
147	30/8/1945–9/12/1949	4/9/1945	GCD 143
148	11/3/1945–18/11/1945	18/9/1945	GCD 144
149	20/9/1945–2/10/1945	2/10/1945	GCD 144A
150	4/10/1945–24/1/1950	16/10/1945	GCD 145
151	17/10/1945–30/10/1945	30/10/1945	GCD 146
152	2/5/1944–16/1/1946	11/12/1945	GCD 147
153	10/1/1946–22/11/1946	22/1/1946	GCD 148
154	10/1/1946–5/2/1946	5/2/1946	GCD 149
155	6/2/1946–19/2/1946	19/2/1946	GCD 150
156	20/2/1946–5/3/1946	5/3/1946	GCD 151
157	12/3/1946–26/3/1946	26/3/1946	GCD 152
158	17/4/1946–23/4/1946	23/4/1946	GCD 153
159	16/5/1946–23/5/1946	23/5/1946	GCD 154
160	25/5/1946–6/8/1946	4/6/1946	GCD 155
161	6/6/1946–25/6/1946	25/6/1946	GCD 156
162	11/7/1946–12/11/1946	23/7/1946	GCD 157
163	29/5/1946–20/8/1946	20/8/1946	GCD 158
164	26/9/1946–1/10/1946	1/10/1946	GCD 159
165	18/10/1946–20/1/1950	29/10/1946	GCD 160
166	15/11/1946–5/1/1949	3/12/1946	GCD 161

18   New Year and Birthday Honours Lists

18.1 INTRODUCTION

Outside of wartime, the most significant announcements concerning honours, especially since the early 20th century, have always been the New Year and Birthday Honours Lists. Sometimes known as the 'Half Yearly' or 'Periodic' honours, twice a year large numbers of individuals have been honoured by the State for their contributions to it and to the Empire or Commonwealth.

In order to ascertain if an honour you are researching falls into the category of New Year or Birthday Honours, it is very important to see what is said in the heading announcing the award in the *London Gazette*. New Year Honours are usually published in the *London Gazette* on the last working day of the year, but some awards are published up to the second week in January. The variation in publication date makes reading the *London Gazette* headings very important.

The Birthday Honours Lists are published to celebrate the Sovereign's birthday and whilst they are currently announced in June, in the past the date varied slightly. Once again, read what the announcement says in the *London Gazette*.

The awards announced in the New Year and Birthday Honours Lists are primarily for meritorious service, but awards for gallantry can be announced in the same lists. Between the two World Wars, many military awards for valuable service in minor military operations were announced in the New Year and Birthday Honours Lists.

18.2 THE RECORDS

There are a number of different ways to identify records concerning recommendations for New Year or Birthday Honours.

Initially, the quickest way to find a file at the National Archives is to keyword search the Catalogue, using the term 'New Year' or 'Birthday' and 'award*' or 'honour*' and the date(s). If you know that the recipient was in the armed forces, you may wish to add the appropriate Departmental code: ADM for the Royal Navy and

Royal Marines, AIR for the RAF and WO for the Army. An example of a search, such as the one described above, indicates that, according to the AIR 2 catalogue, there are 40 files containing recommendations for New Year Honours and 43 files for Birthday Honours.

Recommendation for civilians whose awards appeared in either the New Year or Birthday Honours Lists are dispersed across a wide range of different records series, the most significant being PREM 2.

At the British Library many of the recommendations for New Year and Birthday Honours are in the series L/PS/15, with some Indian Army recommendations in L/MIL/7.

18.3 DETAILED LISTS

The following document references all contain recommendations or lists of awards granted in either the New Year or Birthday Honours List. The vast majority of records listed in PREM 2 are from either of these two types of list, but the series also includes a number of other Honours Lists. Rather than separate out all of the different lists, the whole of the PREM 2 is listed below.

CO 323/756/59	Proposals for New Year Honours 1918	
DO 35/427/2A	New Year Honours List 1931	
DO 35/427/6	New Year Honours List 1931: Archbishop Carter	
DO 35/432/4	New Year Honours List 1932	
DO 35/433/9	New Year Honours List 1932	
DO 35/436/1	New Year Honours 1932: Australian quota	
DO 35/1126	List of South Africans in Ministry of Works and Transport recommended for Honours	1943–6
L/MIL/7/1338	OBEs Birthday and New Year Honours Lists	1923–4
L/MIL/7/1339	Military CBEs	1924–5
L/MIL/7/1340	Birthday Honours List	1929
L/MIL/7/1341	Birthday and New Year Honours Lists	1930
L/MIL/7/1342	Birthday Honours List	1931
L/MIL/7/1343	OBEs: New Year	1932
L/PS/15/51 file H 2	Indian Honours List New Year 1921	1921

PREM 2

1	1916	Birthday Honours (BH)
2	1916	Mr Asquith's Resignation
3	1916	Distribution of War Decorations to Allied Forces

4	1917	New Year Honours (NYH)
5	1917	BH
6	1917	British Empire Honours List: 1st Gazette
7	1918	NYH
8	1918	British Empire Honours List: 2nd Gazette
9	1918	BH
10	1918	British Empire Honours List: 3rd Gazette
11	1918	Honours for Army and Navy Commanders
12	1918	Corporation of London Honours
13	1915–18	Order of the British Empire: Proposals for the Order
14	1919	NYH
15	1919	New Ministry List
16	1919	BH
17	1919	Corporation of London Honours
18	1920	NYH
19	1920	BH
20	1920	British Empire Honours List
21	1920	Corporation of London Honours
22	1921	NYH
23	1921	British Empire Honours List for staff of Ministries of Shipping, Munitions and Food on termination of Dept.
24	1921	BH
25	1921	Honours given on opening of Ulster Parliament
26	1921	Honours given on termination of post-war work of the Ministry of Transport
27	1921	Corporation of London Honours
28	1922	NYH
29	1922	British Empire Honours (Allenby's List)
30	1922	BH
31	1922	Mr Lloyd George's Resignation List
32	1922	Corporation of London Honours List
33	1923	NYH
34	1923	Mr Bonar Law's Resignation List
35	1923	BH
36	1923	Honours given to Southern Rhodesia on achieving self-government
37	1923	Corporation of London Honours
38	1923	Setting up of Political Honours Scrutiny Committee
39	1924	NYH
40	1924	Mr Baldwin's Resignation List
41	1924	British Empire Exhibition Opening List
42	1924	BH

43	1924	Royal Lifeboat Institute Centenary Honours
44	1924	Mr MacDonald's Resignation List
45	1924	Corporation of London Honours
46	1922–4	Royal Commission on Honours
47	1925	NYH
48	1925	Railway Centenary Honours List
49	1925	BH
50	1925	Corporation of London Honours
51	1926	NYH
52	1926	British Empire Exhibition Closing List
53	1926	Honours given in connection with HRH the Prince of Wales's visit to South America
54	1926	BH
55	1926	Corporation of London Honours
56A	1927	NYH
56B	1927	Visit of HRH the Duke of York to Australia
57	1927	BH
58	1927	Corporation of London Honours
59	1928	NYH
60	1928	BH
61	1928	Honours awarded on the opening of the Sarda Canal
62	1928	Corporation of London Honours
63	1929	NYH
64	1929	BH
65	1929	Mr Baldwin's Resignation List
66	1929	Corporation of London Honours
67	1930	NYH
68	1930	BH
69	1930	Corporation of London Honours
70	1931	NYH
71	1931	BH
72	1931	Dissolution Honours List
73	1931	Corporation of London Honours
74	1932	NYH
75	1923–32	Future of the Order of St Patrick
76	1932	Honours awarded at the opening of the Sukkur Barrage
77	1932	BH
78	1932	Corporation of London Honours
79	1933	NYH
80	1933	BH
81	1933	Corporation of London Honours

82	1934	NYH
83	1934	BH
84	1934	Corporation of London Honours
85	1935	NYH
86	1935	BH
87	1935	Quetta Earthquake Honours (which it isn't!) OIOC
BL		
88	1935	Corporation of London Honours
89	1936	NYH
90	1936	BH
91	1936	Corporation of London Honours
92	1937	NYH
93	1937	Coronation and Birthday Honours List
94	1937	Mr Baldwin's Resignation List
95	1937	Honours for relief work at Rabaul
96	1937	Corporation of London Honours
97	1938	NYH
98	1938	BH
99	1938	Corporation of London Honours
100	1939	NYH
101	1939	BH
102	1939	Corporation of London Honours
103	1940	Change of Administration List
104	1940	Institution of the George Cross and George Medal
105	1940	Gallantry Awards
106	1941	NYH
107	1941	BH
108	1941	George Cross and George Medal Warrants
109	1941	Corporation of London Honours
110/1	1941	Gallantry Awards
110/2	1941	Gallantry Awards
111	1941	Strengthening of Labour Party in the House of Lords
112	1942	NYH
113	1942	BH

The following lists for 1943 and 1944 contain detailed recommendations for the British Empire Medal to both civilians and military personnel.

114	1943	New Year Honours (NYH)
115	1943	Birthday Honours (BH)
116	1944	NYH
117	1944	BH

118	1945	NYH
119	1945	BH
120	1946	NYH
121	1946	BH
122	1947	NYH
123	1947	BH
124	1948	NYH
125	1948	BH
126	1949	NYH
127	1949	BH
128	1950	NYH
129	1950	BH
130	1951	NYH
131	1951	BH
132	1952	NYH
133	1952	BH

All of the above pieces are open for scrutiny. Some of the following are closed for 75 years from creation, the opening dates being noted.

134	1953	New Year Honours (NYH) Open 01/01/2029
135	1953	Birthday Honours (BH) Open 01/01/2029
136	1954	NYH Open 01/01/2030
137	1954	BH Open 01/01/2030
138	1955	NYH
139	1955	BH
140	1956	NYH Open 01/01/2032
141	1956	BH
142	1957	NYH
143	1957	BH Open 01/01/2033
144	1958	NYH Open 01/01/2034
145	1958	BH
146	1959	NYH
147	1959	BH
148	1960	NYH
149	1960	BH Open 01/01/2036
150	1961	NYH
151	1961	BH Open 01/01/2037
152	1962	NYH Open 01/01/2038
153	1962	BH Open 01/01/2038
154	1963	NYH Open 01/01/2039
155	1963	BH Open 01/01/2039
156	1964	NYH Open 01/01/2040

157	1964	BH Open 01/01/2040
158	1965	NYH Open 01/01/2041
159	1965	BH Open 01/01/2041
160	1966	NYH Open 01/01/2042
161	1966	BH Open 01/01/2042
162	1967	NYH Open 01/01/2043
163	1967	BH Open 01/01/2043

Further 'Half Yearly' Honours Lists can be found in the series T 305. The Lists cover the period 1936–70, but unfortunately they are all closed for 75 years from creation.

The vast majority of New Year and Birthday Honours Lists for Army personnel are in the series WO 373, where they are described as 'Half Yearly' Lists, and the list for them has been extracted from the remainder of the WO 373 catalogue. Although the Lists start in 1943, they do not all survive.

WO 373

156	1943	NYH 1943 and BH 1943
157	1945–8	NYH 1945, BH 1945 (CBE Only), NYH 1947, BH 1947, NYH 1948
158	1948–51	BH 1948, BH 1949, NYH 1950, BH 1950, NYH 1951
159	1951–2	BH 1951, NYH 1952
160	1952–3	BH 1952, NYH 1953
161	1953–4	BH 1953 (Coronation Honours), NYH 1954
162	1954–5	BH 1954, NYH 1955
163	1955–6	BH 1955, NYH 1956
164	1956–7	BH 1956, NYH 1957
165	1957–8	BH 1957, NYH 1958
166	1958–9	BH 1958, NYH 1959
167	1959–60	BH 1959, NYH 1960
168	1960–1	BH 1960, NYH 1961, BH 1961
169	1962–3	NYH 1962, BH 1962, NYH 1963
170	1963–4	BH 1963, NYH 1964, BH 1964
171	1965–6	NYH 1965, BH 1965, NYH 1966
172	1966–8	BH 1966, NYH 1967, BH 1967, NYH 1968
173	1968–70	BH 1968, NYH 1969, BH 1969, NYH 1970, BH 1970
174	1970–3	NYH 1971, BH 1971, NYH 1972, BH 1972, NYH 1973
175	1973–5	BH 1973, NYH 1974, BY 1974, NYH 1975, BH 1975

176	1976–8	NYH 1976, BH 1976, NYH 1977, BH 1977, NYH 1978
177	1978–80	BH 1978, NYH 1979, BH 1979, NYH 1980
178	1980–3	BH 1980, NYH 1981, BH 1981, NYH 1982, BH 1982, NYH 1983
179	1983–5	BH 1983, NYH 1984, BH 1984, NYH 1985, BH 1985
180	1986–8	NYH 1986, BH 1986, NYH 1987, BH 1987, NYH 1988
181	1988–90	BH 1988, NYH 1989, NYH 1990, BH 1990

A stray file concerning recommendations as Knight Grand Cross (GCB) of the Order of the Bath for the New Year and Birthday Honours Lists of 1946 can be found in WO 32/12112.

19 Foreign Awards to Britons and British Awards to Foreigners

19.1 INTRODUCTION

Even before 1793, grateful foreign nations were bestowing their awards upon British nationals who had helped them in some way. Initially, it was the most important individuals who were the usual recipients of such honours. Over the last 200 or so years, however, the number of awards has increased and the status of the recipients has become more representative of the social spectrum.

Even as Britons have become grateful recipients of foreign awards, so the British nation has recognized the deeds of many thousands of foreigners by giving them an award. There were a number of different government departments that needed to be consulted when a foreign award was to be bestowed upon a Briton and, in most cases, the same departments were involved when a foreigner was to be recognized by Britain. The Foreign Office Treaty Department and the Home Office took part in the decision-making process about the acceptance of foreign awards. Recipients of foreign awards often had to apply for a warrant, usually approved by the sovereign, giving them permission to accept and wear a foreign honour in the British Empire.

When researching foreign awards to Britons and British awards to foreigners in the *London Gazette*, note that while foreign awards to Britons are announced in the *London Gazette*, British awards to foreigners are not. However, there are exceptions to this rule. During the 20th century, especially in the two World Wars, a large number of Britons received a foreign award that was not announced in the *London Gazette* and there are a number of reasons for this. Firstly, there were cases when large numbers of low status foreign awards were granted to Britons and not all of the proper authorities were involved in the process. Secondly, although the individual was given permission to accept the award, they were given restrictions about when and where they could wear the foreign award. Where restrictions were applied to the acceptance of a foreign award, the award was quite often not announced in the *London Gazette*.

19.2 THE FOREIGN OFFICE

The Foreign Office's involvement in foreign awards to Britons and British awards to foreigners is very important, as in many cases it is the only place where information about an award can be found.

The Treaty Department of the Foreign Office dealt with most of the protocols regarding awards, from making sure that the right parts of government were involved in the process and kept informed, to the correct form of language to be used when either offering an award to a foreign national or accepting an award on behalf of a Briton.

The records of the Treaty Department up to 1905 are in the series FO 83 and the files concerning orders, decorations and medals are listed below.

FO 83

Decorations, etc.: British

584	1813–76	Knighthood: Correspondence
606	1861–79	Star of India: Correspondence
769	1839–82	Gallantry Medals for Saving Life at Sea: Correspondence
935	1865–78	St Michael and St George: Correspondence
936	1879–80	As above
	1865–80	Register and index to above in FO 802/233

937	1840–55	Order of the Bath (Military): Correspondence
938	1856	As above
939	1857–62	As above
940	1864–80	Order of the Bath (Civil): Correspondence
941	1864–75	As above
942	1876–80	As above
943	1825–64	Order of the Garter: Correspondence
944	1865	As above
945	1866–77	As above
946	1878–82	As above
1654	1898	British and Indian Orders: Proposed Amalgamation under one Chancery
2540	1896–1914	Royal Victorian Order: Correspondence

Medals: Military

605	1846–79	Correspondence
690	1855–61	French troops (Crimean War): Correspondence
691	1858–63	Turkish (Crimean War): Correspondence
692	1855–64	Turkish, Sardinian and Miscellaneous Troops (Crimean War): Correspondence
693	1842–77	Austria, China, Denmark, France and Hanover: Correspondence
694	1865–76	Germany: Correspondence
695	1847–77	Italy, Papal States, Portugal, Russia, Spain and Turkey: Correspondence
696	1878–9	Austria, China, France, Germany, Italy, Netherlands, Roumania, Russia, Turkey: Correspondence

Decorations: Foreign Orders

468	1822–75	Titles of nobility: Correspondence
688	1812–70	Order and Medals: Regulations
947	1866–86	Regulations: Proposed alterations etc.
638	1812–19	Entry book of Correspondence
639	1819–23	As above

Some of the following pieces have information regarding more than one country. The list is in alphabetical order by country, giving the date range of the record relevant to that country.

Some countries have more than one file because they bestowed a larger number of awards upon British subjects when we were their

allies during a war. This is especially so of France and Turkey, for
example, as Britain fought alongside them against Russia.

FO 83		
2115	1897–1905	Abyssinia: Correspondence
2115	1897–1904	Afghanistan: Correspondence
640	1814–41	Austria: Correspondence
641	1832–79	As above
2116	1897–1905	Austria-Hungary: Correspondence
2117	1901–5	Baden: Correspondence
640	1810–22	Bavaria: Correspondence
641	1855–76	As above
2117	1898–1905	Bavaria: Correspondence
640	1833–41	Belgium: Correspondence
642	1845–78	As above
2117	1898–1905	As above
640	1826–41	Brazil: Correspondence
642	1841–78	As above
2117	1897–1905	Bulgaria: Correspondence
643	1865–78	China: Correspondence
2118	1897–1905	As above
2119	1899–1905	Coburg: Correspondence
2119	1900–2	Corea (Korea): Correspondence
640	1838–41	Denmark: Correspondence
642	1846–74	As above
2119	1897–1905	As above
2120	1897–8	Egypt: Correspondence
2121	1899–1900	As above
2122	1901–2	As above
2123	1903	As above
2124	1904–5	As above
644	1815–41	France: Correspondence
645	1826–55	As above
646	1856	As above
647	1856	As above
648	1857	As above
649	1858–63	As above
650	1863–80	As above
2125	1897–1905	As above
652	1842–1875	German States: Correspondence
2126	1897–1900	Germany: Correspondence
2127	1901–3	As above

2128	1904–5	As above
651	1834–41	Greece: Correspondence
652	1842–79	As above
2129	1898–1905	Greece
653	1837–41	Hanover: Correspondence
654	1842–61	As above
2129	1901–4	Hesse-Darmstadt: Correspondence
656	1863–80	Italy: Correspondence
2130	1897–1902	As above
2131	1902–5	As above
643	1875–9	Japan: Correspondence
2132	1897–1903	As above
2133	1904–5	As above
2134	1899–1905	Liberia: Correspondence
657	1854–67	Mexico: Correspondence
658	1830–79	Miscellaneous: Correspondence
2134	1897–1905	As above
659	1817–41	Netherlands: Correspondence
660	1842–78	As above
2134	1897–1905	As above
659	1818–41	Persia, Afghanistan, Punjab: Correspondence
661	1842–80	Persia only
2135	1897–1905	As above
659	1837	Peru: Correspondence
662	1815–36	Portugal: Correspondence
663	1837–41	As above
664	1847–56	As above
665	1857–79	As above
2135	1897–1905	As above
659	1817–41	Prussia: Correspondence
666	1842–78	As above
655	1842–79	Rome (Vatican): Correspondence
2137	1898–1905	Roumania: Correspondence
667	1813–41	Russia: Correspondence
678	1842–80	As above
2137	1897–1905	As above
668	1815–39	Sardinia: Correspondence
669	1842–60	As above
668	1820–41	Saxe-Coburg and Saxony: Correspondence
2138	1898–1903	Saxony: Correspondence
2138	1899–1905	Serbia: Correspondence

643	1862–80	Siam: Correspondence
2138	1897–1905	As above
668	1811–31	Sicily: Correspondence
655	1849–61	As above
670	1814–36	Spain: Correspondence
671	1837–8	As above
672	1839–41	As above
673	1842–9	As above
674	1850–2	As above
676	1853–80	As above
2139	1897–1905	As above
677	1813–38	Sweden: Correspondence
678	1850–77	As above
2140	1897–1905	As above, and Norway
2140	1905	Tunis: Correspondence
679	1835–54	Turkey: Correspondence
680	1855	As above
681	1856	As above
682	1856	As above
683	1857	As above
684	1858	As above
685	1858	As above
686	1859–70	As above
687	1871–81	As above
2141	1897–1901	As above
2142	1902–5	As above
677	1817–41	Tuscany: Correspondence
655	1847–65	As above
2143	1898–1901	Venezuela: Correspondence
677	1816	Wurtembeg: Correspondence
2143	1900–5	As above
2144	1897–1900	Zanzibar: Correspondence
	1901–5	As above (see FO 97/612)

From 1906 onwards, the Treaty Department records are FO 372. There is a card index covering the period 1906–19. From 1920–53, there are yearly index books. You can search both types of index by name or subject, either by the name of the recipient, by the name of the country or the term 'Decorations' and then the name of the country.

The two FO general correspondence indexes require different approaches and the one for 1906–19 is the more complex. Once you have found a card of interest, it is usually necessary to use FO 566 to identify the correct file in FO 372. There is an information leaflet on how to go about this.

If you have difficulty converting the FO reference into a TNA FO 372 reference, for the period 1906–19, you can always look at all of the appropriate files for the specific year and country. Please note, however, that the records in FO 372 cover more than just medals, so you must always find the ones listed under decorations. Don't be fooled by the term 'prizes' as this relates to ships and money! You may not find what you want using this technique, but you will come across some very interesting files.

The Foreign Office index books of general correspondence for the period 1920–53 are much easier to use. The easiest approach is to search by name of recipient. The references found in the index books take the form of alpha-numeric references, with the letters and numbers denoting which Foreign Office department dealt with the correspondence, the file and paper number, and which country it came from. The way in which the Foreign Office indexed these letters changed over the life of the index books; two examples are given below.

Foreign Office: *General Correspondence Index R–Z*, 1921

Stewart, Alexander, Pipe-Major
Japanese Decoration. T9762/5578/323D

T	denotes Treaty Department of the Foreign Office
9762	is the paper within the File
5578	is the File
300	is the Treaty, added to which is the Country code, so
23	is Japan
D	denotes Decorations

By applying all of this data to the FO 372 paper catalogue, it will be seen that the file will be in FO 372/1814.

Stewart's Japanese award can be seen in PLATE 20.

Foreign Office: *General Correspondence Index E–L*, 1948

Hunt, Bernard Francis

Netherlands Decoration. T23396/321/372

T	denotes the Treaty Department of the Foreign Office
23396	is the paper number within the File
321	is the File
372	is the Treaty plus country code

This file can be found in FO 372/6296.

Hunt's Dutch award can be seen in PLATE 23.

The medals to which the above two index entries refer and reasons why the recipients received them, are discussed at the end of this chapter at 19.12.

Apart from the records in FO 83 and FO 372, there are other files concerning the subjects of British awards to foreigners and foreign awards to Britons. The following are some examples.

FO 141/693/3	Award of British Medals and Decorations to Egyptian and Sudanese Nationals: Part 1	1932
FO 141/693/4	Part 2	1932
FO 141/693/4	Part 3	1932
FO 369/3590	Awards to Crews of foreign ships who rendered Services to torpedoed British ships	1946
FO 371/43387	Awards to Members of the Soviet forces	1944
FO 371/54076	Awards to Helpers of escaped Prisoners of War	1946
FO 371/59546	Recognition of Yugoslav Helpers of British and American Escapers and Evaders: General question of Awards	1946
FO 371/77701	Awards to Stalin on his 70th birthday	1949
FO 371/83572	Awards for Service rendered in the Yangtze Incident	1950
FO 371/83656	Report about the wounding of Captain Stewart Richardson in Indo-China and the French Award of the Croix de Guerre	1950
FO 660/105	Awards for Gallantry	1943
FO 898/96	Awards and Decorations	1944–5
FO 954/6A	Proposed honorary OBE to an Ethiopian	1941
FO 954/12B	Recommendation for Mr Knabenshue, US Minister in Baghdad, for a KCMG for assistance to British subjects during the rebellion	1941
FO 1032/658	Honours and Awards: Policy towards Germans	1946–9

19.3 THE HOME OFFICE

The Warrant Books, which record the warrant by which an individual was granted permission to accept and wear a foreign order, are in the series HO 37 and HO 38.

The Warrant Books in HO 37 cover the period 1777–1863 and the Warrant Books in HO 38 cover the period 1782 to 1969.

HO 37

1	1777–1837	Foreign Orders
2	1838–63	Foreign Orders

Each Warrant Book in HO 38 covers a specified period and they are internally indexed up to 1953 (HO 38/1–77).

For the period 1926–67, there is a specific run within HO 38 that concerns nothing but foreign order warrants. This run is arranged in alphabetical order.

HO 38

84	1926–67	Names A–B
85	1926–68	Names C
86	1926–67	Names D–E
87	1926–67	Names F–G
88	1926–67	Names H–I
89	1926–68	Names J–L
90	1926–67	Names M–N
91	1926–68	Names O–R
92	1926–67	Names S
93	1926–67	Names T–Z

19.4 THE ADMIRALTY

In the 19th century, naval officers in receipt of foreign decorations are annotated as such in the Navy List, but as naval ratings are not mentioned in the Navy List, it is necessary to use archival sources. There are a number of Admiralty records series where information about foreign awards to naval recipients and British awards to foreign naval personnel may be found.

The vast majority of files concerning foreign awards to naval personnel are in the records series ADM 1. Prior to 1914, it is necessary to use ADM 12, the Admiralty Index and Digest, in order to locate the appropriate records in ADM 1. The techniques need to access ADM 12 and how to translate the references are discussed in CHAPTER 25 on Research Techniques.

The alternative method to finding a file concerning foreign awards from 1914 onwards is to keyword search the catalogue of ADM 1 online. By using the terms, such as the name of the bestowing country or the name of the award, you may find the file you require.

The majority of files concerning foreign awards in ADM 1 are quite well described; below are some examples.

ADM 1 *Examples include:*

1/8425/177	Officers and Men of the Royal Navy recommended for the Croix de Guerre in Silver	
1/8448/33	Decorations conferred by France on Officers and Men of the Royal Marines serving in the Royal Naval Division	
1/8482/44	Japanese Honours to British Officers	
1/8511/17	Awards to Brazilian Officers	
1/8530/194	British Nominations for French Awards 1918	
12407	Dutch Awards to British Naval personnel	1942–4
12409	Greek Decorations Awarded to personnel of the Mediterranean fleet	1942
12448	Awards to Norwegian Merchant Navy personnel	1941–3
14478	Russian Honours for British personnel	1943
14552	Landing of Free French personnel in enemy territory: French Awards to British Naval personnel	1943

ADM 116 *Examples include*:

1102	Messina Earthquake – Awards by the King of Italy	1909–12
1493	Russian Awards, principally for Jutland	1916–17
1576	Croix de Guerre and Silver and Bronze Al Valore Militari	1917

The majority of rolls in ADM 171 concern Campaign and Long Service and Good Conduct medals, but a few pieces of the series, either in part or whole, contain information about foreign awards.

ADM 171/61 contains information about foreign awards granted to members of the Royal Navy and Royal Marines from countries such as Denmark, France, Greece, the Netherlands, Norway, USA and USSR. The complete roll of the Messina Earthquake Medal 1908 can also be found here.

Angels in Blue Jackets: the Navy at Messina 1908 by J.W. Wilson and Roger
Perkins (Picton, 1985)

ADM 171/67 is a roll of Foreign Orders awarded to Naval Officers for the
period 1905–18.

ADM 171/76 contains the names of foreign Officers recommended for British
Decorations for the period 1914–18.

ADM 171/172 contains another list of Royal Navy and Marine Officers
holding foreign Awards and this covers the period 1905–22.

19.5 THE AIR MINISTRY

Although there are no consolidated indexes concerning foreign
awards to members of the Royal Flying Corps and Royal Air
Force, there are a large number of files concerning honours and
awards to the flying services from 1914 onwards. Until such time
as the Honours and Awards index is transferred to AIR 81,
researching foreign awards to the RFC and RAF for the First
World War is not as effective as it could be.

The majority of files concerning honours and awards in AIR 1
are arranged by unit and it is important to know not only in which
squadron an individual served, but also the Brigade or Wing.
Many of the honours and awards files in AIR 1 do not mention
foreign awards by name in their descriptions; they are frequently
described just as 'Recommendations for awards'. However, there
are a few files with the term 'French Decorations' in the description, an example being:

AIR 1/775/204/4/377   Award of French Decorations to RFC
                             personnel, September–November 1914

After the First World War, the majority of Air Ministry files concerning honours and awards can be found in the series AIR 2. The
easiest way to search AIR 2 for files concerning foreign awards
is, once again, to keyword search the AIR 2 catalogue online. You
can search by the name of the country bestowing an award or the
name of the country of the foreign national, whichever is more
appropriate.

There is, however, an easier way to locate a foreign award to the
RAF or even a British award to a foreigner connected with avia-

tion. A private individual has indexed all of the surviving RAF files concerning honours and awards from 1939 onwards and he is able to provide the AIR 2 file reference for any award from 1939 onwards. Interested individuals are asked to contact:

Mr P Baillie
14 Wheatfields
St Ives
Huntingdon
CAMBS
PE17 6YD
paulbaillie@tiscali.co.uk

Examples of files in AIR 2 concerning foreign awards and British awards to foreigners include:

AIR 2

2844	Russian Decorations awarded to 26 Officers prior to the Revolution	1918–21
2845	Italian Decorations awarded to British Officers	1918–19
4798	Russian Awards to RAF personnel	1941–5
5904	Proposed Award of the George Medal to Mlle. Andree de Gough	1945–7
6304	Proposed Awards to Dutch personnel	1941–8
8742	Recommendations for Awards to Allied and neutral Citizens 1945	
9641	USA Awards to RAF personnel	1944–8
9642	Dutch Awards for Operations at Arnhem	1944–51

The Air Ministry controlled the committee that met to consider awards of the King's Medal for Courage in the Cause of Freedom, and three files containing recommendations for this award can be found in AIR 2/8742, 9288 and 9294.

19.6 SPECIAL OPERATIONS EXECUTIVE (SOE)

Some information about honours and awards to members of the Special Operations Executive will be found in CHAPTER 15 on Second World War Awards. The records discussed here relate to those men and women of the SOE who were foreign nationals.

The most significant source for honours and awards to SOE is the card index in HS 12/1. This index provides name, rank, number, parent unit, SOE section, by whom the award was recommended and when it was announced in the *London Gazette*.

Amongst the records of SOE in the different HS records series are a number of files concerning honours and awards. If you know the name of the operation or organization, you can search the National Archives Catalogue by that name and you may well find a file concerning awards. The following files concern awards to SOE members.

HS 1 *SOE: Far East*

| 258 | Operation Jaywick: Citations and Awards | 1943–6 |

HS 2 *SOE: Scandinavia*

| 246 | Honours and Awards to Norwegians | 1942–5 |
| 247 | Honours and Awards to Norwegians | 1945 |

HS 3 *SOE: Africa and Middle East*

| 29 | Madagascar:Honours and Awards | 1942–5 |
| 93 | Postmaster: Recommendations for Awards and Decorations | 1942–4 |

HS 4 *SOE: Eastern Europe*

| 267 | Honours and Awards: Polish, Czech and Hungarian | 1944–5 |

HS 5 *SOE: Balkans*

105	Honours, Awards and Citations	1944–5
169	Personnel: Supply, Postings, Awards	1943
302	A.A. Pallis; Archbishop Damaskinos: Awards and Assistance to people who helped British escapees and others who worked for the Allies	1944–5
347	Washington Operation: Awards to Asopos party	1943
367	Personnel: Awards	1943
380	Personnel: Greek Awards	1943
652	Commitments: Greek Agents and Collaborators: Awards	1944–5
801	Romanian Collaborators: Honours and Awards	1942–6

HS 6 *SOE: Western Europe*

| 466 | Recommendations for Awards to Z Group Agents | 1944 |
| 895 | British Awards to Italian personnel | 1945 |

HS 8   *SOE: Headquarters*

387	Citations for French Nationals: A–Bid
388	Citations for French Nationals: B
389	Citations for French Nationals: C
390	Citations for French Nationals: D
391	Citations for French Nationals: E–F
392	Citations for French Nationals: G
393	Citations for French Nationals: H–L
394	Citations for French Nationals: M–O
395	Citations for French Nationals: P–R
396	Citations for French Nationals: S–Z
397	Citations for French Nationals: Nominal roll
398	Certificates for Persons without personal files: A–K
399	Certificates for Persons without personal files: L–R
400	Certificates for Persons without personal files: S–Z
401	Citations for Foreign Nationals (excluding France): Africa, America, Austria and Belgium
402	Citations for Foreign Nationals (excluding France): Corsica, Czechoslovakia and Denmark
403	Greek Force 133: A–F
404	Greek Force 133: G–P
405	Greek Force 133: R–Z
406	Holland
407	Citations for Noreign Nationals (excluding France): Countries I–Z
987	Compilation of SOE subject file index: SOE Honours and Awards
994	Force 136: Nominal roll; Honours and Awards
995	Romania: Disposal of agents; Awards; Symbols and Pseudonyms

FO 643/74 contains further Recommendations for Force 136.

The personal files of SOE agents in HS 9 should be consulted, provided that they be open. HS 9 can be searched by name. Many of the files in HS 9 are closed. In order to access a closed file in HS 9, it is necessary to request a review of the file, which can be done by clicking on the 'request review' button on the online catalogue entry. Most HS 9 files are closed for 100 years from the date of birth of the individual.

19.7 THE WAR OFFICE

Very few files concerning foreign awards to members of the British army before the First World War are preserved at the War Office. In most cases, it is necessary to consult FO 83. One obvious pre-1914 file concerning foreign awards to British soldiers is in WO 100/375, French Military War Medal: NCOs and Soldiers selected for recommendation, 1856.

The records in WO 32 (Code 50A) contain some files about foreign awards, including both policy issues and recommendations for specific awards.

WO 32 *Examples include*:

5389	Report of the Greene Committee on distribution of War Decorations to the Allies	1915
5403	Military Mission to USA; Recommendations for Awards	1917
5406	Award of OBE for Intelligence Services performed by Mademoiselle Louise de Bettignies (dated 1915)	1918–19
5407	Award of OBE to Prince and Princess de Croy, and Royal Red Cross to Princess M. de Croy for Services in aiding escaping British troops	1919–21
9950	Award of Norwegian Military Cross and Medal	1941–3
9951	Award of British Decorations to the Greek Army	1941–4
10453	Soviet military personnel: Awards	1942–9
10542	Chinese military personnel: Awards	1942–51
10544	USA Awards to British Officers and Other Ranks	1942–4
11046	Inter-allied Awards	1944–51

A register of honorary appointments to the Distinguished Service Order between July 1915 and October 1943 can be found in WO 390/13.

At the end of the First World War, the British government decided to grant a special award for those men and women who had aided the Allied cause. The Allied Subjects Medal was issued in both Silver and Bronze, but unfortunately it was not named. The medal roll for the Allied Subjects Medal can be found in WO 32/5571. See also FO 372/1523, WO 32/5573 and WO 32/5574. A list of French, Belgian and Dutch secret service agents, honoured for their work in the First World War, can be found in WO 106/6192.

Lists of foreign awards granted to British Army personnel and British awards granted to personnel of Allied armies during the First World War can be found in the series WO 388. The series is available on microfilm. The lists in WO 388 are arranged in alphabetical order of the name of the country bestowing the award, or the name of the country in which a foreign soldier who was receiving a British award served. Each country list is then in chronological order and then by type of award.

Also to be found in WO 388 are two alphabetical indexes of French awards and Belgian awards given to British soldiers. Each index gives the date when the award was announced in the *London Gazette*.

Recommendations and lists relating to foreign awards to Britons and British awards to foreigners for the Second World War onwards are in the records series WO 373.

The following WO 373 references give the name of the bestowing country and the *London Gazette* date(s) when the award was announced, where appropriate. Each file covers more than one gazette date. The list is split into Foreign to British and British to Foreign.

WO 373

Foreign to British

PIECE NO.	COUNTRY FROM	GAZETTE DATE(S)	REMARKS
107	Abyssinia	05/05/1942	
		01/03/1945	
		10/01/1948	
		19/11/1948	
		28/01/1949	
		25/03/1949	
		27/05/1949	
		14/10/1949	
124	Austria	27/11/1962	UN Ops in Congo
111	Belgium		Recommendations from 21 Army 1945
112	Belgium	06/04/1943	
		08/11/1945	
		15/08/1946	

		17/10/1946	
		16/01/1947	
		23/05/1947	
		18/07/1947	
		25/09/1947	
		14/11/1947	
		14/03/1948	
		17/09/1948	
		19/11/1948	
112	Belgium	28/01/1949	
		25/03/1949	
		29/07/1949	
		14/10/1949	
113	Belgium	10/03/1950	
		15/02/1952	
		29/08/1952	
		15/09/1953	
		26/02/1954	
		11/01/1957	
142	Belgium		For Ops in Korea
124	Belgium	30/11/1962	UN Ops in Congo
145	China	29/12/1942	
		02/03/1943	
		30/04/1943	
		02/11/1943	
		28/03/1944	
		08/11/1945	
		23/05/1947	
		15/05/1948	
		27/05/1949	
143	Czechoslovakia	10/07/1942	
		23/07/1943	
		02/06/1944	
		24/05/1945	
		02/08/1945	
		30/05/1946	
		15/08/1946	
		17/10/1946	
		16/01/1947	
		20/03/1947	

		23/05/1947	
		14/11/1947	
		16/01/1948	
		14/05/1948	
		23/07/1948	
		27/05/1949	
108	Denmark	02/08/1945	
		17/10/1946	
		20/03/1947	
		14/11/1947	
		16/01/1948	
		14/05/1948	
		23/07/1948	
		14/10/1949	
		10/03/1950	
		10/07/1951	
185	France		Various Awards for the
			period 10/5/1940–17/3/1958
		20/10/1944	21 Army Group
124	France	15/04/1958	For Suez
110	Greece	09/05/1941	
		28/10/1941	
		10/04/1942	
		05/05/1942	
		18/08/1942	
		29/12/1942	
		16/02/1943	
		24/09/1943	
		20/06/1944	
		15/03/1945	
		02/08/1945	
		15/08/1946	
		17/10/1946	
		20/03/1947	
		23/05/1947	
		18/07/1947	
		14/11/1947	
		16/01/1948	
		14/05/1948	
		23/07/1948	
		19/11/1948	

		28/01/1949
		25/03/1949
		27/05/1949
		29/07/1949
		14/10/1949
		10/03/1950
		10/07/1950
		15/02/1952
		12/09/1952
		05/12/1952
		24/05/1953
	Iran	10/03/1944
107	Iraq	
145	Jordan	25/09/1947
		18/10/1949
		28/02/1950
		20/06/1952
		10/11/1953
		09/11/1954
		10/01/1956
		28/01/1958
107	Luxembourg	25/07/1944
		02/08/1945
		15/08/1946
		17/10/1946
		23/05/1947
		27/05/1949
		15/09/1953
144	Netherlands	26/06/1942
		15/01/1943
		15/02/1944
		28/07/1944
		08/11/1945
		21/02/1946
		15/08/1946
		17/10/1946
		16/01/1947
		20/03/1947
		23/05/1947
		18/07/1947

		14/11/1947	
		16/01/1948	
		14/05/1948	
		28/01/1949	
		25/03/1949	
		10/07/1951	
		15/02/1952	
		10/06/1952	
		01/07/1952	
		14/11/1952	
125	Netherlands	29/03/1955	
		02/09/1955	
109	Norway	04/08/1942	
		11/08/1942	
		19/03/1943	
		17/08/1943	
		26/11/1943	
		29/08/1944	
		24/05/1945	
		21/06/1945	
		17/10/1946	
		20/03/1947	
		23/05/1947	
		19/03/1948	
		17/09/1948	
		19/11/1948	
		25/03/1949	
		27/05/1949	
		10/03/1950	
		10/07/1951	
		26/02/1954	

92	Oman	Sultan's Accession Medal
		As Sumwood Medal 1975
		Peace Medal: 10th Anniversary Medal
172	Oman	
182	Oman	

124	Papal	25/08/1964	UN Ops in Congo
143	Poland	22/07/1941	
		19/08/1941	
		23/09/1941	

		01/05/1942
		15/05/1942
		13/08/1942
		08/10/1943
		14/12/1943
		25/02/1944
		20/06/1944
		31/10/1944
		21/11/1944
		07/12/1944
		22/02/1945
		24/05/1945
		31/05/1945
		21/06/1945
		02/08/1945
145	Portugal	12/04/1949
108	Tunis	
119	USA	

Many of the following recommendations include troops from Australia (AUS), Canada (CAN) and New Zealand (NZ).

147	USA	28/07/1942
		23/02/1943
		23/07/1943
		10/08/1943
		13/08/1943
		20/08/1943
		21/09/1943
		22/10/1943
		15/02/1944
		10/03/1944
		14/04/1944
		21/04/1944
		26/05/1944
		20/06/1944
		28/07/1944
		14/09/1944
		19/09/1944
		07/11/1944
		14/11/1944
		21/11/1944

		07/12/1944	
		28/12/1944	
		04/01/1945	
		25/01/1945	
		15/02/1945	
		15/03/1945	
		05/04/1945	
		12/04/1945	
		24/05/1945	
		21/06/1945	
		02/08/1945	
		08/11/1945	
		24/01/1946	
		04/04/1946	
		30/05/1946	
		15/08/1946	
		17/10/1946	
		16/01/1947	
		20/03/1947	
148	USA	23/05/1947	
		18/07/1947	
		25/09/1947	
		14/11/1947	
		16/01/1948	
		14/05/1948	
		23/07/1948	
149	USA		WW2 Awards to AUS, CAN and NZ
149	USA	27/05/1949	
		29/07/1949	
		14/10/1949	
		10/03/1950	
		21/07/1950	
119	USA	16/02/1951	
		08/06/1951	
149	USA	10/07/1951	
125	USA	12/10/1951	
119	USA	18/12/1951	
		05/02/1952	
149	USA	15/02/1952	
142	USA	Korea Ops	
107	USSR	16/01/1947	

145	Yugoslavia	23/06/1944
		02/11/1944
		16/01/1947

WO 373/125, 183 and 184 contain various foreign awards to British soldiers, but they were given restricted permission to accept them.

WO 373
British to Foreign
Not all of the following dates are gazette dates. In most cases, the dates relate to the correspondence or the date the awards were submitted for approval. I have attempted to list them in chronological order, and this may mean that the WO 373 reference is repeated more than once.

PIECE NO.	COUNTRY	DATE(S)	REMARKS
187	Belgium	Various dates 1942–6	
153	Belgium	10/10/1944	
		30/11/1944	
		19/12/1944	
		30/12/1944	
		04/01/1945	
		29/01/1945	
		03/02/1945	
		25/06/1945	
		16/07/1945	
		18/12/1945	
		05/02/1946	
		11/11/1946	
145	China		
143	Czechoslovakia		
187	Czechoslovakia		
108	Denmark		
145	Egypt		
154	France	31/03/1943	
		01/07/1943	
		12/08/1943	
		17/10/1943	
		13/11/1943	
154	France	18/09/1945	French troops in North

		West Europe	
		21/09/1945	1944–5
153	France	17/10/1945	
154	France	27/10/1945	
153	France	29/11/1945	
154	France	18/12/1945	
154	France	03/01/1946	
155	France	17/05/1946	
153	France	13/06/1946	
155	France	31/07/1946	
153	France	13/08/1946	
154	France	15/01/1947	
		31/06/1947	
153	France	06/08/1947	
155	France	10/12/1947	
		12/07/1948	
111	Greece		
187	Greece		
107	Iraq		
187	Iraq		
107	Luxembourg		
187	Luxembourg		
145	Nepal		Various dates in 1945
187	Nepal		
155	Netherlands	10/10/1944	
		04/01/1945	
		21/01/1945	
		03/02/1945	
		07/03/1945	
		29/03/1945	
		16/07/1945	
		31/08/1945	
		03/01/1946	
		05/02/1946	
		05/09/1946	
		25/01/1949	
187	Netherlands		Various dates 1945–9
108	Norway		

187	Norway		
143	Poland		
146	Poland		
187	Poland		
145	Portugal		
187	Sudan		Various dates 1943–50
145	Trans-Jordan		
155	USA		American Field Service
149	USA	Awards approved: 17/06/1943–13/03/1945	
149	USA	Awards approved: 07/04/1945–25/06/1945	
150	USA	Awards approved: 10/07/1945–27/02/1946	
151	USA	Awards approved: 10/07/1945–27/02/1946	
152	USA	Awards approved: 16/05/1946–24/06/1949	
152	USA		Undated Awards
187	USA		Non-combat Gallantry
184	Various	Various dates 1941–53	For Special Service
142	Various	1950–3	For Korea
145	Yugoslavia		

19.8 THE TREASURY

The granting of orders, decoration and medals carries with it the cost of both manufacture and administration. The Treasury was responsible for a number of aspects regarding British awards to foreigners.

T 303 contains 9 files about the regulations on the acceptance and wearing of foreign decorations by British Military personnel. Included in the series is information about the temporary changes made concerning foreign awards during the Second World War.

T 303

1	General	1939–51
2	Belgium	1941–54
3	France	

	(including some civilians)	1939–54
4	Greece	1941–9
5	Netherlands	1941–6
6	Poland	1940–6
7	USA	1942–54
8	Soviet Union	1941–5
9	Yugoslavia	1942–54

T 313 is concerned with policy decisions regarding the bestowal of British orders, decorations and medals to foreigners during the Second World War. The series is arranged over 12 files and covers Allied military and civilian personnel and a number of specified Allied nations.

T 313

1	Allied Military personnel	1939–42
2	Allied Military personnel	1942–4
3	Allied Military personnel	1944–5
4	Allied Military personnel	1945–50
5	Allied Civilian personnel	1939–64
6	Belgium	1941–9
7	France	1939–49
8	Italy	1944–84
9	Poland	1941–5
10	USA	1941–5
11	USA	1944–6
12	Soviet Union	1941–5

The records series T 339 is concerned with the bestowal of the King's Medal for Service in the Cause of Freedom (KMS) to foreigners for their services towards the Allied cause. Many of the awards were for charitable and fund raising acts on behalf of British civilians.

The series is full of recommendations for the award of the KMS.

T 339

1	Arabia (Cyrenaica)	1946
2	Argentina	1945–6
3	Armenia	1946
4	Austria	1946
5	Belgium	1945–6
6	Brazil	1945–6
7	Cuba	1946

8	Czechoslovakia	1945
9	Denmark	1945–8
10	Egypt	1945–7
11	Estonia	1945–6
12	France	1943–7
13	Greece	1945–9
14	Guatemala	1945–6
15	Honduras	1945
16	Iceland	1945–7
17	Iran	1945–6
18	Iraq	1945–8
19	Lebanon	1945–6
20	Luxembourg	1945–6
21	Netherlands	1945–7
22	Norway	1946
23	Palestine	1945–6
24	Panama	1939–45
25	Poland	1945–6
26	Portugal	1946–51
27	Spain	1945–6
28	Stateless	1945
29	Sudan	1949
30	Sweden	1945–7
31	Switzerland	1945
32	Syria	1939–45
33	Trans-Jordan	1945–6
34	Turkey	1945–6
35	USA: Names A–E	1945
36	USA: Names F–J	1939–45
37	USA: Names K–O	1947
38	USA: Names P–S	1945
39	USA: Names T–Z	1945–7

19.9   OTHER GOVERNMENT DEPARTMENTS

After the Foreign Office and Colonial Office amalgamated to form the Foreign and Commonwealth Office, so the Treaty Department of the Foreign Office gained a new name: the Protocol Department. The records of this new department are in the series FCO 57 and, apart from the occasional recommendation, the series consists mainly of policy files.

It is possible to find honours and awards files in the records of other government departments. Of these, the most significant are the records of the Board of Trade (BT) and the Ministry of Transport (MT), both of which have files concerning awards to foreign sailors. The records in BT 261 contain registers of foreign awards to Britons and vice versa. For further information see CHAPTER 21 on Gallantry (Life Saving) Awards.

Records in MT 9 date back to 1856 and there are numerous files concerning awards. Prior to 1903, the files are dispersed across the series. From 1903, MT 9 is coded and the code for awards is code 6.

19.10 INDIA OFFICE RECORDS (BRITISH LIBRARY)
A small number of files concerning foreign awards to members of the Indian Army can be found in the records of the India Office at the British Library.

L/MIL/7/4037	Russian and Serbian Decorations announced in the *London Gazette* on 15 May 1917	
L/MIL/7/4038	Receipts for above Awards	
L/PS/15/43 file H144	Indian Orders: Awards to Chinese Officials for Services rendered during the war	1919

19.11 ASSORTED OTHER RECORDS
Parliamentary Papers are available at the National Archives on microfiche and amongst them are a number of papers concerning orders, decorations and medals. Of these, the most significant are the lists of those British servicemen who were granted foreign awards for service in the Crimean War. Not only do these lists provide the names of the individuals, they also describe the deed for which the award was granted.

To find Parliamentary Papers at the National Archives, you can use the index available via the OPERA link on the Public Pages on the National Archives in-house terminals. You can then search the index of Parliamentary Papers, using the term 'awards' or 'honours'. The papers themselves are on microfiche in the Microfilm Reading Room.

19.12 CASE STUDIES
Pipe Major Alexander Stewart

Very little is known of Alexander Stewart since his record of service is not available. Although he received the Territorial Force Efficiency Medal for service in the Scottish Horse in 1913, it appears that he did not serve with them in South Africa in the Boer War.

On 23 May 1921, Crown Prince (later Emperor) Hirohito of Japan visited Great Britain. He visited Scotland and stayed with

T.9672/5578/323.D.

The Under Secretary of State for Foreign Affairs presents his compliments to The King's Private Secretary, and is directed by the Secretary of State to inform him that His Majesty has been pleased to grant restricted permission to the under-mentioned members of the Staff at Blair Castle to accept and wear the decorations indicated against their names, conferred upon them by the Emperor of Japan, on the occasion of the visit of the Crown Prince of Japan to the Duke of Atholl:-

Sergeant-Major MacArthur) 7th Class of the Order of
Pipe-Major Alexander Stewart) the Rising Sun.

Pipe Corporal Robert Irvine) 8th Class of the Order of
Private Sinclair   ) the Rising Sun.

It is accordingly requested that the customary formal letters acquainting the recipients of these decorations of the grant of such restricted permission may be prepared and forwarded to this Office for transmission to them, and that this Memorandum may be marked below as having been acted on and returned to the Treaty Department, Foreign Office, for record

Foreign Office, S.W.1.
August 22nd, 1921.

Date of Letter sent *Aug. 25. 1921*

Initial of Private Secretary .. *Gw* ...

FIG 20. *A typical Foreign Office letter concerning a foreign award being bestowed upon a British national, and the protocols followed* [FO 372/1814]

the Duke of Atholl at Blair Castle. During his visit, the Crown Prince presented a small number of the Duke's staff with various grades of the Order of the Rising Sun, and Pipe Major Stewart was one of them.

The Foreign Office letter listing Alexander Stewart's award is shown in FIGURE 20 and his two medals in PLATE 20.

Bernard Francis Hunt

Bernard Francis Hunt joined the British Army on 11 August 1914, aged 18 years and 5 months. Serving with 21 London Regiment, he went to France on 16 March 1915, thus qualifying for a 1914/15 Star, British War Medal and Victory Medal.

According to his record of service, Hunt was wounded twice, once by shrapnel on 18 March 1916 and then by a gun shot wound to the chest on 23 May 1916. He was invalided back to the UK on 21 June 1916 and invalided out of the army on 16 October 1917.

By August 1919 Bernard Hunt was working for a company called Gysleman and Stemp in the Dutch East Indies. Although

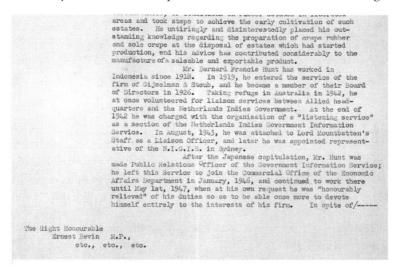

FIG 21. A letter from the Dutch government detailing why Bernard Hunt was granted the Order of Orange Nassau [FO 372/6296]

very little is known of his time in the Dutch East Indies, Hunt initially left the area when the Japanese invaded it in 1941 and returned in 1942 to set up a wireless service. It was for this that the Dutch government awarded him the Order of Orange Nassau, announced in the *London Gazette* on 23 September 1949.

The official Foreign Office correspondence concerning Hunt's award, and his medals are illustrated in FIGURE 21 and PLATE 23 respectively.

20   Military Awards Post-1945

Since the end of the Second World War the British Armed Forces have been involved in many military operations, and are indeed still heavily involved today.

20.1   THE *LONDON GAZETTE*

The *London Gazette* is still the first place to start when researching a post- Second World War award. Capturing the information regarding name, rank, number, service award, operational theatre and gazette date should ensure that any research is started from the best position. For further information on the *London Gazette* see CHAPTER 7.

20.2   THE RECORDS

The majority of records series containing recommendations for honours and awards for the three armed services have already been discussed in previous chapters. The two biggest problems about post-1945 honours records relate to survivability and disclosure. Very few post-1945 honours files for the RAF survive and those that do are in the series AIR 2. They are easily located by keyword searching on the Catalogue.

Records of Admiralty recommendations are mostly in the series ADM 1 and ADM 116, but they do not all survive. Due to administrative changes made to the Royal Navy, there are a number of

Plate 21 (*previous page, left*)
An Army Long Service and Good
Conduct Medal awarded during
the reign of Queen Victoria

Plate 22 (*previous page, right*)
The Rocket Apparatus Volunteer
Long Service Medal awarded to
Richard Richards in 1911

Plate 23 (*facing page, left
to right*) The medals of
B.F. Hunt: 1914/15 Star, British
War Medal, Victory Medal and
Dutch Order of Orange Nassau

Plate 24 (*below*) The Special
Constabulary Medal, its box
and envelope as received by
George Spencer

Plate 25 (*facing page*) Consul A. J. Hill's medals, the British War Medal for his service in the RNR and the 1937 Coronation Medal

Plate 26 (*right*) The author's South Atlantic Medal for service in the Falklands in 1982

Plate 27 (*above top*)
Admiralty Digest and Index
1857   ADM 12/627

Plate 28 (*above*) Admiralty
Correspondence concerning
Henry Cooper's VC
ADM 1/5685

Plate 29 (*facing page*)
Admiralty Correspondence
concerning Henry Cooper's
VC   ADM 1/5388

Plate 30 (*right*) Henry
Cooper VC

Plate 31 (*following page, left to right*) The medals of Air
Marshal Sir Bertine Sutton
KBE, CB RAF comprising DSO,
MC, 1914/15 Star, British War
Medal, Victory Medal with
MiD oakleaf, IGS 1908–35
with clasp MOHMAND 1933
and MiD oakleaf, Defence
Medal 1939–45, War Medal
1939–45, 1935 Jubilee Medal,
1937 Coronation Medal and
Belgian Croix de Guerre

War Office

22nd June 1857

Victoria Cross.

Crimea

War Office
9th April
1857
received

Admiralty
13. Feb 1857

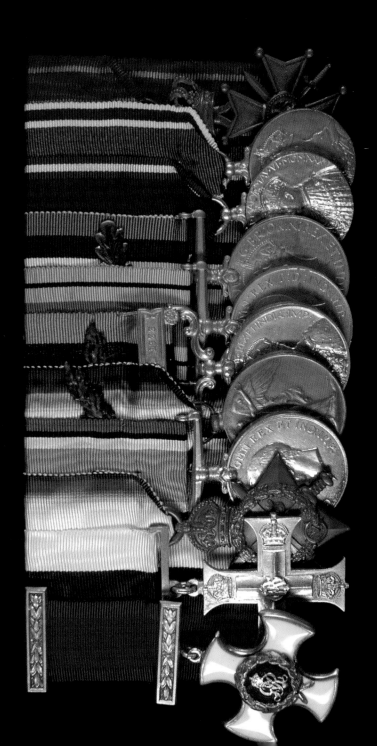

Admiralty recommendations for awards in the series DEFE 49, but some are still closed.

All surviving recommendations for the Army are in WO 373 and these are listed in CHAPTER 11 on Awards by Operational Theatre. They include the recommendations from post-war Palestine to awards for the Falklands in 1982 in WO 373/188, to the Lebanon in 1984 also in WO 373/188, and awards for non-combat gallantry from 1939 to 1990 in WO 373/183. Due to the sensitive nature of the operational theatre, recommendations for awards for Northern Ireland are still retained by the Ministry of Defence.

The Series T 351 contains recommendation for civil gallantry awards to military personnel. Most of the recommendations concern the George Cross, George Medal and British Empire Medal.

For those researching men and women who had a Mention in Despatches (MiD), it is worth looking at *Above and Beyond* by Alexander N. Palmer (1993).

All future transfers of military honours and awards files will be into the series DEFE 74.

21 Gallantry (Life Saving) Awards

21.1 INTRODUCTION

This chapter is concerned with awards of the Royal Humane Society, Royal National Lifeboat Institution and other non-government bodies.

There are a number of files held by the National Archives and in the Oriental and India Office Collections (OIOC) at the British Library concerning the award of medals and lesser awards of the Royal Humane Society (RHS) and the Royal National Lifeboat Institution (RNLI). The majority of the files fall into two distinct types: those with details concerning deeds for which an individual was recommended for an RHS award, and those giving just the names of recipients of such awards.

Researchers looking for information about RNLI awards can do no better than to consult *Lifeboat Gallantry* by Barry Cox (Spink, 1998).

21.2 RECORDS HELD AT THE NATIONAL ARCHIVES

ADM 171/65 and ADM 171/66 contain the names only of those officers and men of the Royal Navy and Royal Marines who received RHS and RNLI awards. These lists are not complete and only cover the periods 1833–1918 and 1917–48 respectively.

There are a large number of files in the ADM 1 series that contain correspondence between the Admiralty and the Royal Humane Society. Many of these files can be identified by using the Admiralty Index and Digest of Correspondence in the records series ADM 12 (see CHAPTER 25 on Research Techniques). However, it is possible to search the catalogue to identify some of the files. Some are listed below and are arranged in chronological order

1898	ADM 1/7390	
1904	ADM 1/7778	
1906	ADM 1/7906	
1907	ADM 1/7965	January–June
1907	ADM 1/7966	June–December
1908	ADM 1/8024	

Individual case files in ADM 1, rather than correspondence between the Admiralty and the Royal Humane Society, are given below.

ADM 1/10830 Altmark incident. RHS Bronze Medal and Testimonial given to members of the Crew of HMS *Cossack*. 1940

ADM 1/12347 RHS Bronze Medal to Surgeon Lieutenant J.D. Kidd, RNVR. 1942

ADM 1/29413 RHS Bronze Medal to Lieutenant F.E. Walton, RNVR. 1944

ADM 1/29613 RHS Testimonial to Lieutenant D. Lewis, RCNVR. 1944

ADM 1/30319 RHS Testimonial to Able Seaman R.F. Barton, US Army Transport Corps. 1944–5

ADM 1/26237 RHS Award to Ordinary Seaman T.A. Rossiter. 1955

ADM 1/26407 RHS Awards to Marines R. Hindmarsh and S. Oliver. 1955

ADM 1/28047 RHS Silver Medal to Marine S. Crystal. 1962

AIR 2/2838, AIR 2/6101 and AIR 2/16181 all contain policy information about the granting of RHS awards to RAF personnel. The files cover the periods 1918–20, 1940–8 and 1962–7 respectively.

The series BT 261 and BT 238 both concern awards to merchant seamen and they are listed and discussed in CHAPTER 10 on Civilian Awards.

The series CUST 49 also contains some recommendations for awards.

Awards to members of the army for life saving were considered as non-combat gallantry. Recommendations for non-combat gallantry are in a specific section in WO 373.

The armed services were not the sole recipients of awards from the Royal Humane Society. Many civilians in our overseas colonies were also awarded for their bravery. Files from the Colonial Office and Dominion Office are listed below. Some of the files mention one or two individuals, so where possible the names are given. However, some files contain the names of many individuals and it has not been possible to list them all.

CO 717/76/11 RHS Bronze Medals to Police Constables Mall Singh and Dost Mohamed. Federated Malay States. 1930–1
DO 35/748/12 RHS Silver Medal to Mr Samuel Fowlow. 1939–41
DO 35/35/846/2 Includes details relating to RHS Bronze Medals awarded to Mafuta, Kunda and George. 1939
DO 119/59 RHS Bronze Medal to Mr D.C. de Waal of the Cape Parliament. 1891

The Treaty Department of the Foreign Office was responsible for handling correspondence from embassies and consulates overseas and its records can be found in FO 83 and FO 372. Only one obvious file contains information about an RHS award and that is given below. There will undoubtedly be others (see CHAPTER 25 on Research Techniques).

FO 372/6423 Award of RHS Bronze Medal to Lance Corporal Hamdoun, Sudan Defence Force. 1948

Those employed either on or near the sea became recipients of awards given by the Royal Humane Society. Records of the Board of Trade, Customs and the Ministry of Transport all contain recommendations for awards, and correspondence between the respective department and the Royal Humane Society. Known files are given below.

BT 238/97 RHS: Recommendations for Awards with details of action and award presentation. 1963–84
BT 238/213 RHS Bronze Medal to Junior Engineer A.J. Pretorious. 1967
BT 238/214 RHS Stanhope Gold Medal to Junior Engineer J.M. Easton. 1966–8
CUST 49/830 RHS Medal Award to Mr Alexander Carson. 1925
CUST 49/1179 RHS Testimonial to Mr Herbert Harding Foster. 1930
CUST 49/2068 RHS Testimonial to Mr E.E. Anderson. 1936
CUST 49/2237 RHS Testimonial to Mr Eric L.G. Goddard. 1937
CUST 49/2367 RHS Testimonial to Mr John Sims Mitchell. 1938
CUST 49/2461 RHS Testimonial to Mr John G. Cowie. 1939
CUST 49/2611 RHS Testimonial to Mr Stanley J. Dorey. 1942

The following 3 reports all contain the names of those granted medals in the reporting year, together with the deeds that resulted in their awards. The reports also give a list of names of those who had received awards in the preceding years.

MT 9/353 The Humane Society of the Commonwealth of Massachusetts, Report, 1889
MT 9/409 The Humane Society of the Commonwealth of Massachusetts, Report, 1891
MT 9/445 The Humane Society of the Commonwealth of Massachusetts, Report, 1892
MT 9/1969 RHS Testimonial to C. J. de Groot. 1930–1
MT 9/2870 RHS Bronze Medal to 2nd Officer R.H. Robertson. 1938

21.3 RECORDS IN THE ORIENTAL AND INDIA OFFICE COLLECTION

In the Oriental and India Office Collections there are a large number of files full of recommendations for awards in the L/PJ/6 series. Within each specific piece of L/PJ/6 file, there are numbered files containing the information. It is not necessary to use the file part of the reference when ordering the document of the ordering computer.

The following is a list of pieces, giving the names where known and the date. All pieces should be prefixed L/PJ/6. For convenience only, the piece number and file (f) number are given. The first reference would thus be L/PJ/6/4.

4, f 168   Presentation of the Stanhope Gold Medal of the RHS accompanied by a note of thanks to Baubu Kristo Chunder Chuckerbutty. 3 February 1880

23, f 1389   Award of an honorary silver RHS Medal to Native Police Constable Nizam Din. 2 October 1880

30, f 70   RHS Medal for Constable Futteh Shere, Shakpur District. 10 January 1881

53, f 1563   Native Head Constable Mahomed Ghouse, Salem District. 31 August 1881

55, f 1705   As above. 5 November 1881

57, f 1823   Presentation of RHS Bronze Medal to Mahomed Ghouse. 25 November 1881

78, f 1174   Award of RHS Medal to Native Constable Ramaswami, North Arcot District. 11 July 1882

93, f 422   RHS Bronze Medal to a Boatman named Nur. 6 March 1883

116, f 181   Gallant Conduct of Native Constable Parsatharathi. 8 January 1884

117, f 233   Gallant Conduct of Garikana Masenu. 15 January 1884

119, f 381   Awards of the RHS to Natives of India for Gallant Conduct in saving life. 26 February and 1 March 1884

146, f 233   RHS Silver Medal to Saral Din. 5 February 1885

149, f 492   RHS Bronze Medals sent to India for Mr McLeod and Sepoy Dhan Singh. 16 March 1885

153, f 784   RHS Bronze Medal to Constable Ram Sarap, Pellundar District Police. 20 April 1885

164, f 2106   RHS Medal and Certificate to Mr A.H. Harrington. 10 November 1885

168, f 139   RHS Medal and Certificate to Pandit Mansa Ram. 27 January 1886

170, f 287   Loss of RHS Medal and Certificate awarded to Mr A.H. Harrington. 2 February 1885

184, f 1454   Papers sent to RHS concerning Native Constable Jodh Ram, Rawalpindi Police. 3 September 1886

185, f 1536   Application for Grant to Mr W.F. Sinclair and Mr T. Foster for rescuing the brigantine *Flora*. 14 September 1886

186, f 1677   Mr W.F. Sinclair and Mr T. Foster. Rescue not within the conditions prescribed by the RHS. 20 October 1886

187, f 1734   RHS Medal and Certificate for Native Constable Jodh Ram. 28 October 1886

198, f 514   RHS Medal for Constable Ram Singh, Kangra Police. 22 February 1887

202, f 753   RHS Testimonial to Ram Singh, Kangra Police. 30 April 1887
206, f 1165   Application on behalf of Constable Karim Bakhsh, Lahore Police. 9 June 1887
208, f 1368   RHS Medal awarded to Constable Karam Bay, Lahore Police. 2 August 1887
211, f 1624   Application for recognition by the RHS of the conduct of pilot Simon Baroni. 16 August 1887
212, f 1705   Application from Burma for recognition by the RHS. 21 September 1887
215, f 2011   RHS Medal awarded to Lilladhur Dharsee. 4 November 1887
216, f 2158   Application on behalf of Constable Piran Ditta, Lahore District Police. 10 November 1887
218, f 60   RHS Medal for Constable Piran Ditta, Lahore District Police. 9 January 1888
229, f 1065   RHS Medal and Testimonial for Mr John Robinson, Assistant Engineer BNW Railway. 23 July 1888
240, f 1792   Papers relating to the saving of life for transmission to the RHS. 5 November 1888
242, f 12   RHS Medal and Certificate to Pogono Kirasami. 2 January 1889
256, f 1122   RHS Medal and Certificate to Ishar Das. 5 July 1889
259, f 1339   RHS Medal and Certificate to Mr John Fox, Deputy Superintendent, Alipore Jail. 6 August 1889
270, f 261   Application for the award of an RHS Medal. 8 January 1889
271, f 315   Re-application for an RHS Medal. 24 February 1889
273, f 592   RHS Medal and Certificate for a Native of India. 1 April 1889
280, f 1101   Application from Bombay recommending Frasis Saloo of Savadi. 4 June 1890
280, f 1134   RHS acknowledges receipt of Government of Bombay's application. 1 July 1890
283, f 1319   RHS Medal and Certificate for Frasis Saloo. 1 August 1890
285, f 1585   RHS Medal awarded to Rura, Traffic Jamadar on the Rajputana Malwa Railway. 11 September 1890
288, f 1808   Application on behalf of Colonel J.W.S. Butler. 13 September 1890
290, f 2035   RHS Bronze Medals and Certificates awarded to Mr T.C. Anderson and two native Indians. 27 November 1890
301, f 805   Application for the RHS Medal for Foot Constable Nur Muhammad, Shahpur District. 22 April 1891
301, f 914   RHS Medal and Certificate awarded to Nur Mihammad. 2 June 1891
310, f 2030   Recommendation of Police Constable Kalidas Amarsing of Surat for the RHS Medal. 27 November 1891

311, f 2073 Papers relating to Mr I.C.A. Browne, Telegraph Department. 30 November 1891

312, f 10 Application for Award to Constable Bahadur Khan, Rawalpindi District. 16 December 1891

314, f 239 RHS Bronze Medal awarded to Police Constable Kalidas Amarsing of Surat. 11 February 1892

316, f 401 RHS Awards to E.C.A. Browne and Constable Bahadur Khan. 4 March 1892

316, f 463 Report of death of Police Constable Kalidas Amarsing of Surat. 23 February 1892

317, f 499 Award of RHS Medal to Constable Fatteh Khan, Rawalpindi District. 2 March 1892

320, f 728 RHS Medal and Certificate awarded to Police Constable Fattah Khan. 4 May 1892

321, f 849 Shaik Isib walad Shaik Abdulla recommended for an RHS Bronze Medal or Certificate. 5 May 1892

322, f 893 As above. 31 May 1892

323, f 1085 RHS Award to Shaik Isib walad Shaik Abdulla. 7 July 1892

326, f 1299 Application from Burma for an Award to Mr J. Bevan, Inspector of Police. 19 July 1892

331, f 1868 Application for an RHS Award to Maulvi Abdul Aziz. 16 October 1892

334, f 2056 As above. 16 December 1892

334, f 2073 Recommendation for Police Constable Kalu, Jhelum District. 30 November 1892

337, f 152 RHS Medal and Certificate awarded to Police Constable Kalu, Jhelum District. 26 January 1893

338, f 210 Application for an Award to Police Constable Rajwali, Peshawar District. 18 January 1893

340, f 355 RHS Medals and Certificates. 24 February 1893

347, f 931 Application for RHS Medals for four men of the 39th Garhwal Rifles. 19 April 1893

351, f 1272 RHS Bronze Medal to Ridsat Ali of Asadpur. 29 June 1893

352, f 1333 Recommendation for Police Constable Nand Singh, Rawalpindi District. 20 June 1893

353, f 1450 RHS Bronze Medal to Police Constable Nand Singh, Rawalpindi District. 28 July 1893

356, f 1849 Recommendation for Lt C.P.G. Griffin, 1st Bengal Cavalry. 5 September 1893

360, f 2140 Recommendation for Mr H.E. Newton. 11 October 1893

361, f 2189 Recommendation for Colour Sergeant J. Kellie. 18 October 1893

362, f 2218 RHS Silver Medal awarded to Lt C.P.G Griffin, 1st Bengal

Cavalry. 9 November 1893

363, f 2331 RHS Bronze Medals awarded to Mr H G Newton and Colour Sergeant J. Kellie. 23 November 1893

365, f 13 RHS: Award of Medal to Foot Constable Imam Bakhsh, Muzaffargarh District Police. 13 December 1893

365, f 14 Application for an Award to Foot Constable Nanak of Lahore District Police. 13 December 1893

366, f 126 Application for an Award to Pte R. Williamson. 3 January 1894

366, f 177 RHS Testimonials for two Indian Police Constables. 2 February 1894

368, f 322 Applications for RHS Medals. 24 January 1894

368, f 341 RHS Testimonial for Pte Williamson, 1st East Kent Regiment. 26 February 1894

368, f 357 RHS: Recognition of the Conduct of Lascar Rustum Khan. 9 February 1894

370, f 567 RHS: Awards of Medals and Certificates to Natives of India. 2 April 1894

376, f 1127 The Royal Humane Society's Award. 27 June 1894

379, f 1438 Recognition by the RHS of the Conduct of Lt F.L. Oman and Pte Hakabir Rae. 21 July 1894

383, f 1854 RHS Bronze Medals to Lt F.L. Oman and Pte Hakabir Rae. 23 October 1894

388, f 2217 RHS: Grant of Medal to Jot Ram. 12 December 1894

391, f 210 RHS: Honorary Testimonial for Jot Ram. 6 February 1895

392, f 389 Application for an RHS Award to a Warder for saving a prisoner from drowning. 20 February 1895

393, f 415 Application for an RHS Bronze Medal to Pte Parker and a Certificate to Pte Hodson. 19 February 1895

393, f 497 Award of the RHS Bronze Medal to a Warder for saving a prisoner from drowning. 27 March 1895

396, f 703 RHS Testimonials awarded to Ptes Parker and Hodson. 2 May 1895

398, f 911 Application for Recognition by the RHS of the Conduct of Mr Duncan McMurchie. 10 May 1895

399, f 1069 RHS Bronze Medal to Mr Duncan McMurchie. 28 June 1895

400, f 1194 Application for award of RHS's Medal. 2 July 1895

402, f 1340 Application for an RHS Award to Galab of Khanpur. 23 July 1895

403, f 1435 RHS Awards. 26 August 1895

406, f 1729 Application for an RHS Award to Mr J.P. Algie, Assistant Deputy Superintendent of Police. Burma. 25 September 1895

407, f 1891 RHS Testimonial to Mr Dexter, 1st Class Engine Driver, RIMS

Comet. 4 November 1895

408, f 1975 RHS Bronze Medal awarded to M. R. Ry N. S. Tirumalai Aiyangar and M. R. Ry C. Subramania Aiyar. 24 October 1895

409, f 2087 RHS Bronze Medal awarded to Mr J.P. Algie, Deputy Assistant Superintendent of Police, Burma. 30 November 1895

412, f 13 RHS medal awarded to Mr T. Aiyangar and Subramamia Aiyar, native of Madras. 1 January 1896

418, f 643 Gallant conduct of Lascar Shaik Ebrahim to be brought to the notice of the RHS. 25 March 1896

422, f 976 RHS Bronze Medal awarded to Lascar Shaik Ebrahim, RIMS Lawrence. 27 May 1896

428, f 1542 Case of a Sepoy of the Lashio Military Police. 11 August 1896

432, f 1953 RHS Bronze Medal awarded to Sepoy Faiz Ali Khan, Lashio Military Police. 30 October 1896

433, f 2016 RHS recognition asked for the conduct of Mutta (Rawalpindi) and Maung Shwe Geve (Burma). 21 October 1896

434, f 2145 RHS Awards to Mutta (Rawalpindi) and Maung Shwe Geve (Burma). 28 November 1896

437, f 99 RHS Awards to Gajebdra Thapa and Llbi Gurung. 14 January 1897

449, f 1132 RHS Medals in respect of the wreck of the *Warren Hastings*. 4 June 1897

452, f 1413 Application for Recognition by the RHS. 29 June–12 July 1897

453, f 1561 Case of Gangji Prema. 3 August 1897

454, f 1641 Case of Lt G.H. Baldock. 28 July 1897

455, f 1770 Case of Namdar Jamiyat. 13 August 1897

456, f 1835 RHS Bronze Medals to Captain G H.H. Couchman, Somerset Light Infantry and Syce Raju. 9 September 1897

458, f 2021 Case of Pte William Starling. 23 September 1897

462, f 2292 RHS Medals. 15 November 1897

471, f 246 Papers regarding Bhil, Ganji Prema. 22 January 1898

472, f 301 Application for an Award to Gunner Indar Singh, No 3 (Peshawar) Mountain Battery. 3 February 1898

475, f 696 RHS Awards. 5 April 1898

481, f 1071 Case of Mr H.C. Boswell. 7 May 1898

483, f 1259 RHS medal for Mr H.C. Boswell, Abkari Inspector in Bombay. 21 June 1898

487, f 1660 Recommendations for Corporal G.S. Hill and Lance Corporal A.A. Murray. 4 August 1898

490, f 1929 Application for an Award to Gunner Havildar Ganda Singh. 15 September 1898

490, f 1933 Papers on the Case of Abdul Kadar Ali Khan. 17 September 1898

494, f 2205 RHS Awards. 12 November 1898

496, f 2288 RHS Certificate awarded to Major Grantham. 19 November 1898

497, f 2393 RHS Awards. 7 December 1898

499, f 16 Two Cases for the RHS. 15 December 1898

501, f 213 RHS Awards. 30 January 1899

510, f 940 Case of Mr C.J. Deefholts. 27 April 1899

512, f 1119 Application for an Award to Palit Sasibhusan. 22 May 1899

513, f 1203 RHS Bronze Medal to Mr C.F. Deefholts. 23 June 1899

516, f 1467 Award of the RHS to Sasibhushan Palit. 4 August 1899

517, f 1593 Case of Military Policeman Phula Singh. 3 August 1899

518, f 1666 RHS Award to Baraji Jasaji. 31 August 1899

522, f 2024 RHS Bronze Medal to Military Policeman Phula Singh, Rangoon. 25 October 1899

522, f 2029 Request for a replacement RHS medal. 12 October 1899

523, f 2163 Application for an RHS Award to Driver Stephen O'Brien, RHA. 26 October 1899

525, f 221 Duplicate RHS medal for Punjab Police Sergeant. 22 November 1899

527, f 2414 RHS Award to Driver Stephen O'Brien, RHA. 20 December 1899

543, f 1167 Application for an Award to Private Chinasami, 26th Madras Infantry. 7 June 1900

544, f 1350 RHS Medal to Private Chinasami, 26th Madras Infantry. 25 July 1900

554, f 2114 RHS Medal awarded to a Sepoy of the 24th Punjab Infantry. 13 November 1900

556, f 2257 RHS Bronze Medal to Captain G.H.G. Mockler. 7 December 1900

557, f 2331 Case of Mr G.W. MacMillan. 5 December 1900

593, f 269 RHS Bronze Medal to Kashar Bhikaji. 8 February 1901

593, f 278 Application for an Award to Police Constable Bostan. 23 January 1902

595, f 450 RHS Medals and Certificates. 5 March 1902

595, f 471 Case of Sepoy Ahmed Khan. 20 February 1902

597, f 619 Case of Kaikharu Rastamji Datal. 15 March 1902

597, f 637 RHS Bronze Medal to Sepoy Ahmed Khan. 3 April 1902

599, f 881 RHS Medal to Mr K. R. Dalal. 6 May 1902

601, f 991 Conduct of Privates Murray, Strickland and Emery. 8 May 1902

604, f 1310 RHS Awards. 1 July 1902

604, f 1351 Application for an Award to Pte J. Edney. 19 June 1902

606, f 1454 Duplicate Medals awarded to Colonel H.N. McRae. 26 July 1902

606, f 1497 Case of Native Soldier Tikaram Thopa. 10 July 1902

613, f 1966 Recommendation for Jemandar Abdul Karim Khan. 28 Aug. 1902

616, f 2307 Awards of the RHS. 18 October 1902

618, f 2435 Award to Jemandar Abdul Karim Khan. 30 October 1902

622, f 2913 Award of RHS Testimonial to Captain A.P. Browne. 30 Dec. 1902

628, f 426 Three Cases recommended by the Government of India. 12 February 1903

630, f 627 Recommendation for Captain V.E.H Lindsay. 12 March 1903

631, f 691 Awards of the RHS. 4 April 1903

634, f 919 RHS medal to Captain Lindsay, Indian Medical Service. 8 May 1903

640, f 1348 Recommendation for Pte Denis Butler, 4th (Queen's Own) Hussars. 18 June 1903

643, f 1703 Recommendation for Maung Shwe Lin, Clerk in the office of the Assistant Political Office, Karenni. 30 July 1903

644, f 1789 RHS Award to Pte Dennis Butler, 4th Hussars. 25 August 1903

645, f 1835 Recommendation for three men of the 24th Baluchistan Infantry. 13 August 1903

645, f 1840 Recommendation for Police Constables Rahim Abdullah and Anup Bechar. 15 August 1903

647, f 1971 Recommendation for Ram Sahai, Warder of Damoh District Jail. 27 August 1903

648, f 2102 Recommendation for Burmese Coolie Maung Kyun Bin. 10 September 1903

653, f 2607 RHS Awards to Police Constables Rahim Abdulla and Anup Bechar. 20 November 1903

655, f 2798 RHS Award to Lt W. L.O. Twiss. 9 December 1903

656, f 29 Recommendation for Basawan Ganesh. 19 December 1903

661, f 241 Awards of the RHS. 2 February 1904

661, 275 Recommendation for Lascar Somir Alli, Customs Department. Moulmein. 21 January 1904

670, f 501 RHS Award to Lascar Somir Alli, Customs Department, Moulmein. 1 March 1904

671, f 593 Recommendation for Captain J.R. Nuttall. 25 February 1904

676, f 865 Recommendation for Lt A.D. Connor and Jamadar Shaikh Khadir. 31 March 1904

678, f 992 Recommendation for Native Constable Dad Balaji, Bombay. 2 April 1904

678, f 1078 RHS Award to Captain J.R. Nuttall, 8th Gurkhas. 10 May 1904

680, f 1262 Recommendation for Ghulam Muhammad. 12 May 1904

684, f 1566 RHS Awards. 30 June 1904

690, f 1566 Recommendation for Lance Naik Fatteh Khan. 11 August 1904

692, f 2231 Application for recognition of Constable Bir Singh, Ambala District Police. 25 August 1904

692, f 2315 RHS Awards to Lts W.L.G. Pitcher and H.W.S. Keighley, 39th Central India Horse. 25 September 1904

694, f 2416 Recommendation for Babu Mauji Ram Jandan. 15 September 1904

697, f 2586 RHS asks for further details on the case of Constable Bir Singh. 19 October 1904

697, f 2612 Applications on behalf of Constables Vireshvar Amiram and Tukaram Nana, Bombay Police. 8 October 1904

700, f 2797 Recommendation for Loka Singh and Wali Muhammad. 27 October 1904

700, f 2798 As above. 27 October 1904

701, f 2854 Recommendation for Native Constable Daji Govind. 5 Nov. 1904

702, f 2924 Awards of the RHS. 1 December 1904

705, f 81 RHS Awards. 11 January 1905

707, f 265 Duplicate Medal for Sepoy Sher Khan. 1 February 1905

713, f 719 Recommendation for an RHS Award. 2 March 1905

713, f 720 Information for the RHS on the Case of Constable Bir Singh, Ambala District Police. 2 March 1905

714, f 805 Recommendation for Babu Hari Charan Bhattacharjee. 9 March 1905

716, f 988 Recommendation for an RHS medal. 5 April 1905

720, f 1262 RHS Awards. 2 May 1905

727, f 1954 RHS Bronze Medal for Constable Ladu Sadoji, Bombay. 4 July 1905

731, f 2509 RHS Bronze Medal for Babu Janendra Candra Banerji and Testimonial on Vellum to Lt A.H. Hopwood. 16 August 1905

734, f 2888 RHS Bronze Medal for Rifleman Namdabir Rana, 3rd Gurkhas and Testimonial on Vellum for Bugler Musaddi, 37th Dogras. 18 September 1905

738, f 3492 Application for Native Constable Babaji Raoji, Bombay. 28 October 1905

740, f 3657 Case of Lt Mackworth. 30 November 1905

743, f 91 Submissions for Awards to the RHS. 9 January 1906

744, f 243 Application for Recognition of Constable Shaikh Raj Muhammad. 11 January 1906

748, f 557 Cases for the RHS. 8 February 1906

748, f 558 As above. 8 February 1906

750, f 787 A Case for the RHS. 1 March 1906

759, f 1311 Case of Native Constable Rama Yesu, Bombay. 21 April 1906

760, f 1375–8 Cases for the RHS. 26 April 1906

763, f 1505 RHS Awards. 21 May 1906

763, f 1560 Recommendation for Bombay Constable Ebrahim Alibux. 12 May 1906

766, f 1852 RHS Testimonial for Native Constable Rama Yesu, Bombay. 20 June 1906

768, f 2001 Application for RHS Awards. 14–16 June 1906

769, f 2149 RHS Awards. 4 June 1906

772, f 2409 Application for the RHS. 12 July 1906

772, f 3022 Awards of the RHS. 12 September 1906

778, f 3162 Cases of Corporal J. Goulden and Private W.E. Moulton. 6 September 1906

782, f 3544 Case for the RHS. 6 October 1906

789, f 4131 RHS Awards to Samano Khanderanoo, Corporal J. Goulden and Private W.E. Moulton. 12 December 1906

792, f 80 Applications for RHS Medals. 7 January 1907

806, f 1021 Application for Recognition of Private Alfred Simmons, Middlesex Regiment. 14 March 1907

806, f 1027 Case of Native Constable Govind Hiraji, Mahi Kantha Agency Foot Police. 16 March 1907

806, f 1080 Recommendation for Abani Mohan Das of the Sonthal Parganas Police. 21 March 1907

807, f 1407 RHS Awards. 4 May 1907

811, f 1570 Rescue of a boy from Narbada River. 2 May 1907

817, f 2183 RHS Bronze Medal to Seth Baddi Lal and Testimonial on Vellum to Jhita. 5 July 1907

819, f 2408 Application for Mr J. S. Trench. 4 July 1907

822, f 2596 Application for Sapper Zaman Ali. 18 July 1907

822, f 2597 Case of Mr R.A.B. Chapman. 18 July 1907

823, f 2693 Case for the RHS. 27 July 1907

827, f 3207 RHS Bronze Medal to Mr J.S. Trench, E Bengal State Railway. 17 September 1907

828, f 3257 Application for Havildar Atmaram Thapa and Rifleman Bale Thapa. 5 September 1907

834, f 3827 Application for an 8 year old boy who rescued his sister from a well. 17 October 1907

835, f 3971 Conduct of Lance Naick Pahar Singh. 31 October 1907

836, f 4046 Awards of the RHS to be forwarded to India. 21 November 1907

838, f 4169 RHS Bronze Medal to Sourendra . Bhattacharjee. 5 December 1907

838, f 4194 Case of Police Constable Amriji Samji. 23 November 1907

840, f 4445 Awards of the RHS. 31 December 1907

841, f 33 Case for the RHS. 19 December 1907

847, f 384 Conduct of Thaggai Mallah. 16 January 1908

852, f 770 Case of Aya Khan. 13 February 1908

854, f 856 Cases for the RHS. 4 March 1908

855, f 910 RHS Bronze Medal for Aya Khan. 1–12 March 1908

855, f 969   RHS Bronze Medal for Aya Khan. 27 February 1908

866, f 1563   Request for a duplicate Medal for Constable Natha Singh, Amballa. 5 March–7 May 1908

867, f 1637   Recognition of Lt A.R.G. Willock, Royal Indian Marine. 16 April 1908

867, f 1705   RHS Award to Mr H. Holman Hunt. 13 May 1908

873, f 2147   Application for Recognition of Soldiers of the 30th Lancers. 28 May 1908

878, f 2487   Case of Commander C.B. Henley and Lt H.M. Salmond, RIM. 18 June–19 July 1908

886, f 2926   Cases for the RHS. 23 July 1908

886, f 2983   Awards of the RHS. 13 August 1908

888, f 3111   Case of Police Constable Abdul Rahman, Kangra District. 6 August 1908

897, f 3774   Case for the RHS. 26 September 1908

908, F 4517   RHS Awards. 3 December 1908

L/MIL/7/19476   Recommendations for Awards for the 1935 Quetta Earthquake

L/PS/13/483   As above 1935–40

21.4   THE ROYAL HUMANE SOCIETY

The Royal Humane Society was established in 1774; it still exists and continues to grant awards. It is possible to obtain information from the Society, but please remember that it is a charity.

The Royal Humane Society is at:

Brettenham House
Lancaster Place
London
WC2E 7EP
www.royalhumanesociety.org.uk

For online information, look at the website of the Life Saving Awards Research Society, which contains information about RHS awards. For further information, see CHAPTER 26 on Online Information.

PART TWO

Long Service and
Good Conduct Awards;
Coronation and
Jubilee Medals;
Commemorative and Miscellaneous
Medals

22   Long Service and Good Conduct Awards

22.1   INTRODUCTION

Long Service and Good Conduct awards date back to 1830 when the Army Long Service and Good Conduct Medal (LSGC) was instituted. The following year, an Order in Council was passed creating a similar award for the Royal Navy.

Since 1831, a large number of awards for long service and good conduct have been created. Medals for the armed forces, both regular and part time have been instituted, as well as awards for civilians. Not all of these awards have records relating to recipients, especially civilian awards. What records are known to exist at the National Archives and in the Oriental and India Office Collection at the British Library are given below.

Beyond the qualification of consistent good conduct, there has always been a length of service element attached to each LSGC medal. The length of time element has varied from service to service, civilian organization to organization. In the case of parttime servicemen, service in wartime, i.e. mobilized service, counted double towards the award of the appropriate long service medal.

22.2   ARMED FORCES LONG SERVICE AWARDS

As with many records there are inconsistencies, all three armed services doing things differently, and this is reflected in the records. There are medal rolls for the Army award from 1831 to 1975, but the Royal Navy rolls don't start until 1912. The records concerning the RAF LGSC medal do not take the form of a medal roll at all!

22.3   ADMIRALTY RECORDS

The surviving rolls for Long Service and Good Conduct Medals (LSGC) issued by the Admiralty are in the records series ADM 171. The records within this series relate to the RN (Royal Navy) LSGC, the RNR (Royal Naval Reserve) LSGC, the RNVR (Royal Naval Volunteer Reserve) LSGC and the RFR (Royal Fleet Reserve) LSGC. In the case of the RNR LSGC, there are a number of subtle variations that need to be highlighted.

For a very detailed study of all the different types of LSGC given to personnel under the control of the Admiralty, read *The Naval Long Service Medals* by Kenneth Douglas-Morris (London, 1991). Douglas-Morris's book covers all the awards in great detail and includes all the key information required to understand this particular area of medals. Medal rolls for the William IV (Anchor) issue and the Queen Victoria Wide Suspender variety also are contained in the book. A copy is available in the National Archives library.

22.3.1 *RN LSGC*

The earliest medal roll for the Royal Naval Long Service and Good Conduct Medal starts in 1912. There is a useful way to note when an individual received an LSGC Medal prior to that date by looking at his record of service.

ADM 171/73   1912–17   RN LSGC Claims 40276–50994
ADM 171/141   1925–30   RN LSGC Issue Books
   indexed by ADM 171/156
ADM 171/142   1930–3   RN LSGC Issue Books
   indexed by ADM 171/156
   This roll is annotated to the effect that medals with the new King
   George V effigy were first issued from 7 May 1931.
ADM 171/143   1934–7   RN LSGC Issue Books
   Indexed by ADM 171/156 and 157
   This roll is annotated to the effect that medals with the new King
   George VI effigy were first issued from 27 August 1937.
ADM 171/144   1938–42   RN LSGC Issue Books
   indexed by ADM 171/157
ADM 171/145   1942–7   RN LSGC Issue Books
   indexed by ADM 171/157 and 158
ADM 171/149   1925–30   RN LSCG Claims 34900–48939
ADM 171/150   1930–5   RN LSGC Claims 48940–63099
ADM 171/151   1935–40   RN LSGC Claims 63100–77049
ADM 171/152   1940–4   RN LSGC Claims 77050–86679
   Prior to 1947, it is easier to research an RN LSGC medal by using the
   issue books up to ADM 171/145. After that time, it is necessary to search
   the records listed below, which takes longer.
ADM 171/153   1944–54   RN LSGC Claims 86680–98529
ADM 171/154   1954–62   RN LSGC Claims 98530–110379
ADM 171/155   1962–70   RN LSGC Claims 110380–122289

22.3.2 RNR and RNVR LSGC and Variations

One of the confusing issues about the Royal Naval Reserve and Royal Naval Volunteer Reserve Long Service and Good Conduct Medals was the fact that wartime service counted double towards qualifying for the award. Kenneth Douglas-Morris's book, mentioned above, covers all of the key facts concerning these awards.

The medal rolls for the RNR and RNVR LSGC Medals are in the records series ADM 171 and the rolls include the Long Service and Good Conduct Medals of the RNR, RNVR, RNASBR and the RNAWR. The rolls are arranged in chronological order. If a recipient qualified for a bar to their medal, the entry of the first awarded is usually annotated to that effect.

ADM 171/70	1909–12	Reserve Long Service Medal: Recipients
ADM 171/71	1912–37	Reserve Long Service Medal: Recipients
ADM 171/72	1938–49	Reserve Long Service Medal: Recipients

22.3.3 RFR LSGC

The medal rolls for the Royal Fleet Reserve Long Service and Good Conduct medal are also in ADM 171.

ADM 171/146   1921–32   RFR LSCG Medal – in alphabetical order
   This roll is annotated to the effect that medals with the new King George V effigy were first issued from 23 April 1931.

ADM 171/147   1933–1942   RFR LSGC Medal – in alphabetical order
   This roll is annotated to the effect that medals with the new King George VI effigy were first issued from 27 August 1937.

ADM 171/160   1935–52   RFR LSGC Claim Book 20000–29999,
   indexed by ADM 171/162

ADM 171/161   1953–72   RFR LSGC Claim Book 30000–32990,
   indexed by ADM 171/163

22.3.4 Other Admiralty Records

There are numerous policy files concerning long service awards in ADM 1, very few of which mention individuals. Of those that do, one is listed below.

ADM 1/25250 Imperial Service Medal: Award to Participants in General Strike
   of 1926

22.4   AIR MINISTRY RECORDS

There are no rolls for the RAF Long Service and Good Conduct Medal or the Air Efficiency Award.

The RAF Long Service and Good Conduct Medal was announced in Air Ministry Orders (AMOs), copies of which can be found in the records series AIR 72. The medal was announced in AMOs from 1919 until 1941, and then for a number of years after the Second World War until the early 1960s. The announcements in the AMOs held at the National Archives only cover the period 1920–35.

Although there is no roll of the Royal Observer Corps Medal, information about it can be found in *The Plane Spotters* by H.J.G. Dartnall (Roberts, 1995).

22.5   WAR OFFICE RECORDS

The War Office records concerning Long Service and Good Conduct awards take a number of different forms, such as index cards, rolls and registers. Information about the Meritorious Service Medal can be found in CHAPTER 9 on advice for researching gallantry and meritorious service awards.

The medal rolls for Army LSGC Medal are in the series WO 102 and these cover awards from 1831 to 1975. The Register of the Volunteer Decoration is in WO 330/3–4 and covers the period 1892–1932.

The medal rolls for the King's African Frontier Force and West African Frontier Force LSGC Medals are in WO 102/24 and 26. Please be aware that the earlier roll is WO 102/26 and not WO 102/24.

The records of the issue of the Volunteer Force Long Service Medal, the Territorial Force Efficiency Medal, Territorial Efficiency Medal and the Efficiency Medal (Territorial) and variations are in both WO 102 and online. The awards are also announced in Army Orders, with some lists in WO 123.

The following army long service rolls include the LSGC Medal for the regular army, for the Imperial Yeomanry, Militia, Special Reserve, West African Frontier Force, King's African Rifles, and the Territorial Efficiency Medal and Efficiency Medal (Territorial) and derivatives of the latter.

WO 102 *Army Long Service and Good Conduct Awards*

1	1859–67	Guards, Cavalry, Foot Guards and Infantry
2	1865–70	Horse Guards, Cavalry, Foot Guards and Infantry, Rifle Brigade, West India Regiment, Army Hospital Corps, Ceylon Rifles, Cape Mounted Rifles, Royal Malta Fencible Artillery, Canadian Rifles, School of Musketry, Commissariat, Royal Military College, Corps of Military Labourers, Military Store Staff Corps
3	1870–74	Horse Guards, Cavalry, Foot Guards and Infantry, Rifle Brigade, West India Regiment, Army Hospital Corps, Ceylon Rifles, Cape Mounted Rifles, Royal Malta Fencible Artillery, Canadian Rifles, School of Musketry, Commissariat, Royal Military College, Army Service Corps, Army Schoolmasters, Bengal Unattached List, Armourers
4	1870–75	Horse Guards, Cavalry, Foot Guards and Infantry, Rifle Brigade, West India Regiment, Army Hospital Corps, Ceylon Rifles, Cape Mounted Rifles, Royal Malta Fencible Artillery, Canadian Rifles, School of Musketry, Commissariat, Royal Military College, Army Service Corps
5	1875–82	Horse Guards, Cavalry, Foot Guards, Infantry 1st–40th Foot
6	1875–85	Infantry 41st –109th Foot, Rifle Brigade, West India Regiment, Royal Malta Fencible Artillery, Military Regiment of Labourers, Army Hospital Corps, Army Service Corps, School of Musketry, Royal Military College
7	1881–1901	Horse Guards, Royal Artillery, Cavalry, Royal Engineers, Foot Guards and Infantry, Corps
8	1886–1902	Royal Artillery
9	1831–48	All arms of the Service
10	1831–59	Royal Artillery
11	1868–72	Royal Artillery
12	1872–6	Royal Artillery
13	1877–80	Royal Artillery
14	1850–66	Cavalry, Foot Guards and Infantry
15	1860–62	Royal Artillery (in order of Brigades)
16	1866	Royal Artillery
17	1901–12	All arms of the Army (digitized on DocumentsOnline)

18	1913–19	All arms of the Army (digitized on DocumentsOnline)
19	1902–12	Royal Artillery
20	1913–19	Royal Artillery
21	1902–35	Imperial Yeomanry LSGC
22	1908–30	Militia LSGC
23	1908–53	Special Reserve LSGC
24	1918–50	West African Frontier Force and King's African Rifles LSGC Vol 2

The following are piece references for rolls that are in course of transfer from the Ministry of Defence.

25	1909–25	West African Frontier Force and King's African Rifles: Issue Book of LSGC Medals and DCMs, Vol 1
26	1920–32	Royal Artillery
27	1920–32	All arms of the Army (except Royal Artillery)
28	1933–49	All arms of the Army
29	1950–75	All arms of the Army

Territorial Force Efficiency Medal (TFEM), Territorial Efficiency Medal (TEM) and Efficiency Medal (Territorial) (EM(T)) and derivatives: Photocopies of Army Orders.

30	1908–18	TFEM
31	1919–20	TFEM and TEM
32	1921–3	TEM
33	1924–32	TEM and EM(T)
34	1933–7	EM(T)
35	1938–44	EM(T)

Copies of Army Orders for the EM(T) and derivatives.

WO 102

36	June 1945–March 1946
37	April 1946–December 1946
38	1947–8
39	1949–55
40	October 1953–November 1968
41	January 1969–January 1979

22.6 ORIENTAL AND INDIA OFFICE COLLECTION RECORDS (BRITISH LIBRARY)

All LSGC medals awarded to the forces of the Honourable East India Company, Indian Army and Auxiliary Forces of India were announced in General Orders and Indian Army Orders. These can be found in the series L/MIL/17/1 British Army, L/MIL/17/2 Bengal Army, L/MIL/17/3 Madras Army, L/MIL/17/4 Bombay Army and L/MIL/17/5 Indian Army.

A collection of lists of Long Service and Good Conduct Medal and Meritorious Service Medal annuitants living in England can be found in L/MIL/7.

L/MIL/7/7916	List of Annuitants	1892–5
L/MIL/7/7917	As above	1896–7
L/MIL/7/7921	As above	1897–9
L/MIL/7/7923	As above	1899–1900
L/MIL/7/7924	As above	1900–2

22.7 CIVILIAN AWARDS

The most commonly seen long service medals to civilians are the Special Constabulary Medal, the Police Long Service and Good Conduct Medal and the Imperial Service Medal. Beyond files concerning the creation of the first two medals, there are no medal rolls for them held at the National Archives. Although central government created the policy by which the awards could be granted, any records concerning recipients are the responsibility of the constabularies.

22.7.1 The Imperial Service Order and Imperial Service Medal

The Imperial Service Medal (ISM) and the Imperial Service Order (ISO) were instituted in 1902 as rewards for long and faithful service in the Civil Service. Both awards are announced in the *London Gazette*, although the ISO is no longer awarded in the United Kingdom. The ISO and ISM could be awarded to civil servants of the Colonial Service and records concerning these awards can be found in CO 524 and CO 834. These awards are also announced in the appropriate colonial gazette (see CHAPTER 8 for further information). The gazette announcements usually give you the occupation and place of employment of the recipient.

There are numerous files concerning the Imperial Service Order (ISO) and Imperial Service Medal (ISM) amongst the records at the National Archives. The majority concern policy issues, such as the qualifications for the awards, but occasionally you may find a file concerning a recipient of one of the awards. The records of the Home Office in HO 45 contain a number of files about the ISO and ISM.

Amongst the files concerning the ISM are:

AIR 2/6352	Award of ISM to Air Ministry Employees	1941–6
CO 524/14/2	ISO and ISM: Recommendations	March 1928
CO 524/14/3	ISO and ISM: Recommendations	June 1928
CO 524/14/4	ISO and ISM: Recommendations	September 1928
CO 524/14/6	ISO and ISM: Recommendations	March 1929
CO 524/14/7	ISO and ISM: Recommendations	1929
CO 524/14/8	ISO and ISM: Recommendations	Birthday Honours 1929
CO 524/14/9	ISO and ISM: Recommendations	March 1930
CO 524/14/10	ISO and ISM: Recommendations	June 1930
CO 524/14/11	ISO and ISM: Recommendations	Birthday Honours 1930
CO 524/14/12	ISO and ISM: Recommendations	March 1931
CO 524/14/13	ISO and ISM: Recommendations	June 1931
CO 524/14/14	ISO and ISM: Recommendations	Birthday Honours 1931
CO 524/14/15	ISO and ISM: Recommendations	Birthday Honours 1931
CO 524/14/16	ISO and ISM: Recommendations	December 1931
CO 524/14/18	ISO and ISM: Recommendations	1932
CO 524/14/19	ISO and ISM: Recommendations	June 1932
CO 524/14/20	ISO and ISM: Recommendations	Birthday Honours 1932
CO 524/14/22	ISO and ISM: Recommendations	September 1932
CO 537/1489	ISO: Recommendations	1946
CO 834/1	ISO: Register	1902–18
CO 834/2	ISO: Register	1919–26
CO 835/1	ISO: Register of Out Letters	1902–25
CO 825/2	ISO: Register of Out Letters	1926
DO 35/425/15	Recommendations for ISM: Queensland Police	1930
MAF 226/47	Award of ISM: Policy	1926–61
MAF 227/48	Award of ISM: Policy	1961–6
OS 1/750	ISM: Regulations	1902, 1926–8 and 1939–59
PCOM 7/620	ISM: Presentation and Eligibility	1905–23

Recent lists of the Imperial Service Medal from 2003 to 4 can be found at **www.honours.gov.uk/lists/**. Announcements of the Imperial Service Medal are published in the *London Gazette* at **www.gazettes-online.co.uk**.

There are a number of files in the India Office series L/PS/13 and L/PS/15 concerning the Imperial Service Order and Imperial Service Medal.

L/PS/13

363	Awards of the ISO and ISM: Correspondence Recommendations, Recipients, etc.	1925–37
364	ISO and ISM awards	1937–49
427	List of Recipients in India of the ISM	1922–45
428	List of Members of the ISO	1924–42

L/PS/15

34		ISO and ISM	1910–16
36	file H104	Receipt of 20 ISMs for the Govt of India	1917
36	file H107	List of ISM Recipients	1917
36	file H129	List of Members of the ISO	1917
36	file H160	ISM	1913–23
40	file H76	ISO: Birthday Honours	1918–20
41	file H177	List of Members of the ISO	1918
41	file H179	List of the Recipients in India of the ISM	1918
48	file H207	ISO and ISM: King's Birthday Recommendations	1920
54	file H184	ISO and ISM: Appointments June 1921	1921
59	file H136	ISO Appointments made on 2 June 1923	1923–4
60	file H117	ISO and ISM: Birthday Honours 1924	1924–5

A further list of holders of the Imperial Service Medal in India from 1925–41 is available at the British Library, under the reference V25/72/2.

22.7.2 *The Rocket Apparatus Volunteer Long Service Medal*

The Rocket Apparatus Volunteer Long Service Medal was instituted in 1911 as a reward for 20 years' service with the Rocket Apparatus Volunteers. When the award was instituted, it was decreed that recently retired members who met the criteria for the award were also eligible. The medal roll for this medal is in BT

167/84 and covers awards bestowed between 1911 and 1935. Many of the awards granted in 1911 went to men who had only recently retired from the Rocket Apparatus Volunteers.

The Rocket Apparatus Company Records in BT 167/87–97 contain the names of those members of a company at a given time. Each volume is arranged in alphabetical order by place name. Amongst the details recorded about each member of the company was whether they held the Rocket Apparatus Volunteer Long Service Medal. These company records cover the period 1923–33 and any member who was awarded their medals between those two dates should be found.

Reports detailing the activities of the Rocket Apparatus Companies were published on a yearly basis, but not all of them survive. The reports usually mention those who were awarded bravery awards.

Surviving reports are in MT 9 and Parliamentary Papers (PP).

1907	Report PP LXVII.119	Fiche 113.627
1911	Report PP LXXII.299	Fiche 117.679
1912–13	Report PP LXXVI.979	Fiche 118.718
1914	Report PP XLVII.837	Fiche 120.480
1914–16	Report PP XXXV.219	Fiche 121.336
1916	Report PP XV.513	Fiche 122.119
1916–20	Report PP XXV.33	Fiche 126.254
MT 9/1677	Life Saving Apparatus Reports 1922/1925	

22.7.3 Civil Defence Long Service Medal

The Civil Defence Long Service medal was instituted in 1961 and whilst the National Archives holds information about the creation of the award, there are very few records concerning individual recipients. HO 322/572 contains some information about a number of civil servants who received the award between 1967 and 1984. One problem with the medal, however, was the fact that it was issued unnamed.

22.7.4 St John's Ambulance Service Medal

Details of awards of the St John's Ambulance Service Medal and bars made to members of the mining industry for the period

1957–8 can both be found in COAL 74/8708.

22.7.5 Special Constabulary Medal

Instituted in 1919, the Special Constabulary Medal can be difficult to research as there are no medal rolls for it held at the National Archives. The most effective way to research these medals is to have something that will provide the constabulary or geographical region where the individual served. In most cases, the box and envelope in which a medal was issued can usually provide the key to other areas of research. Should the individual have received a Coronation or Jubilee Medal from 1935 onwards, the medal rolls will provide you with the constabulary or geographical key to further research.

22.7.6 Royal Household Faithful Service Medal

The best source for information about these medals is *Royal Service, Volume III* by David Stanley (London, 2001).

22.8 USING ONLINE RESOURCES

It is possible to find announcements relating to the Territorial Decoration and other long service decorations that were announced in the *London Gazette*.

You can search **www.gazettes-online.co.uk** by name of the recipient. If you search using the term 'efficiency decoration' that should also produce results.

Another online resource worth using is the *The Times* newspaper, as many of the *London Gazette* announcements were also produced in *The Times*. In the 19th century, a large number of articles mentioning the award of LSGC medals to soldiers and sailors appear in *The Times*, especially when the medals were presented by an important person.

22.9 CASE STUDIES

There is always the possibility that no trace of the medal can be found or that the information on it may be slightly inaccurate or may provide you with a false trail. The following cases fall into these categories.

Thomas Sidwell

According to his Army Long Service and Good Conduct Medal, Thomas Sidwell served in the 3rd Royal Surrey Militia. Unfortunately there is no entry amongst the medal rolls for the Army LSGC medal in WO 102. By looking at the design of the medal and the unit title, the medal is what is known as a small letter reverse LSGC. As the army regimental titles were changed in 1881, the medal had to have been awarded between 1855 and 1881.

By looking for a muster for the 3rd Royal Surrey Militia in WO 13, it was easy to pin down Sidwell's presence in the unit as a Permanent Staff Sergeant. The big problem when researching Permanent Staff of the Militia is knowing which regular army regiment they came from, in order to find their record of service. Unfortunately there is no entry in the musters of the 3rd Royal Surrey Militia saying where Thomas Sidwell came from.

As the medal must have been awarded prior to 1881, I decided to search the census to see if I could find him. According to the 1871 census, Thomas Sidwell was serving at Chatham in the 1st Depot Reserve Infantry Battalion. The census entry also stated that he was born in Coventry.

By looking at Hart's Army List for 1871, I found that it was recorded that the 1st Depot Reserve Infantry battalion fed recruits to the 7th, 24th, 35th and 77th Regiments of Foot. By looking through the discharge papers of all of the regiments in WO 97 for the years 1855–72, I found Thomas Sidwell in the records of the 35th Foot. According to his papers, the Long Service and Good Conduct Medal was his only award. Sidwell's medal can be seen in PLATE 21. Use all available sources to find a person, even the non-military records.

James Martin/Galway

The Army Long Service and Good Conduct Medal awarded to 1604 Private J. Martin 1/21st Regiment appears quite correct – and it is. Finding the service record for this man proved the importance, once again, of using all available sources.

According to the medal roll for his Army Long Service and Good Conduct Medal in WO 102/4 (see FIGURE 22), James

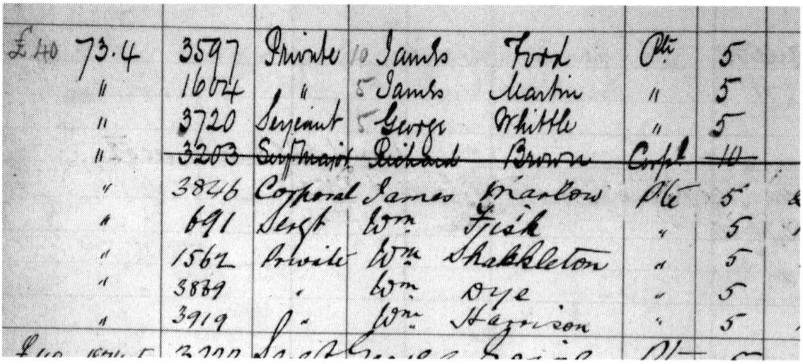

£40	73.4	3597	Private	10 James	Ford	Pte	5
	"	1604	"	5 James	Martin	"	5
	"	3720	Serjeant	5 George	Whittle	"	5
	"	~~3203~~	~~Serjt Major~~	~~Richard~~	~~Brown~~	Corpl	~~10~~
	"	3846	Corporal	James	Marlow	Pte	5
	"	691	Sergt	Wm	Fisk	"	5
	"	1562	Private	Wm	Shackleton	"	5
	"	3889	"	Wm	Dye	"	5
	"	3919	"	Wm	Harrison	"	5

FIG 22. *The Army Long Service and Good Conduct medal roll for James Martin 1/21 Foot, later James Galway* [WO 102/4]

Martin was awarded his medal on 14 March 1874. At the time that Martin's medal was awarded, he must have served for at least 18 years with long service and good conduct.

Taking the date the medal was awarded into account, an estimate of when Martin was likely to have been discharged with a full service pension (22 years+) worked out to be c.1878. As the records of service in WO 97 are arranged in chronological batches, the discharge period of 1873–82 for the infantry, with surnames including Martin, was consulted. Looking at the WO 97 box for the name 'Martin' produced no results, and it was therefore necessary to look elsewhere.

The Muster and Pays Lists for the army for the period 1874 are in the series WO 12. By looking at the muster for 1/21st Foot for the period when Martin got his Long Service and Good Conduct Medal confirmed his details. Moving through the subsequent Muster and Pay List, an important change was noted. Although 1604 Private James Martin had kept his rank, number and Christian name, he had changed his surname to Galway!

By looking at WO 97/1964 1873–82 Infantry including the name Galway, James Galway's (formerly Martin) record of service was discovered. According to his record of service, James Galway joined the 81st Foot in 1854. He transferred to the 34th Foot in 1864, the 38th Foot in 1866 and finally the 1/21st Foot in 1871. James

Galway was discharged to pension in 1876. The Long Service and Good Conduct Galway received was his only medal. An example of the medal Galway was awarded can be seen in PLATE 21.

Richard Richards
The Rocket Apparatus Volunteer Long Service Medal to Richard Richards was awarded in 1911, when the medal was first instituted. According to the roll in BT 167/84, Abbott served in Cornwall with the Coverack Company (see FIGURE 23).

Although nothing is known about Richard Richards, the Coverack Company did attend one famous wreck, but they were unable to do anything. A ship called the *Mohegan* ran aground on rocks called the Manacles, but she was too far out for the rockets to get a line to her. The ship was wrecked in 1893, so Richard Richards was almost certainly present.

The Rocket Apparatus Volunteer Long Service Medal awarded to Richard Richards can be seen in PLATE 22.

George Spencer
Although not a particularly important medal in numismatic terms, the Special Constabulary Medal awarded to George Spencer is very important as a practical example because it is still accompanied

Year.	Name of Recipient.		Date of Presentation.	Presented by	M. Registered Number.	Whe
19 11/12	Richards	Richard	15 Feb.	Mr P. D. Wms	21116/11	
1913/14	Bastian	John.	13 April 14	D. O.	25856/13.	
	Lawrence	Wm.	6·10·21	,,	1687/21	
	Bowden	Alexander	,,	,,	,,	
	Richards	Sidney	10·10·21	,,	,,	

FIG 23. *Medal roll for the Rocket Apparatus Volunteer Long Service Medal for recipients based at Coverack in Cornwall, including Richard Richards* [BT 167/84]

by its box of issue and the envelope bearing Leicestershire Constabulary. The medal is important to me because it was earned by my great-grandfather,and George Spencer's special constabulary medal can be seen in PLATE 24.

23   Coronation and Jubilee Medals

23.1   INTRODUCTION

Coins, medals or tokens commemorating the coronation or jubilee of a sovereign date back to the coronation of King James I. However, it was not until Queen Victoria was proclaimed Empress of India in 1877 that a medal in a form recognizable today was instituted. Medals were awarded not just for coronations and jubilees, but also for other specific connected events such as durbars and royal visits.

Prior to Queen Elizabeth II Golden Jubilee in 2002, the number of people who received a medal commemorating a sovereign's coronation or jubilee was much more limited. Unlike the 2002 Golden Jubilee, where over 350,000 medals were issued, the number of medals awarded for each coronation or jubilee between 1887 and 1977 never exceeded 129,000.

The approximate numbers of medals awarded for coronations and jubilees between 1887 and 1977 are given below.

1887	JUBILEE (Police Issue)	
	Metropolitan Police	14,000
	City of London Police	900
1897	JUBILEE	4,003
1897	JUBILEE (Mayor and Provost Issue)	526
1897	JUBILEE (Police Issue)	
	Metropolitan Police	7,481
	City of London Police	535
	Police Ambulance	210
	St John's Ambulance Brigade	910
	Metropolitan Fire Brigade	950
1900	VISIT TO IRELAND	2,285

1902	CORONATION	9,547	
1902	CORONATION (Police Issue)		
	Metropolitan Police	16,760	
	City of London Police	1,065	
	LCC Fire Brigade	1,000	
	St John's Ambulance Brigade	912	
	Police Ambulance Service	204	
1903	DELHI DURBAR	2,707	
1903	VISIT TO SCOTLAND	2,957	
1903	VISIT TO IRELAND	7,757	
1911	CORONATION	15,901	
1911	CORONATION (Police Issue)		
	Metropolitan Police	19,783	
	City of London Police	1,400	
	County and Borough Police	2,565	
	London Fire Brigade	1,374	
	Royal Irish Constabulary	585	
	Scottish Police	2,800	
	Royal Parks	119	
	Police Ambulance Service*		
	St John's Ambulance Brigade*		
	St Andrew's Ambulance Corps*	2,623*	Combined
1911	DELHI DURBAR	30,200	
1911	VISIT TO IRELAND	2,477	
1935	JUBILEE	85,234	
1937	CORONATION	90,000	
1953	CORONATION	129,000	
1977	JUBILEE	60,000	

23.2   MEDAL ROLLS AND RECOMMENDATIONS

The most readily available records concerning the award of a coronation or jubilee medal, durbar or royal visit medal, are the numerous medal rolls. There are, however, a number of sources that are not just lists of names of those who received one of these awards, but are concerned with giving the reasons why such individuals should receive them.

Prior to 2002, people who received a coronation or jubilee medal were specifically selected or recommended. In the case of military and police personnel, they were individuals who usually took part in a specific event associated with the celebration.

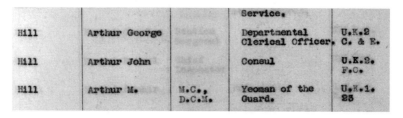

Hill	Arthur George			Departmental Clerical Officer,	Service. U.K.2 C. & E.
Hill	Arthur John			Consul	U.K.2. F.O.
Hill	Arthur M.	M.C., D.C.M.		Yeoman of the Guard.	U.K.1. 23

FIG 24 *1937 Coronation Medal roll entry for Consul A.J. Hill*

Military recipients included the most senior officers and the longest serving other ranks. Holders of the Victoria Cross and George Cross usually received the medals. Many service personnel were chosen by ballot.

There are numerous files held by the National Archives and the Oriental and India Office Collections of the British Library concerning coronation, jubilee and durbar medals. Although some are policy files, many contain details about the recipients beyond just their names.

A page from the 1937 Coronation Medal roll can be seen in FIGURE 24.

Listed below are the known files at the National Archives and British Library relating to each medal and a description of their contents.

1887 Jubilee

WO 100/42 one Royal Artillery recipient only, Gunner J. Parsons.

1897 Jubilee

ADM 171/61 folios 25–33 contains a roll of Naval Officers who received this Medal.

MEPO 5/66 contains a partial roll for the St John's Ambulance Brigade.

WO 100/42 Three Royal Artillery recipients: Master Gunner J.H. Rowley, who received the Medal in silver; Corporal J. Taylor, who received the Medal in bronze and Gunner J. Parsons, who received an 1897 Clasp for his 1887 medal

WO 100/111 contains the Army medal roll on folios 13–63 and includes Officers and Other Ranks, and the names of men from the colonial rifle teams of Victoria, Queensland, Natal and the Cape.

1902 Coronation

ADM 171/61 contains a Medal roll for Officers from folio 34–9 and Naval Ratings from folio 41–5.

ADM 116/628 concerns the issue of the 1902 Coronation Medal in bronze to Naval Ratings.

WO 100/111 folios 64–108 contains a roll for Officers; folio 109 is the roll for His Majesty's escort, folios 110–15 contains another roll for Officers, folios 115–82 is the roll for the Overseas Contingents and folios 183–213 is the roll of Officers and Men of British Army Units.

1903 Delhi Durbar

L/MIL/5/126 is a roll of Military and Civilian recipients.

WO 100/339 is a copy of L/MIL/5/126.

1911 Coronation

ADM 171/59 contains a roll of Officers and Men of the Royal Marine Artillery who received the Medal.

ADM 171/61 folios 120–183 is an A–Z list of Naval Officers who received the Medal, folios 186–98 contains the roll of Naval Ratings and folios 202–20 is the roll of the Colonial Contingents of Canada, Australia, Newfoundland and the South African RNVR.

HO 45/19195 contains rolls for Lord Lieutenants, High Sherrifs and Chairs of County Councils.

HO 45/19196 contains rolls for the Royal Parks Police, Buckinghamshire Constabulary, Berkshire Constabulary, Portsmouth Police, Cardiganshire Police, Merionethshire Police, Norwich Police, Windsor Police, 5 London County Council representatives, Norfolk Police, Dover Police, Caernarvonshire Police and deputations presenting loyal addresses.

HO 45/19197 contains rolls for Home Office staff, Lord Lieutenants and their wives, High Sherrifs, Chairmen of County Councils, Lord Mayors and Mayors and the Royal Irish Constabulary.

HO 45/19198 contains the medal roll for the County and Borough Police who received the Medal.

WO 330/1 contains the medal roll for Army personnel, starting with ADCs to the King and including the Corps, Chaplains, Army Schools, the National Reserve, Officers Training Corps and Cadets.

WO 330/2 contains the Army medal roll for all of the Cavalry and Infantry, both regular and territorial.

WORK 21/29/28 contains another roll for the Royal Parks issue.

1911 Delhi Durbar

ADM 171/61 folios 204–5 is the Naval Officers roll; folios 206–9 the naval ratings roll.

L/MIL5/127 Army recipients only

WO 100/111 folios 373–89 contains a list of Officers who received the medal.

WO 100/400 is described as 'Medal Rolls of the Army in India'.

1935 Jubilee

There are a number of medal rolls held in the library at the National Archives. There is an A–Z list of British recipients, a roll for Australia, a roll for India and Burma, a Colonial Roll, a roll for Newfoundland, Southern Rhodesia, Swaziland, Basutoland, and the Bechuanaland Protectorate. There is also another roll for India that is arranged in the different categories according to employment, both military and civil.

ADM 171/68 is the roll of Naval and Marine personnel who received the Medal.

DO 35/136/2 contains lists of individuals from Basutoland, Bechuanaland, Swaziland, Southern Rhodesia and Newfoundland who received the Medal. The file also contains a few Recommendations for other people connected with the Dominions Office.

FD1/4206 contains the names of 10 individuals connected with the Medical Research Council who received the 1935 Jubilee Medal.

HO 144/20003 contains rolls for the Home Office and Prison Commissioners and a list of Advisers to the Home Office.

L/PS/15/264 Index to the nominal rolls of recipients A–K

L/PS/15/265 Index to the nominal rolls of recipients L–Z

MEPO 2/2830 contains lists of those personnel of the Metropolitan Police who received the Medal. Apart from a roll of recipients, the file contains lists of the Metropolitan Police Special Constabulary who received the Medal and a specific list of Officers employed at Buckingham Palace and Windsor Castle.

PCOM 9/202 contains a list of those employees of the Prison Commissioners who received the 1935 Jubilee Medal. The list shows at which prison the individual was working at.

POST 62/94 is a list of Post Office employees recommended for the Medal, giving name and position. The list is corrected to August 1935. This file is held by the Post Office Archives.

WO 100 The British Army roll for the 1935 Jubilee Medal will shortly be added to this series.

1937 Coronation

There are a number of medal rolls held in the library at the National Archives. There is an A–Z list of British recipients, a roll for Australia, a roll for Colonial issues, a roll for Burma, a roll for Newfoundland,

Southern Rhodesia, Swaziland, Basutoland and the Bechuanaland Protectorate.

ADM 171/69 is a roll of Naval and Marine personnel who received the Medal.

ADM 116/3601–3602 contains a list of Admiralty Civil Staff recommended for the Medal. Details of Service of the Staff are enclosed.

DO 35/536/5 contains a miscellaneous roll of recipients who were Advisers to the Government.

DO 35/536/6 contains rolls for Southern Rhodesia, Newfoundland, Basutoland, Bechuanaland Protectorate and Swaziland. The file also contains a copy of the New Zealand Gazette of 28 May 1937, listing the awards for New Zealand.

HO 45/17121 contains the roll for the Prison Service and Home Office Staff and Advisers.

HO 45/19499 contains rolls of Jersey and Guernsey recipients.

HO 45/19500 contains rolls for the Belfast Fire Service, Local Authorities in Northern Ireland, the Royal Ulster Constabulary and Ulster Special Constables.

L/PS/15/261 Nominal rolls of Recipients in India, volume I

L/PS/15/262 Nominal rolls of Recipients in India, volume II

L/PS/15/263 Nominal rolls of Recipients in India, volume III

WO 100 The British Army medal roll will shortly be added to this series.

1953 Coronation

Once again, there are a number of medal rolls held in the library at the National Archives. There is an A–Z list of British recipients, a roll for Ceylon (Sri Lanka) and a roll of Colonial recipients.

CO 967/186 contains the Recommendations for 26 non-State advisers who were connected with the Colonial Office.

DO 35/2149 contains the medal roll for non-State advisers who have given the State outstanding service or assistance.

FD 1/4206 This file contains names of individuals recommended for the 1953 Coronation Medal by the Medical Research Council.

POST 62/93 and 95 list Post Office employees recommended for the medal, giving name and position. These files are held by the Post Office Archives.

POWE 10/508 contains detailed Recommendations from the Ministry of Fuel and Power for a number of individuals employed within the industry.

WO 100 The British Army medal roll for the 1953 Coronation Medal will shortly be added to this class.

1977 Jubilee

There are two rolls for this medal held in the library of the National Archives. There is an A–Z list of British Recipients and a roll for

Overseas Territories.

WO 100 The British Army roll for the 1977 Jubilee Medal will shortly be added to this class.

23.3 COLONIAL AND DOMINION GAZETTES

The names of recipients of Coronation and Jubilee Medals in the dominions and colonies of the British Empire and later the Commonwealth were usually announced in the appropriate gazette. A full list of the CO and DO series for these gazettes is given in CHAPTER 8.

23.4 CASE STUDY
Arthur John Hill

Arthur John Hill was born in September 1887 and, at the outbreak of the First World War, he was serving in the Board of Trade as Deputy Superintendent of the Mercantile Marine Office. In November, Hill was appointed Acting Vice Consul in Calais and, at the same time, he was given a commission as a Paymaster Sub Lieutenant in the Royal Naval Reserve (RNR). It appears that he spent the whole war based in Calais. For his service in the RNR, Hill was awarded a single British War Medal and the medal roll for this can be found in ADM 171/92.

After the war, Arthur Hill left the RNR and joined the Foreign Office. After serving in various places around Europe, he was eventually posted to Central America. By 1936, Hill was serving as Consul and Chargé d'Affairs in San Salvador. It was in this capacity that Hill received the 1937 Coronation Medal.

Arthur Hill died on 25 February 1941 whilst on leave, as a result of wounds received during an air attack on Exeter. He was 54.

Hill's medals are shown in PLATE 25.

24   Commemorative and Miscellaneous Medals

This chapter is a catch-all for those medals that do not fall into any of the more clearly defined medal categories covered in previous chapters. This is not to say that the medals discussed here are less important.

24.1   MEDALS FOR ARCTIC AND POLAR DISCOVERIES AND EXPLORATION

The medal rolls for the Arctic Discoveries Medal 1818–55 can be found in ADM 171/9 and 10. The medal roll for the Arctic Medal 1875–6 for service on HM ships *Discovery*, *Alert* and *Pandora* can be found in ADM 171/38.

Information concerning the Polar Medal 1904 and those who received it can be found in ADM 171/61 and a number of other files dispersed throughout ADM 1. There is a copy of the current medal roll showing all awards from 1904 to 2002 in the library at the National Archives. Awards of the Polar Medal are now announced in the *London Gazette*.

British Polar Exploration and Research: A Historical and Medallic Record with Biographies 1818–1999 by N. Poulsom and J. Myres (Savannah, 2000) is the most recently published book about those men and women who have been awarded the Polar Medal, a copy of which is in the library at the National Archives.

ADM 1

8367/21	1914	Award of Polar Medal to Officers and Men of the Scottish Antarctic Expedition 1902–4
8760/230	1932	Request for information on the history and early awards of the Polar Medal
8768/104	1933	Investiture of the Watkins British Arctic air route Expedition 1930–1 with the Polar Medal
11501	1941	Award of Polar Medal in Silver to members of Oxford University Arctic Expedition 1935–6
10434	1939–40	Grahamland Antarctic Expedition: Award of Polar Medal and Clasp to Members

26461   1954–6   Polar Medal: Awards to certain Members of British-Norwegian-Swedish expedition to Antarctic 1949–52

The only example of a file concerning the Polar Medal amongst the Air Ministry files in AIR 2 is:

AIR 2/4911   1942–3   Proposed award of Polar Medal: Spitzbergen flights

24.2 THE HONG KONG PLAGUE MEDAL

Awarded to a number of service personnel and civilians for service in Hong Kong during a major plague outbreak in 1894, the most comprehensive roll is in *The Whitewash Brigade* by J.J. Platt, M.E. Jones and A.K. Platt (Dix, Noonan and Webb, 1998).

24.3 MEDALS FOR SHOOTING

Skill with a rifle or naval gun has always been very important. Although the basic precepts of the Army award for the Champion Shot have remained the same, the Naval Good Shooting Medal has changed.

Between 1903 and 1914, the Royal Navy held annual gunnery competitions and awarded the best crews with the Naval Good Shooting Medal. The medal roll for this medal is in ADM 171/57. The results of each competition were published as Parliamentary Papers and, apart from the score, the names of the crews are mentioned.

Parliamentary papers are available at the National Archives on microfiche. Below are the fiche numbers for each year's results.

Results of Gunlayer's Competition in His Majesty's Fleet

Year	Fiche number	Session	Volume and page
1903	110.477	1904	LIII.177
1904	111.445	1905	XLVIII.183
1905	112.648	1906	LXX.199
1906	112.648	1906	LXX.215
1907	114.707	1908	LXV.851

1908	115.521	1909	LIII.651
1909	116.572	1910	LXI.771
1910	116.573	1910	LXI.799
1911	117.462	1911	XLVIII.763
1912	119.383	1913	XLIII.545
1913	120.532	1914	LIV.241
1914	121.377	1914–16	XL.383

The Naval Good Shooting Medal was reinstituted in 1953 along similar lines to the Army Best Shot Medal, i.e. an award for shooting with small arms and not ship-borne guns.

The Naval Good Shooting Medal 1903–1914 by R.J. Scarlett (London, 1990)

Although I have found no rolls for either the Army Best Shot Medal or the Queen's Medal for Champion Shots of the Royal Air Force, some information concerning recipients was published in early editions of *British Battles and Medals* by L.L. Gordon. Information announcing winners of these medals was published in Army Order and Air Ministry Orders as appropriate. A file concerning the King's Medal for best shot in the Territorial Army for the period 1934–6 can be found in WO 32/3425.

24.4 THE ORDER OF THE LEAGUE OF MERCY
The medal roll for the Order of the League of Mercy can be found in MH 11. MH 11/1 is the roll of the Order from 1902–24 and MH 11/2 the roll for 1925–47.

24.5 THE DICKIN MEDAL (THE ANIMAL VC)
Founded by the People's Dispensary for Sick Animals as an award for brave animals, there are two files held by the National Archives containing recommendations for the Dickin Medal.

AIR 2/5036	1943–6	Pigeons: Awards of the Dickin Medal for gallantry
MEPO 2/7738	1946–7	Award of Dickin Medal to three Metropolitan Police horses

For further information about the award see **www.pdsa.org.uk**.

25 Research Techniques

Here is a collection of pointers to help researchers find the information they seek.

25.1 USING THE MEDALS

Medals can tell you a lot. A historian works with names, places and dates. An identified and attributable medal can usually give you the name of the recipient, the place (if it is a campaign medal) and the date.

The design of the medals and ribbons, and how they are named (if appropriate) are all important. The obverse royal effigy or cipher and the reverse design both tell you something by which you can identify and date the medal. For those medals awarded over a wide chronological period, such as the Indian General Service Medal 1854–94, the naming of the medal can also help you in your quest.

The most readily available books to assist identification are *British Battles and Medals* by E. Joslin, A. Litherland and B. Simpkin (Spink, 1988) – a 7th edition is due very soon – and *The Medal Yearbook* published by Token Publishing. The first covers all British campaign medals, including all those from 1793 to the time of publication. It illustrates the medals and their associated ribbons, and will tell you the units that qualified for them.

The *Medal Yearbook* covers all orders, decorations, campaign medals, coronation and jubilee medals and a large number of other medals awarded to British and Commonwealth forces and civilians. Although the book is primarily a price guide, it does provide very useful information about most of the medals you are likely to research at the National Archives or British Library.

A third useful book when researching campaign medals is *Collecting Medals and Decorations* by Alec A. Purves (Seaby, 1978). Apart from being an extremely good book on the subject, the section on the different styles of medal naming is very useful.

25.2 USING DOCUMENTS

Discharge documents, Soldier's Pay (small) books, certificates which were often found in the boxes of coronation and jubilee medals, and boxes in which medals were issued can all tell you something to aid your research since most of them have a typed label with the recipient's details on them.

The records of soldiers and Royal Marines usually tell you which medals an individual qualified for. If a man received more than one campaign medal and you are researching just one, then the record of service may tell you whether you have a man's full entitlement or something is missing.

25.3 MAKING THE RECORDS WORK FOR YOU

In order to get the information you really want, it may be necessary to use one record to gain access to another. There are a large number of cases where one record can access another, but here are some of the most useful.

25.3.1 *RN Ratings Records in* ADM *188*

Prior to c.1885, naval medal rolls do not have service numbers on them, so trying to find a record of a naval rating between 1873 and 1885 can be difficult. Now that the records of RN ratings in ADM 188 have been digitized and made available on DocumentsOnline, it is possible to search by name for a record of service. There are however a number of ways of assisting your search.

If you have looked at a medal roll in ADM 171 for a naval campaign medal, it is important to note both the name of the ship and the man's ship's book number or ship's list number that is usually found alongside the man's name or rate. The number is usually in two parts: the book or list number and then the man's entry within that book or list. From the medal roll, you should now have the name of the man, his ship's book number, the name of the ship and a very good idea of the date relevant to the campaign.

When you search for an ADM 188 on DocumentsOnline, you will have information that will set one man apart from another. All you have to do when reading a record is to look for the ship's name and ship's book number taken from the medal roll in ADM 171.

Of all the items noted on an ADM 188, the most significant medal related item is that relating to the RN Long Service and Good Conduct Medal (LSGC). As there are no rolls for the RN LSGC prior to 1912, the record of a man who received the medal should either be annotated 'Traced M or Medal' and a date. More recent records in ADM 188 are stamped to that effect.

25.3.2 RN LSGC Medals (Narrow Engraved Variety 1875–7)

Although it is possible to look for a record of service of an RN rating in ADM 188 by searching a database, and the above technique of using information from a campaign medal roll will help you narrow the possibilities down, if all that the man received was an LSGC Medal, then the search may be more protracted.

If a man received an RN LSGC Medal of the narrow suspension variety with engraved naming (1875–7), there is one technique I would recommend. For the period 1875–7, the men of each ship and a number of shore establishments were listed in ships' ledgers, and these can be found in ADM 177. You can search the catalogue by the names of the ships or establishment, including 'Naval Barracks'. If you find the name of the recipient of the medal in the ledger, his entry will give you the man's official number and this can be applied to ADM 188 to get the record of service.

The same technique as above can be used for the musters in ADM 38 for campaign medals issued between 1853 and 1874. If you look at a medal roll and it tells you the name of the ship and date where and when the medal was sent, look for that ship in ADM 38. You should search specifically for those musters marked 'D' for description in the catalogue, as these musters are more likely to show the continuous service number for records of service in ADM 139 or the official number for records of service in ADM 188.

25.3.3 The Military General Service Medal 1793–1814 (MGS)

Although there are two very good published rolls of the MGS – Kingsley Foster and Mullen – there are two things the original roll in WO 100 will tell you that the published rolls will not. Firstly, the rolls in WO 100 note the clasps that were refused and secondly, each roll for the other ranks contains men listed under two headings,

'Pensioners' and 'Non-pensioners'. This will give you an idea of length of service and whether a man was discharged with a length of service pension or a disability pension.

25.4   USING ADM 12: THE ADMIRALTY INDEX AND DIGEST

The most effective way to trace an award granted to a member of the Royal Navy, Royal Naval Reserve, Royal Naval Volunteer Reserve, Royal Marine Light Infantry, Royal Marine Artillery, Royal Marines, Royal Naval Air Service or Fleet Air Arm is to trace the correspondence containing the recommendation for the award.

Since at least 1793, the Admiralty has been indexing all of its correspondence. Using alpha-numeric codes, departmental titles and abbreviations, the Admiralty has given a unique reference to each item of correspondence and recorded them in ADM 12.

For each given year or range of years, a number of volumes of ADM 12 record all the letters and reports. The Index for each year records names of ships, people, countries, etc. To help cross-reference the correspondence, it was also recorded in the Digest by giving numerical codes to subjects, which in the case of honours and awards and medals was 85 or 85a.

Each Index volume of ADM 12 is arranged in three major columns on each page. The left-hand column is usually related to Officers, the middle column to ships and the right-hand column to 'Promiscuous' (Miscellaneous).

Each major column division is then split into three columns again, the date on the left, the most important of which is headed 'How and where to be found' in the middle and 'Branch' on the right. The important references to record are in those in the date column and under 'How and where to be found' as these should lead you to the records in ADM 1, ADM 7, ADM 116, ADM 137 or ADM 199.

Each Digest volume is arranged differently from the Index. Instead of being in three columns spread across each page, a Digest page contains a précis of the correspondence on most of the page from left to right. The 'How and where to be found' and date columns are to the right of the précis.

The types of references found in ADM 12 vary according to

where the Admiralty filed it. For the period 1793–1913, most of the references fall into two distinct types, the alpha-numeric and departmental title type, and these should be found in ADM 1. Any references that have the term 'Case' and a number are Case files, where a number of Admiralty files on the same subject are gathered together; these will be found in ADM 7, but mostly in ADM 116. If you find a reference 'Min' or 'Minutes' and a date, these are in ADM 3.

During the First World War period for the years 1914–19, there are two ADM 12 volumes for each range of the Index or Digest, and it is necessary to search both.

The First World War style references in ADM 12 are still very similar to previous years, but there are number of key points about where to look for the files. In ADM 12, if a file has the date in full, e.g. 31 May 1916, then the file will almost certainly be in ADM 1, where you can look for the date in full down the right-hand side of the catalogue page. All Case papers are still in ADM 116.

Any other surviving ADM 12 references for the period 1914–18 will be in ADM 137. In order to find a reference in ADM 137, it is necessary to use the ADM 137 Key. The Key is arranged in chronological order and each year is then arranged in alphabetical order, with each heading listing the files that survive. Alongside each of the surviving references should be a number, most of which will be under a heading 'HS', but some could be 'HAS' or 'HSB'. The HS, HSA or HSB number then needs to be converted into an ADM 137 reference.

From 1918 to 20, a small number of files concerning awards can be found in ADM 137, but to describe them is very complicated due to their nature, so ask the staff at the National Archives.

During the period 1921–30 most of the awards files are described adequately in either ADM 1 or ADM 116.

For the Second World War period, the volumes in ADM 12 usually cover two years at a time. The arrangement is similar to previous years and, once again, most of the records are in ADM 1. The majority of awards files have the Admiralty branch prefix H&A (Honours and Awards), a number, and / and the year. Most of these files are in ADM 1. References to Cases are in ADM 116. If you find WH or War History Case and number, these records are in ADM 199.

The listing of ADM 1 post-1946 is such that awards files are easiest found by keyword searching ADM 1 on the online catalogue.

There is a 'How to Use ADM 12' guide available in the Research Enquiries Room at the National Archives.

25.5 USING THE CATALOGUE AT THE NATIONAL ARCHIVES

Keyword searching the National Archives' online catalogue can often produce the item you seek very quickly. There are a few tips that may be of help.

If you are unsure of whether to use a word in full or not, shorten it and add an * at the end, so 'awards', 'award' or 'awarded' will all be covered if you use 'award*'.

To combine two words, use AND in capitals between the two terms.

There are thousand of files concerning medals, so you may wish to narrow the date range a little.

When searching, use terms such as medals, decorations, honours, bravery, gallantry or orders. If you know the type of award, try searching under that.

There is a facility on the public terminals at the National Archives at Kew to search an ongoing project called Access to Archives or A2A. This provides access to the catalogues of participating archives in England. You can get to it via www.a2a.org.uk.

25.6 CASE STUDY
Henry Cooper

Boatswain Henry Cooper was awarded the Victoria Cross for service in the Crimea, the award being announced in the *London Gazette* on 24 February 1857. How can this be researched using ADM 12?

The citation for Cooper's award states that the award was earned in 1855, so the two important years are 1855 and 1857. I looked at ADM 12/595 and 627 for the letter C for 1855 and 1857, respectively. In the latter volume, under the Promiscuous

Column, appeared the entry Henry Cooper, Boatswain, VC. In the column 'How and where to be found' were two references: '13 February, Admiralty and 22 June, War Office'. These two references (see PLATE 27) and their dates were then applied to the ADM 1 Series for the year 1857.

The Admiralty letter of 13 February 1857 is in ADM 1/5685 and the War Office letter of 22 June 1857 can be found in ADM 1/5688.

The specific parts of each letter relating to Henry Cooper are illustrated in PLATES 28 and 29. A picture of Boatswain Henry Cooper VC wearing his Victoria Cross and other medals can be seen in PLATE 30.

26   Online Information

26.1   INTRODUCTION

The most important online medal resource is the *London Gazette* and this is covered in CHAPTER 7. What follows here are the most important internet resources where information may be gathered either for use with the archival sources mentioned in other chapters of this guide or as sources of information to stand on their own.

There are a number of commercial websites where, by paying a subscription or a fee for a single item, it is possible to download medal-related information. These sites are not mentioned. Here we are concentrating on key government or free sites.

There are many websites with complete or partial medal rolls based on the records held at the National Archives or British Library. How you use these resources is your choice. If you are far away from the National Archives or British Library and are unable to visit, then online resources may be the only way to obtain the information. If you are going to employ a researcher to research a medal or medal group and you have found something on the net, you should tell the researcher what you have found.

It is not the intention here to talk about how to use a search engine, but just to advise you to use all the information you have at your disposal when searching the net. You can search by the type of medal, the unit or the name of the recipient – the possibilities are endless.

26.2 THE MINISTRY OF DEFENCE

In the News section of the Ministry of Defence (MOD) website **www.mod.uk**, you will always find lists of those service personnel honoured in the New Year and Birthday Honours Lists as they are published. Any other awards announced outside of the New Year and Birthday Honours Lists, are also posted on the News section.

The Veterans Agency, which can be accessed via the MOD site, provides contact information for the Ministry of Defence Medal Office.

26.3 THE CABINET OFFICE

Details about the current British honours system, how it works, how to recommend an individual and recently announced honours can be found at **www.honours.gov.uk**. Honours lists from 2003 to date are published on this website at **www.honours.gov.uk/lists/**.

26.4 *THE TIMES* DIGITAL ARCHIVE

The Times newspaper has been digitized; it is available at selected sites around the country as it is only available via subscription beyond the financial reach of individuals. Access to *The Times* is available at the National Archives.

It is possible to search the paper by keyword and so discover many medal-related articles. Apart from items concerning *London Gazette* announcements, it is possible to find out about long service- and good conduct medals being awarded and presented, obituaries of medal recipients, and accounts of incidents that have led to gallantry awards.

One of the most useful sections of *The Times* is the 'Court and Social' section. During the First World War, it was quite common for the names of those being invested with their awards by the King to be listed on the day the investiture took place. If you find an article of interest, it is possible to print it.

26.5 AUSTRALIAN WAR MEMORIAL

The website of the Australian War Memorial **www.awm.gov.au** currently has three databases that are of use to medal collectors and researchers. Under the heading 'Biographical Databases', it is possible to access a database of 47,000 gazetted awards, a database of recommendations for awards granted for service in the First World War, and an Honours and Awards Index database of awards for the Second World War, Korean War and the Malayan Emergency.

26.6 LIBRARY AND ARCHIVES CANADA

Library and Archives Canada **www.collectionscanada.gc.ca** is, like many others, always improving and adding new online resources. Currently there are three key collections of note: Soldiers who fought in South Africa 1899–1902; the Canadian Expeditionary Force (CEF) database of soldiers' papers; and the WW1 CEF War Diaries.

The Soldiers who fought in South Africa and CEF databases enable you to search for papers for a particular soldier and if you find any, to view the front and back pages of the attestation papers. You can also order copies of the whole file for any soldier you find.

The CEF War Diaries have been digitized and it is now possible to search for and download any diary of the CEF. The War Diaries are important sources of information for First World War gallantry awards.

26.7 MEDAL.NET

www.medal.net is a portal by which you can access a large number of medal-related websites, including Medal Dealers, Auction Houses and government-based websites, such as the Ministry of Defence. Please be aware that the links to some websites may be out of date and this can be very frustrating.

26.8 DEALERS' WEBSITES

As the web becomes the most frequent way for medals to be sold away from the main medal auction houses, so many medal dealers have their own websites. Not only is it possible to buy medals, many dealers now put images of their stock on their sites. Some dealers put medal-related research articles on their sites, too.

Many medal auction houses have their own websites where it is possible to download auction catalogues for forthcoming sales. One auction house, Dix, Noonan and Webb (**www.dnw.co.uk**), not only places its forthcoming sale catalogue online, but also enables readers to search their database for items sold from their sale of 12 June 1991, to date.

26.9 FORUMS

If you are interested in discussing medal-related matters online, you may wish to join a forum. Three medal forums are the British Medal Forum **www.britishmedalsforum.com**, the medal discussion group available via **www.medal.net**, or the forum available via the Orders and Medals Society of America website **www.omsa.org**.

Appendices

Appendix A: Where to See Medals

Museums

The best places to see medals are the numerous service, regimental and corps museums around the country. For a list all of the military museums in the UK, look at a copy of *A Guide to Military Museums* by Terence Wise.

The key military museums where medals are on display are the Royal Naval Museum in Portsmouth, the National Army Museum in London, the RAF Museum at Hendon, the National Maritime Museum at Greenwich and the Imperial War Museum. In Wales, the Museum of the South Wales Borderers has an excellent display of medals. The Durham Light Infantry Museum in Durham has a very good medal room, as does the Green Howards Museum in Richmond, North Yorkshire.

Not all museums that display medals are military. Many local museums and stately homes have medals on display – and sometimes medals are even on display in churches!

Books and Magazines

The only magazine dedicated to medals that is published in the United Kingdom is *Medal News*, published by Token Publishing. The magazine is available by subscription and at a few retail outlets, one of which is the National Archives.

There are so many books about medals that it is diffcult to know where to begin. There is a list of Published Sources at the end of this book. However, the great strength of the *Medal Yearbook*, published by Token Publishing, is that it is not only liberally illustrated, but that it also has a very helpful bibliography. You will also find a useful list of military museums in it.

Online

The internet is a great place to look at medals. Plenty of medal dealers and auctioneers have pictures on their websites (see CHAPTER 26). If you are looking for images of medals on the net, don't forget the copyright on the image belongs to the person who took the picture.

Appendix B: Medal and Other Societies

As the vast majority of the medals discussed in this guide are British, whether they were given to Britons or to foreign nationals, the societies mentioned below are also biased towards them or toward British military history. Details about joining the societies can be found on the appropriate website.

The Orders and Medals Research Society (OMRS)

Established in 1942, the Orders and Medals Research Society has a worldwide membership of some 2,500. The society has a number of branches around the UK and some overseas. The society does have a website www.omrs.org.uk, and the General Secretary of the society, Mr P. Helmore, can be contacted at PO Box 1904, Southam, CV47 2ZX.

The Orders and Medals Society of America (OMSA)

OMSA has a membership of some 1,500 members in America and 25 other countries. OMSA has its own website at www.omsa.org and this does have its own forum.

The Military Collectors Club of Canada (MCCC)

Founded in 1963 as a society for those interested in all military artefacts, it has 1,000 members in Canada and overseas. You can find out more at www.mccofc.org.

The Birmingham Medal Society (BMS)

The BMS was formed in 1964 for those wanting to promote an interest in orders, decorations, medals and militaria. The current contact number for further information about the society is 01432 870420.

The Life Saving Awards Research Society

Established as society dedicated to the research of awards granted for saving life, the society has just over 100 members worldwide. The society's website can be found at www.lsars.pwp.blueyonder.co.uk and amongst the information about joining the society, you can find information and medal rolls for the Royal Humane Society awards.

Other Societies

There are a number of other non-medal societies that may be appropriate for those interested in a specific campaign or a broader subject area such as the Victorian Military Society www.vms.org.uk, the Crimean War Research Society www.crimeanwar.org, the Society for Army Historical Research www.edboydenphotos.co.uk/Sahr/sahr.html, the Society for Nautical Research www.snr.org, Cross and Cockade International www.crossandcockade.com and the Western Front Association www.westernfront.co.uk.

Appendix C: Published Sources and Further Reading

The following book lists are divided into two sections: medal books and books that will help access the records at the National Archives and the British Library. Neither list is exhaustive, but they are considered to be the most helpful. The majority are available at the National Archives.

Medal Books

Abbott, P.E. *Recipients of the Distinguished Conduct Medal 1855–1909* (Hayward, 1975)

Abbot, P.E. and Tamplin, J.M.A. *British Gallantry Awards* (Dix, 1981)

Arnold, J.L. *The African DCM* (OMRS, 1998)

Asplin, K.J. *China Medal Roll 1856–60* (Savannah, 2004)

Asplin, K.J. *The Roll of the Imperial Yeomanry, Scottish Horse and Lovats Scouts, Second Boer War 1899–1902* (2000)

Asplin, K.J. *Indian Mutiny: Alphabetical Roll of British Units* (1998)

Bate, C.J. and Smith, M.G. *For Bravery in the Field* (Bayonet, 1991)

Begent, P.J. and Chesshyre, H. *The Most Noble Order of the Garter* (Spink, 1999)

Bowyer, C. *For Valour: The Air VCs* (Kimber, 1978)

Carter, N. and C. *The Distinguished Flying Cross and How it Was Won 1918–1995* (Hayward, 1998)

Chatterton-Dickson, W.W.F. *Seedies Rolls of Awards to ...* (Various Dates)

Chhina Rana *The Indian Distinguished Service Medal* (Invicta India, 2001)

Cook, F. and A. *Casualty Roll for the Crimea 1854–55* (Hayward, 1976)

Cooksley, P. *The Air VCs* (Sutton, 1996)

Cooper, A.W. *In Action with the Enemy: The Holders of the Conspicuous Gallantry Medal (Flying)* (Kimber, 1986)

Cox, B. *Lifeboat Gallantry: The complete record of Royal National Lifeboat Institution Gallantry Medals and how they were won 1824–1996* (Spink, 1998)

Dalton, C. *The Waterloo Roll Call* (Hayward, 1978)

Douglas Morris, K.J. *Naval General Service Medal Rolls 1793–1840* (1982)

Douglas Morris, K.J. *Naval Long Service Medals* (Naval and Military Press, London, 1991)

Duckers, P. and Mitchell, N. *Presented by the Queen: The Crimea Medal*

Award Ceremony 18 May 1855 (Jade, 1996)

Duckers, P. and Mitchell, N. *The Azoff Campaign 1855* (Squirrel, 1997)

Everson, G. *The South Africa 1853 Medal Roll* (Sansom, 1978)

Farmery, J. Peter *Police Gallantry 1909–78* (Periter and Associates, Sydney, 1995)

Farrington, A. *Indian General Service Medal 1895 Casualty Roll* (London Stamp Exchange, 1987)

Farrington, A. *The Second Afghan War 1878–1880 Casualty Roll* (London Stamp Exchange, 1986)

Fevyer, W.H. *The Distinguished Service Medal 1914–1920* (Hayward, 1982)

Fevyer, W.H. *The Distinguished Service Medal 1939-1946* (Hayward, 1981)

Fevyer, W.H. *The Distinguished Service Cross 1901–1938* (London Stamp Exchange, 1991)

Fevyer, W.H. and Wilson, J.W. *The 1914 Star Roll to the Royal Navy and Royal Marines* (Naval and Military Press, 1995)

Fevyer, W.H. and Wilson, J.W. *The Naval General Service Medal 1915–1962 to the Royal Navy and Royal Marines* (Naval and Military Press, 1995)

Fevyer, W.H. and Wilson, J.W. *The Queen's South Africa Medal to the Royal Navy and Royal Marines* (Spink, 1983)

Fevyer, W.H. and Wilson, J.W. *The Africa General Service Medal to the Royal Navy and Royal Marines* (London Stamp Exchange, 1990)

Fevyer, W.H. and Wilson, J.W. *The China War Medal 1900 to the Royal Navy and Royal Marines* (Spink, 1985)

Forsyth, D.R. *South African War Medal 1877-8-9: The Medal Roll*

Forsyth, D.R. *British South Africa Company Co Medal 1890–97*

Galloway, P. *The Most Illustrious Order of St Patrick 1783–1983* (Phillimore, 1993)

Galloway, P. *The Order of St. Michael and St. George* (Third Millennium, 2002)

Galloway, P. *The Order of the British Empire* (Spink, 1996)

Galloway, P., Stanley, D. and Martin, S. *Royal Service, Volume One* (Third Millennium, 1996)

Gould, R. and Douglas Morris, K.J.
The Army of India Medal Roll (Hayward, 1974)

Holme, N. *The Noble 24th, Biographical Records of the 24th Regiment in the Zulu War and the South African Campaigns 1877–79* (Savannah, 2000)

Joslin, E., Litherland, A. and Simpkin, B. *British Battles and Medals* (Spink, 1988)

Kamaryc, R.M. *The Military Cross Awarded to Officers and Warrant Officers, 193 –1993* (Harlow, 1993)

Kingsley Foster, Colonel O.N. *The Military General Service Medal 1793–1814* (1947)

Mackay, J. and Mussell, J. *Medal Yearbook* (Token, 2005)

Maton, M. *Honour the Air Forces: Honours and Awards to the RAF and Dominion Air Forces During WWII* (Token, 2005)

McDermott, P. *For Distinguished Conduct in the Field: Register of the DCM 1920-1992* (Hayward, 1994)

McInnes, I. *The Meritorious Service Medal to the Aerial Forces* (Picton, 1984)

McInnes, I. *The Annuity MSM 1847–1953* (Jade Publishing Ltd, 1995)

McInnes, I. *The Immediate MSM 1916–1928* (Jade Publishing Ltd, 1988)

McInnes, I. and Fraser, M. *Ashanti 1895–96* (Picton, 1987)

Medal Yearbook (Token Publishing)

Message, C.S. *Alphabetical Naval General Service Medal 1793–1840* (1995)

Mullen, A. L.T. *The Military General Service Medal 1793–1814* (1990)

O' Moore Creagh and Humphris, E.M. *The Distinguished Service Order 1886–1923* (Hayward, 1978)

Palmer, A.N. *Above and Beyond* (1993)

Platt, J.J., Jones, M.E. and Platt, A.K. *The Whitewash Brigade* (Dix, Noonan and Webb, London, 1998)

Poulsom, N. and Myres, J. *British Polar Exploration and Research: A Historical and Medallic Record with Biographies 1818–1999* (Savannah, 2000)

Purves, A.A. *Collecting Medals and Decorations* (Seaby, 1978)

Risk, J., Pownall, H., Stanley, D. and Tamplin, J. *Royal Service, Vol. II* (Third Millennium Publishing, 2001)

Scarlett, R.J. *The Naval Good Shooting Medal 1903–1914* (London, 1990)

Snelling, S. *The Naval VCs* (Sutton, 2002)

Stanley, D. *Royal Service, Vol. III* (Third Millennium Publishing, 2001)

Stowers, R. *The New Zealand Medal to Colonials: Detailed Medal Rolls for the New Zealand Wars 1845–1872* (Hamilton, New Zealand, 1999)

Tavender, I. *Casualty Roll for the Indian Mutiny 1857–59* (Hayward, 1983)

Tavender, I. *The DFM Registers for the Second World War* (Savannah, 1999)

Tavender, I. *The Distinguished Flying Medal: A Record of Courage* (Hayward, 1990)

Tavender, I.T. *Casualty Roll for the Zulu and Basuto War South Africa 1877–79* (Hayward, 1985)

Tucker, S. and N.L.G. *In Adversity – Exploits of Gallantry and Awards to the RAF Regiment and its Associated Forces 1921–1995* (Jade Publishing Ltd, 1997)

Walker, R.W. *Recipients of the Distinguished Conduct Medal 1914–1920*, (Midland, 1981)

Webb, J.V. *The Abu Klea Medal Rolls* (1981)

Webb, J.V. *Recipients of Bars to the Military Cross 1916–1920 and a List of Warrant Officers awarded the MC 1916 –1919* (1988)

Williamson, H. *The Collector and Researchers' Guide to the Great War* (privately published, 2003)

Wilson, J.W. and Perkins, R. *Angels in Blue Jackets: the Navy at Messina 1908* (Picton, 1985)

Witte, R. *Fringes of the Fleet* (DNW, 1997)

Further Reading

Burke's Peerage, Baronetage and Knightage

Debrett's Peerage and Baronetage

Honours and Awards: Indian Army August 1914–August 1921 (Hayward, 1974)

Honours and Awards: Army, Navy and Air Force 1914–1920 (Hayward, 1979)

Instructions Regarding Recommendations for Honours and Rewards (Naval and Military Press)

Punjab Campaign 1848–9 Casualty Roll

The Army of the Sutlej 1845–46 Casualty Roll

The Dictionary of National Biography (Oxford University Press)

War Office and Associated Records List and Index LIII (List and Index Society, 1962)

Waterloo Medal Roll (Naval and Military Press, 1992)

Who Was Who (A&C Black)

Who's Who (A&C Black)

Guides to the Archives and Museums

Bevan, A. *Tracing Your Ancestors in the National Archives* seventh edn. (TNA, 2006)

Farrington, A. *Guide to the Military Records of the India Office Military Department* (London, 1982)

Pappalardo, B. *Tracing Your Naval Ancestors* (PRO, 2003)

Spencer, W. *Air Force Records for Family Historians* (PRO, 2000)

Spencer, W. *Army Service Records of the First World War* (PRO, 2001)

Wise, T. *A Guide to Military Museums* (Imperial Press, 2001)

Key Primary Source Descriptions

All references from the National Archives usually consist of three elements: Department, Series and Piece e.g. ADM 171/73

Most references from the India Offce Collection at the British Library consist of four elements e.g. L/MIL/5/55

ADM 1 Admiralty, and Ministry of Defence, Navy Department: Correspondence and Papers 1660–1976

ADM 7 Admiralty: Miscellanea 1563–1956

ADM 12 Admiralty: Digests and Indexes 1660–1965

ADM 116 Admiralty: Record Office: Cases 1852–1965

ADM 137 Admiralty, Historical Section: Records used for Official History, First World War 1860–1937

ADM 171 Admiralty, and Ministry of Defence, Navy Department Medal Rolls 1793–1975

ADM 199 Admiralty: War History Cases and Papers, Second World War 1922–1968

AIR 1 Air Ministry, Air Historical Branch: Papers (Series 1)

AIR 2 Air Ministry and Ministry of Defence: Registered Files 1887–1985

AIR 30 Air Ministry: Submission papers to Sovereign 1918–72

AIR 72 Air Ministry: Air Ministry Orders 1918–74

BT 167 Admiralty and Board of Trade: Registrar General of Shipping and Seamen: Papers etc. 1702–1993

BT 238 Ministry of Transport, Marine Department: Registered Files: Marine Crews (MC series) 1929–92

BT 261 Board of Trade and successors, Marine Divisions: Gallantry at Sea Awards 1856–1981

BT 351 Board of Trade: Registrar General of Shipping and Seamen: Index of First World War Mercantile Marine Medals and the British War Medal 1914–25

BT 395 Registry of Shipping and Seamen: Database of WW2 medals issued to Merchant Seamen 1946–2002

CO 820 Colonial Office: Military Original Correspondence 1927–51

FO 83 Foreign and Commonwealth Office and predecessors, Political and other Departments: General Correspondence before 1906. 1745–1975

FO 372 Foreign Office, Treaty Department and successors: General Correspondence from 1906. 1906–1967

HO 37 Home Office: Miscellaneous warrants 1777–1863

HO 38 Home Office: Warrant Books, General Series 1782–1969

HO 45 Home Office: Registered Papers 1839–1979

HO 207 Home Office and Ministry of Home Security: Civil Defence Regions, Headquarters and Regional Files 1935–57

HO 250 Home Office, Inter-departmental Committee on Civil Defence Gallantry Awards: Minutes and Recommendations 1940–49

HO 286 Home Office: Honours (HON Symbol Series) Files 1927–79

MT 9 Board of Trade and Ministry of Transport and successors: Marine, Harbour and Wrecks (M, H and W Series) Files 1854–1969

PREM 2 Prime Minister's Office: Honours Lists and Papers 1915–67

T 305 Treasury and Civil Service Department: Ceremonial Branch: Submissions to the Prime Minister concerning Half Yearly Honours Lists (HY Series) 1936–70

T 335 Treasury, Ceremonial Branch: Second World War Merchant Navy Awards Files (MN Series) 1939–47

T 336 Treasury, Ceremonial Branch: Second World War Civil Defence Awards Files (GCD Series) 1938–50

T 343 Treasury and Successors, Ceremonial Branch: Order of the British Empire (BE Series) Records 1916–96

T 350 Treasury, Ceremonial Branch: Civilian Gallantry Awards (GCC Series) Files 1941–90

T 351 Treasury, Ceremonial Branch: Civilian Gallantry Awards to Military Personnel (GCM Series) Files 1940–79

WO 1 War Office and predecessors: Secretary-at-War, Secretary of State for War, and Commander-in-Chief, In Letters and Miscellaneous Papers 1732–1868

WO 3 Office of the Commander-in-Chief Out Letters

WO 6 War Department and Successors: Secretary of State for War and Secretary of State for War and the Colonies, Out Letters 1793–1859

WO 32 War Office and successors: Registered Files (General Series) 1845–

WO 54 Ordnance Office and War Office: Entry Books and Registers 1594–1871

WO 100 War Office: Campaign Medal and Award Rolls (General Series) 1793–1949

WO 101 War Office: Meritorious Service Medal: Awards Registers 1846–1919

WO 102 War Office: Long Service and Good Conduct Awards, Registers 1831–1975

WO 104 War Office: Order of the Bath, Returns 1894–1949

WO 105 War Office: Lord Frederick Roberts: Papers 1835–1913

WO 108 War Office: Correspondence and Papers, South African War 1896–1913

WO 373 War Office and Ministry of Defence: Military Secretary's Department: Recommendations for Honours and Awards for Gallant and Distinguished Service (Army) 1935–90

L/MIL/5 Compilations and Miscellaneous 1793–1944

L/MIL/7 Military Collections 1853–1950

L/PS /13 Honours Records of the Political (Internal) Department and its Successors 1931–1950

L/PS/15 Political and Secret Honours Records 1856–1916

Index

Glossary of Abbreviations

AGS Africa General Service (medal)
AM Albert Medal
AMWO Admiralty Weekly Order
AO Army Order
BEM British Empire Medal
DFC Distinguished Flying Cross
DFM Distinguished Flying Medal
DSC Distinguished Service Cross
DSM Distinguished Service Medal
DSO Distinguished Service Order
EM Edward Medal
GC George Cross
GM George Medal
IGS Indian General Service (medal)
KPM King's Police Medal
KSA King's South Africa (medal)
LSGC Long Service and Good
Conduct (medal)
MBE Member of the Most Excellent
Order of the British Empire
MGS Military General Service (medal)
MC Military Cross
MFA Mercantile Fleet Auxiliary

MM Military Medal
MMR Mercantile Marine Reserve
MSM Meritorious Service Medal
NGS Naval General Service (medal)
OBE Officer of the Most Excellent
Order of the British Empire
QSA Queen's South Africa (medal)
RAMC Royal Army Medical Corps
RAOC Royal Army Ordnance Corps
RAPC Royal Army Pay Corps
RASC Royal Army Service Corps
RAF Royal Air Force
RFC Royal Flying Corps
RN Royal Navy
RNR Royal Naval Reserve
RNAS Royal Naval Air Service
RNASBR Royal Naval Auxiliary Sick
Berth Reserve
RNVR Royal Naval Volunteer Reserve
RNWAR Royal Naval Wireless
Auxilliary Reserve
VC Victoria Cross

Picture Acknowledgements

The publishers would like to thank the following for permission to reproduce their material. Every care has been taken to trace copyright holders. However, we will be happy to rectify any omissions in future editions.

Page 71 Dix, Noonan and Webb
Page 115 British Library, Newspaper Library
Page 117 *Hard Lying*, L. B. Weldon

PLATE 1 National Army Museum
PLATE 2 *Kenya Diary*, R. Meinertzhagen
PLATE 3 Keith Steward
PLATE 12 Author's collection
PLATE 14 Keith Steward
PLATE 30 Dix, Noonan and Webb

All other images are found in files at The National Archives and, unless otherwise stated, are © Crown Copyright.